11

Editor: Bill Buford
Assistant Editor: Diane Speakman
Managing Editor: Tracy Shaw
Subscription Promotion: Graham Coster
Executive Editor: Pete de Bolla
Design: Chris Hyde
Editorial Assistants: Michael Comeau, Margaret Costa, Emily
Dening, Michael Hofmann, Cyril Simsa
Editorial Board: Malcolm Bradbury, Elaine Feinstein, Ian
Hamilton, Leonard Michaels
US Editor: Jonathan Levi, 355 Riverside Drive, New York, New
York 10025

Editorial and Subscription Correspondence: Granta, 44a Hobson
Street, Cambridge CB1 1NL. (0223) 315290.
All manuscripts are welcome but must be accompanied by a
stamped, self-addressed envelope or they cannot be returned.

Subscriptions: £10.00 for four issues.

Back Issues: £2.50 for issue 3; £3.50 for issues 5 to 10; issues 1, 2,
and 4 are no longer available. All prices include postage.

Granta is set by Lindonprint Typesetters, Cambridge, and is
printed by Hazell Watson and Viney Ltd, Aylesbury, Bucks.

Granta is published by Granta Publications Ltd and distributed by
Penguin Books Ltd, Harmondsworth, Middlesex, England; Penguin
Books Australia Ltd, Ringwood, Victoria, Australia; Penguin
Books Canada Ltd, 2801 John Street, Markham, Ontario, Canada
L3R 1B4; Penguin Books (NZ) Ltd, 182-90 Wairau Road,
Auckland 10, New Zealand. This selection copyright © 1984 by
Granta Publications Ltd. Each work published in Granta is
copyright of the author.

Cover by Chris Hyde

ISSN 0017–3231   Published with the assistance
ISBN 014–00–   of the Eastern Arts Association

CONTENTS

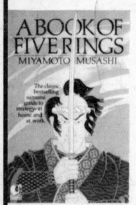

GRANTA

OBSERVATIONS

Save me from this Love
Leonard Michaels

I met a screen-writer at a party in Berkeley. He'd been very success-ful in Hollywood, but he didn't have one good thing to say about the industry or his colleagues. Producers were conniving, direc-tors were bullies, and stars were narcissistic imbeciles. Given his talent and brains, his contempt for his colleagues was under-standable, but he was bitter, he was seething. He went on and on, feeding on negativity, as if to prove that an emotion perpetuates itself. Finally, he told a story. I promised not to repeat it, but I don't feel bound. Others heard him. He was drunk and loud.

He'd been invited to LA to meet a group of wealthy people who wanted him to write a movie on a loathsome subject. This was neither here nor there. Any subject, he said, can be made worthwhile. What mattered was the way it was rendered. I disagreed, but he became impatient, he didn't want to discuss 'art'. He was too upset by life. He'd been offered for writing the movie a stupendous sum, endless cocaine, and a famous beautiful woman. When he said her name his voice leaped, spiralled up with revulsion, as if not to touch her. 'They treated me like an animal.'

'What did you say?'

'What do you think? I said no. I took the next plane home.' With a sullen gaze, he then said, 'You think I'm a schmuck?'

'No, no,' I protested, though I'd ceased to think of him at all. In a dark chamber of my soul, I contemplated the money, cocaine, woman...me.

My own experience wasn't like his. I'd been offered the minimum wage to make my novel, *The Men's Club,* into a film, and I accepted it. It was far more than I could otherwise make so quickly and, since the studio paid option money for my novel, I was rich enough to have my house painted, termite damage repaired, and a drainage system installed in the front yard. There was no beautiful woman and no cocaine, but I was flown first class to New York. A limousine waited for me at JFK. I was put up at the Parker Meridien and taken to good restaurants. At the Russian Tea Room, where one is seen, I was seen. Such treatment wasn't disagreeable. I supposed it was ritual foreplay, crucial to the mood of making movies, but I wasn't used to it and I had an embarrassing apprehension—that I was valuable. Not important, merely valuable, like a woman expensively pampered in expectation of a fantastic return.

When I talked about it to my agent, she didn't share my peculiar excitement and urged me to get out of it. Against her own interest, I thought, but she was a friend. Anyhow, she lived in the world of action. I met classes and graded papers.

My first night in New York, after dinner, I returned to the hotel, collected my key, then went to my room. I found the lamp beside the bed turned on. I didn't remember turning it on. The covers were perfectly smooth, with a corner folded down, exposing a triangle of crisp, clean sheets. I remembered sprawling, messing up the bed trying to recover from jet lag. I backed out, frightened. It wasn't my room. In the corridor, with the door shut, I checked the key again. It *was* my room. At last it occured to me that, when I left for dinner, the room had been restored to good order. Like a bumpkin, I'd been confused and frightened by the ministrations of a classy hotel. I re-entered the room and noticed the radio playing gentle, soporific music. Invisible, subtle, ever-attentive mothers had thought of that, too. I felt loved.

It seemed frightening, being loved this way, with the kind of beautiful and sensuous attention we give to the dead. Loved in the past tense. But I was apprehensive. I was starting a new life. (I see my house now, with its drainage system and bright white paint, and I sometimes think it was OK before. In its decrepitude, its sad vulnerability to the elements, it had a natural, innocent pathos. It was likable. Hard and shining, it stands now like a white iron nurse, ready for any test of its principles.) But it helped a lot when, the next day, I met the producer. Instantly, to the utmost of my abilities, I wanted to please him.

When, for the purpose of a screen-play, he suggested that I change the opening of my novel, I not only made the change, I invented it and elaborated it through fifteen scenes. 'It's much better this way. You understand? A novel is not a movie.' I understood. He was sensitive to feelings I was supposed to have. When it was suggested that I shuffle some scenes in the middle of the novel and put words of one character into the mouth of another, scenes were shuffled, words were snatched from one mouth and thrust into another. As for the ending ... I invented a new ending, introducing new characters, wild events, and an upbeat finale. Somewhat inconsistent with the shape and rhythm of the novel, perhaps, but what novel?

The Men's Club is about seven men talking in a room. 'It's not a movie.' Though it has menace and violence, it represents the spontaneous generation of a value system—that is, the men discover their consanguinity and become ferociously unified. The screen-play has women everywhere. The men are taken out of the room to a party at a whorehouse, where, in a sequence of sexual fantasies, each man is isolated and epitomized. 'It's a movie.' Anyhow, a screen-play. I wrote it. The producer said, 'Ten times better than the novel.' Who knows? In the eyes of God, he might be right.

The producer and I became good friends, bowling around after work in Berkeley, New York, and LA. My three-year-old daughter adored him. I introduced him to my friends and I met his wife and kids. He was part of my life virtually every day for the six months I worked on the screen-play. I was teaching full time. Between classes, between conferences with students, I worked on the screen-play. I worked during weekends and vacations. I worked late at night, night after night. My family recalls the period with hatred.

More than ever before, I went to movies. I was greedy for technical insights, but all I acquired at first was sympathy for movie reviewers, subjected as they are to so much sensational dreck. I mean this very seriously. It is hard to recover from the experience of a movie. That reviewers continue to know good from bad, after the repeated bludgeoning they endure, is inconceivable.

The only interruptions I allowed were phone calls from the producer, sometimes every day for a week, sometimes two hours long. I'd mail him scenes. He'd call to say what worked, what didn't. If he failed to call, I'd worry, though it sometimes destroyed my momentum when he did. 'Why aren't you working?' he'd say, at 9.30 a.m. when I'd been working for over two hours and would continue, after the call, until dinner. I'd never worked harder, not even in my teens when I waited at tables every summer, fourteen hours a day, in Catskill hotels, or when I played basketball in high school and college and tried to make my left hand as good as my right, or when I studied for doctoral examinations and tried to read every important Victorian novel in less than a month, or when I wrote the novel.

Much of the screen-play is supposed to be funny. We laughed a great deal and argued very little. He was usually high on the way it was developing, and yet, after he'd reviewed it scene by scene, line by line, word by word, I found myself revising extensively. This was paradoxical and embittering. I complained. He warned me that it wouldn't end with the screen-play. While a movie is being shot, the need for revisions continues. 'I'll get you a *per diem*.' The point was not the *per diem*, but the absence of any doubt that the movie would be made. In the way he encouraged me, he was always intelligent. An effective boss; literally, a producer. Truly to know the meaning of that word one has to lay aside Karl Marx and go to Hollywood.

The producer had years of experience in show business, a record of success, and strong instinctive critical convictions—the only kind I respect—about what's right and wrong in the tone of a line, the rhythm of a phrase. He demanded good writing, though only such as made money. His standards were absolutely clear. All right. I was writing for money. Cheques came in the mail. Carpenters and painters were all over the house. They joked and shouted and played radios. In the chaos, I seemed to be working for them, as well as the producer. I remember a lecture, given at the university, by a famous writer. It was entitled 'Why I Write.' It intimated, in its simplicity, something desperately personal and fascinating. I thought of it while writing for the drainage system and paint job and producer and money.

Under the producer's microscopic editorial attention, the screenplay developed steadily, with terrible slowness, as if I were working under water, every word issuing from me with increasingly grotesque exertions, while the producer watched from above, in a speedboat. He could speed away any time to Las Vegas. Once, he phoned from there and said it was strangely pleasant standing at the crap tables when the sun came up. I think he heard me whimpering. He said, 'I'm sorry. I know what it's like for you.' Through the watery diffusion that mediated our conversation, I strained to detect the least nuance of his desires. If I wanted to please, I wanted also to be a real writer and do surprising, original things: better than expected. Ultimately, more than anything, I wanted to finish.

*O*ne hot sunny afternoon, near the end, I sat beside the pool at the Beverly Hills Hotel, in my clothes. Other clothed people, associated with movies, were sitting around the pool. I supposed it was a Hollywood moment, where social and business life converged, in relation to nature. In the ambient murmur of conversation, I imagined that heavy deals were being negotiated. In the hot blue light, movies shimmered. Despite appearances, the lassitudinous boiling flesh around the pool contained the burning heart of power. Exactly because I was so close to it, I felt like a peripheral person. I wondered if others in Hollywood ever felt that way. Indeed, I wondered if there were others who didn't at least sometimes feel that way, and many others who never felt otherwise. I remembered meeting an actress who said, with grim sincerity, 'The first thing I had to get straight in Hollywood was that I'm an asshole.'

The producer named some of the men sitting nearby, then told me what movies they'd made. His tone was admiring and affectionate, but then he never sneered at anybody. When talking about deals that had fallen through, he never blamed personal bad luck on others. He seemed amused and happy at the pool, as if the way we all boiled together had a domestic, familial value.

About halfway through the screen-play, I felt pain in my lower back. Not bad pain, simply constant. As the weeks passed, the pain grew tentacles and hauled itself up my spine, then worked into my shoulder, then sank into my right arm where it became bad pain. In the middle of the night I'd wake with it, get out of bed, go to my study, and sit in the dark. A steel fist seemed to have seized my right arm. It squeezed towards the bone. It made me cry. To hurt that much was unreasonable. Unfair. I tried to collect myself and think about this pain, get to know it, make friends with it. I could think only that a force in this world cares nothing for our thinking. Alone in the dark, in agony, I prayed for understanding. At least understanding. I had no hope of relief. The pain would go when it would go. I continued working on the screen-play, but, sooner or later, the pain defeated me and I would end up in a bar, talking to strangers, afraid to be alone.

The screen-play was finished about twelve weeks late, submitted to the studio, and rejected almost immediately.

A Letter
Slawomir Mrozek

*T*o the Highest Council of the Highest Union of the Highest Societies:

I draw your attention to football. The practice of this game threatens the basis of our very way of life. I should explain.

When people watch a game of this sort, they do so, you realize, not knowing what the result will be. It follows that it might very well enter their heads that the HCHUHS also does not know what the result will be. And it further follows that many will come to believe that there is something that the HCHUHS does not actually know. This is not all.

Consider the implications of a match the result of which is unequal. For example, a result that is 'one—nil'. Or another example: a result that is 'nil—one'. People actually believe—it's true—that the team that has scored the most goals is *better* than the team that has scored the least—or has not scored any goals at all. And this of course contradicts a very fundamental principle: that no one is better than anyone else and that only the HCHUHS is better than everyone (unless of course the HCHUHS decides that someone is better than someone else—or at least better until further notice).

This uncontrollable aspect of a football match opens up a yawning gulf through which slips the idea that it is possible to win or lose. Worse, the satisfaction of winning is at the expense of the dissatisfaction of the losing teams. And everybody knows that satisfaction should be distributed equally, and that dissatisfaction shouldn't exist at all.

The very form of the ball in this game is an affront—a veritable contradiction—to our system. For this ball is round; moreover, it rolls; worse, when this football rolls, it may roll here or there—you simply can't know where it's going to roll to next. But everyone knows that our system, which stands firm, rolls nowhere because it is immovable.

I therefore propose a small change: that we abandon the round ball and adopt a square one—in other words, the cube.

There are—I hardly need to point out—many advantages to playing football with a cube, not least that we will never again have the problem of not knowing where a football might go: it won't go anywhere at all.

But there are other, equally important changes that I propose.

First. That the result of each match be fixed in advance by the Central Planning Commission. These results will then be published in the Gazette of Laws and announced at regular intervals through the mass media. This will, in addition, represent a tremendous saving—of both money and energy: for why, ultimately, will we even need to play the match when we already know the result?

Second. Every team declared as the loser will be obliged to display a form of satisfaction. There is of course much variety in forms of satisfaction. There is, for instance, the spontaneous manifestation of joy outside the opposing team's clubhouse. Or letters of thanks can be sent to the HCHUHS. It's obvious that the possibilities are endless. The winning team will of course be required to be equally satisfied in an analogous manner.

Third. The championship of each year's play will be determined by the degree of satisfaction expressed by the individual teams. In this way we eliminate not only the element of competition, but we succeed in channelling it into a healthy and socially constructive form.

With sportive greetings,

Slawomir Mrozek

Certain Thoughts Arising out of being Pointed out by my Two-year-old Son

Raymond Tallis

Whether what follows amounts to a tale is not something I feel especially competent to judge. I have known people who would feel angry and let down if they were sold this piece on the understanding that it was a story. My Great-aunt Nell was one. She has long since passed on, having died in a mental hospital after many years of exile in the absolute solitude of Alzheimer's disease; but while she was alive and daylit she never experienced any difficulty assigning texts she came across to their correct genres. She would have had no use for terms—like 'fictions' or 'factions' or 'fictional essays'—that pander to the uncertainties of pussy-footed intellectuals who have lost confidence in the simple distinction between truth and fiction. As for myself, still alive and apparently sane, I do not share her certainty and shall be quite happy to go along with any reader who would prefer to classify the 'tale' I am about to tell as an 'essay'; or to de-classify it and call it a 'construct'.

*T*he tale begins at a scientific meeting in Yugoslavia. Childless, I am leaning forward at the dinner table to say something or possibly to read the label of my interlocuter to whom I have been introduced but whose name I appear to have forgotten. Someone, unknown to me, takes a photograph. Months later, when the meeting has been wiped from my mind in a flurry of work, my wife's miscarriage, a move into our first house, a very worrying time over a friend who nearly died (but who, I hasten to add, made a complete recovery), an attack of pharyngitis that made me feel very low indeed and an attendance at a complete cycle of *The Ring,* the photograph, along with several others, arrives through the post. Four years later, my two-year-old son and I are looking together at a photograph album. We open the page containing the snaps from the scientific meeting. He sees the one in which, at dinner, I am leaning forward to speak or whatever and, pointing at it with his tiny index finger, exclaims 'Daddy!' A few weeks after this I am travelling by train, stale to the point of nausea, planning to dodge down the pharmacological alleyways offered by several cans of Brewmaster at seventy-five pence a time, when a sudden tingling memory of my toddler pointing me out in the photograph overwhelms me. And so the tale ends.

But is it a tale? And does it end here? Pass on the first question *(vide supra)*. As to the second, I shall make one or two remarks. They will not clinch the matter. Nor will they pacify my Great-aunt Nell or anyone else who can confidently distinguish a tale from mere facts, life's melodies from a mere sequence of notes. But they may be of interest to those who, for personal or professional reasons, can no longer say what separates a story from a pointless accumulation of contingencies.

For some time now, it has been clear to me that organized religion in giving such trivial answers to the profound questions it treats thereby lays waste our mystic powers. The trivializing influence of religion is a result of its attempts to unite the moral and the metaphysical. Of course the two *are* connected—but at a profound and unthinkable level. Nevertheless, it is difficult, one must confess, when discarding religion, not at the same time to lose contact with the profound questions. A person who has a religious outlook, or a religious hunger, but who is deeply repelled by organized religion has to subsist on moments: his spirituality is pared down to its visionary instants. He cannot tide himself over with ritual, appease accidie by organizing the parish jumble-sale, obliterate the absence of God from his heart by volunteering to be a sidesman. Such a person is spiritually only as deep as his most recent visionary experience. Every scrap has therefore to be fastened on, seized hold of and sucked dry for its sense.

Hence this story and the following expository paragraphs which—at the risk of destroying what little effect the tale might have had—I now append.

As I leaned forward to speak (or to look), I was unaware that a lens was trained upon me and that a proportion of light rendering that moment visible was being harvested so it would be seen in the light of future moments. I was also unable to imagine that future years would generate a pair of green-brown eyes which would look at me, a little brain that would recognize me, a small mouth that would re-christen me 'Daddy'. Looking at the photograph of myself leaning forward to speak—I am sure that's what I was doing—I am astounded at my ignorance of what was to come. When we think of them, even our brightest moments in the past seem like a kind of sleep, a dream sealed off in ignorance from that future which is now the ordinary present. Of course, four and a half years ago, my toddler too was asleep—in the profound, dreamless sleep of one who has not yet been conceived. I should like to put it all very romantically and say that my son and I were sealed in different sleeps—his of not being conceived, mine of not conceiving him—and that one day we woke to find ourselves side by side, sharing part, at least, of the same Tuesday. Romance aside, I tingle to see my own face as ignorant of the tiny finger pointing at it as the figure in the thriller is of the gun whose telescopic lenses have their crosswires meet on his heart; my face being pointed at by a tiny index finger whose youth makes me old beyond imagining. (I am times seventeen the age of two of his fingers). The mystery of the photograph is the invisible future that has transcended it, the non-darkness outside its light, the passage of time that has made its dailness the faintest rim of memory.

Who knows who will hold our images and recognize or not recognize us? Supposing these pages are not a tale, neither an essay, nor a faction but another kind of photograph, something else that my son will point at in, say, twenty years' time just before he criticizes its prose style, perhaps to impress the girl who will eventually mother his children—the futures who will point their fingers at him?

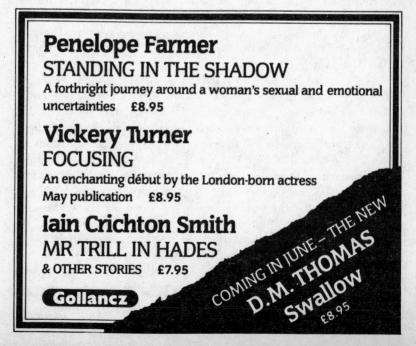

Ian McEwan
An Interview with
Milan Kundera

Milan Kundera was born in Brno in 1929, the son of a famous concert pianist. He joined the Czech communist party in 1947, was expelled in 1950, reinstated in 1956 and expelled once more in 1970. He was a professor at the Prague National Film School until 1969 when he lost his post in the 'normalization' following the Russian invasion of Czechoslovakia. During the next few years the authorities made his life increasingly difficult. In 1975 the University of Rennes offered him a professorship, and since that time Kundera has made his home in France with his wife, Vera.

His first novel, *The Joke* (Faber), appeared in 1967 and was an immediate success and a major event of the 'Prague Spring'. The novel charts the calamitous life that unfolds for a young student who sends his Stalinist girlfriend a playful postcard: 'Optimism is the opium of the people! A healthy atmosphere stinks of stupidity! Long live Trotsky!' The French critic Aragon called it 'one of the greatest novels of the century.' Kundera's fine collection of stories, *Laughable Loves*, also belongs to this period. It was published by Knopf and was included in the excellent series edited by Philip Roth and published by Penguin called 'Writers from the Other Europe'.

During 'normalization', Kundera's work was banned from bookshops and libraries throughout Czechoslovakia, and since that time he has had to write for the translator. Before leaving for France he wrote two more novels, *The Farewell Party* (John Murray) and *Life is Elsewhere*. The latter won the Prix Medicis in France for the best foreign novel of 1973. It is not available in this country. Throughout the seventies Kundera's work was translated extensively. *The Book of Laughter and Forgetting* (Faber), his first novel written in exile, showed Kundera at his best. The wide range of his philosophical and political concerns and the dramas and melodramas of private life (Kundera's 'anthropology') found a new synthesis and succinctness within a more daring, or playful, structure.

His new novel, *The Unbearable Lightness of Being*, was well received in France earlier this year. Like the previous novel, it moves between comic or wistful accounts of the private lives of his characters and wry, paradoxical and sometimes anguished musings on their fates—and on all fates. The French have adopted Kundera as one of their own and he has been besieged by interviewers and profile writers. This may have contributed to his views on journalism here, and to the weariness he clearly felt at having to repeat his views. The worst is still ahead of him, however. In this country and more particularly in the United States, there are plans for a major publishing 'event'; Kundera will have to do a great deal of explaining if he is to avoid the label of 'dissident writer' which he dislikes so much.

The new novel is consistent with the earlier work in its preoccupation with the perils of systematizing human experience into dogma, especially political dogma. That Kundera can devise sexual comedies around these perils is one of his attractions. He cannot leave the Great Questions alone; but the reader is never repelled by cold abstraction. His passionate inquiries remain rooted in and nourished by the lives of his characters whom he treats with an almost parental tenderness. The abuses of power, the political control of the past, the lure of utopias, the nature of history and of existence itself—Kundera's metaphysics—are conjured with the lightest and deftest of touches out of tortuous love affairs and fickle lovers, consuming jealousies, compulsive sexual conquest, the niceties of sexual manners, the limitless comedy of arousal. His treatment of sex borders on the obsessive, and yet his achievement has been to bring both private life and political life into one comic framework and to demonstrate how both take their forms from the same source of human inadequacies. A totalitarian government— that 'realm of uncontested meaning'—generates its own abundant absurdities, its own dark comedy, and Kundera has been both a gleeful and pained debunker of a bureaucracy that does not dare permit its citizens to read their countryman, Kafka.

The interview was conducted in French in an apartment near Montparnasse where Kundera lives with his wife. We began by talking about his exile.

McEwan: Let's talk about exile first of all. Your books are banned in Czechoslovakia and your immediate public is now French. Is it a great loss to be cut off from your native readership?

Kundera: From a general point of view, yes, it is very hard suddenly to lose the public I'd been used to until my forties. But personally it didn't feel all that unpleasant. My books were banned at the time of the Russian invasion, but I continued to live in Prague afterwards. I was fortunate in already having a contract with the French publisher Gallimard so I knew that what I was writing would be published. This alleviated the situation, made it far less cruel. But I wasn't the only one who was banned. It was really almost all of my generation, and some of my colleagues found themselves without any publisher at all. The idea of a French public, though, or the public of any country other than my own, was something abstract, something unknown. Paradoxically, this turned out to be liberating. Your immediate public has its demands, its tastes; it exerts an influence on you without your being aware of it. The public annoys you too, especially in a small country, because all of a sudden it knows you. So in the two novels I wrote after being banned I felt very free. I was free from censorship because I was no longer being published in my own country, and there was no longer pressure from the public.

McEwan: Did you feel uprooted when you left?

Kundera: What does uprooted mean?

McEwan: Well, was the decision to leave a difficult one, or was it clear cut?

Kundera: It was a slow process. Back in '68, the people who wanted to emigrate did so at once. At that time I was one of the people who didn't want to leave, precisely because I thought that a writer couldn't live anywhere else except in his homeland. I remained in Czechoslovakia for seven years after the occupation. At first everything that happened was very interesting, even if sad. For a writer, especially, it was a fascinating experience to live through. But slowly it became, not just very sad, but sterile, too. And gradually it got to be enough. Even at a practical level, it wasn't possible to stay any longer. I'd had it. I'd lost my job at the university. I lost my salary. I couldn't publish any more. So there was no longer any way I could earn my living. . . . I had saved a bit of money so we lasted out for a while. My wife began teaching English, but, as she didn't have permission to teach, she had to do it in secret. My awareness that I could emigrate came— I can remember it very well—in 1973. I had been awarded the Medicis Prize for *Life is Elsewhere*, and, to my surprise, the authorities gave me back my previously confiscated passport and let me go to Paris to collect the prize. We realized then that the regime was not against writers leaving, that in fact it was tacitly encouraging them. I began to think then of emigrating. A little later I was invited to teach at the University at Rennes for two years. During this time things were getting worse in Czechoslovakia, and being in France was a kind of recuperation. And I was struck by the fact that I wasn't nostalgic or homesick in the way I thought I would be. I am very happy here.

McEwan: Exile then is not a form of 'unbearable lightness'.

Kundera: Lightness, yes, perhaps, but more bearable than unbearable.

McEwan: Since you've been living in the West, have you found yourself enlisted in the Cold War? Have people been tempted to manipulate you or your work for their own political purposes?

Kundera: To be completely frank I've never felt that. But what I did feel, especially when I first arrived was that my work was regarded in a simplistic and political way. I had the sense that people read me as a political document; everybody, whether they were on the right or the left. I was angry, and felt offended. I don't think there was any deliberate intention to manipulate me, to make me part of the Cold War. But I do think that modern society encourages journalistic thinking. That's what dominates. Journalistic thinking is fast thinking. It doesn't permit real thought, and its vision of the world is naturally very simplified. If you come from Prague or Warsaw, then automatically you are classed by journalistic non-thought as a political writer. It is not literary critics but journalists who interpret your work. And so in that sense, at first, I did suffer from their interpretations and I had to defend myself against them. And I think I succeeded. Now they seem to understand, more or less.

McEwan: Why exactly are you offended by a political reading of your work?

Kundera: Because it is a bad reading. Everything you think is important in the book you've written is ignored. Such a reading sees only one aspect: the denunciation of a communist regime. That doesn't mean I like communist regimes; I detest them. But I detest them as a citizen: as a writer I don't say what I say in order to denounce a regime. Flaubert detested bourgeois society. But if you read *Madame Bovary* as mainly a denunciation of the bourgeoisie, it would be a terrible misunderstanding of the book.

McEwan: In *The Unbearable Lightness of Being* your character, Tereza, takes photos of Russian tanks and soldiers in the streets of Prague at the time of the invasion. Her pictures will be published abroad. Suddenly she feels strong, fulfilled; she has a purpose. Is there a sense in which you became strong too, at that time? That your subject matter was crystallized for you at the time of the occupation?

Kundera: This is Tereza's affair, not mine. I didn't feel at all strong then. It is a question of private and public life. When public life becomes very intense for Tereza it frees her from her private concerns. It is a paradoxical situation: you suddenly find yourself caught up in dramatic events, threatened with death, surrounded by tragedy, and you feel very good. Why? Because you have forgotten your private sadness.

McEwan: In *The Book of Laughter and Forgetting* you describe two kinds of laughter. The laughter of the devil celebrates the meaninglessness of everything, while the angels' laugh, which has something of a false ring about it, rejoices in how rationally organized and well-conceived everything on earth is. I suppose you would think of Czechoslovakia as being of the Devil's party. The Czechs laugh like devils, the Russians like angels.

Kundera: Absolutely, yes.

McEwan: To belong to a small country has a profound effect on the way you see the world, then?

Kundera: It is very different. Consider, for instance, the national anthem. The Czech anthem begins with a simple question: 'Where is my homeland?' The homeland is understood as a question. As an eternal uncertainty. Or consider the Polish national anthem, which begins with the words: 'Poland has not yet.' And now compare this with the national anthem of the Soviet Union: 'The indissoluble union of three republics, has been joined for ever by the Great Russia.' Or the British 'Victorious, happy and glorious . . . .' These are the words of a great country's anthem—glory, glorious, victorious, grandeur, pride, immortality—yes, immortality, because great nations think of themselves as immortal. You see, if you're English, you never question the immortality of your nation because you are English. Your Englishness will never be put in doubt. You may question England's politics, but not its existence.

McEwan: Well, once we were very big. Now we are rather small.

Kundera: Not all that small, though.

McEwan: We ask ourselves who we are, and what our position in the world is. We have an image of ourselves that was formed in another time.

Kundera: Yes, but you never ask yourselves what will happen when England does not exist any more. It can be asked, but it is terribly abstract. But it is a question that is constantly being asked in these small countries: what will happen when Poland no longer exists? Thirty million people live in Poland, so it is not such a small country. But the feeling is nevertheless true. I remember the opening phrase in a letter between Witold Gombrowicz and Czeslaw Milosz. Gombrowicz wrote, 'In a hundred years—if our country still exists . . . .' No English, American, German or French person could ever write such a phrase.

This feeling of the frailty of existence—this sense of mortality—is linked with a vision of history. Large nations think they are making history. And if you make history you take yourself seriously; you even begin to worship yourself. People say, for instance, history will judge us. But how will it judge us? It will judge us badly. It will judge us . . .

McEwan: Severely?

Kundera: No, not severely, I wouldn't say severely. It will judge us without any authority to do so. Why think that it will judge us justly? The judgement of history is bound to be unjust, perhaps even stupid. To say that history will judge us—which is commonplace enough, everybody says it—means you automatically understand history as rational—with the right to judge, with the right to truth. It is the understanding you find among large nations who, making history, always see it as wise and positive.

If you are a small nation, though, you do not make history. You are always the object of history. History is something hostile, something you must defend yourself against. You feel, spontaneously, that history is unjust, often stupid, and you can't take it seriously. Hence our special humour: a humour capable of seeing history as grotesque.

McEwan: You have written a great deal about what happens when people come to believe in Utopias, when they think they have made a paradise on earth. You see them dancing in a closed circle, their hearts overflowing with an intense feeling of innocence. They are like children. Or they are on a Great March, fists raised, chanting the same syllables in unison. And yet your characters who break away from the circle are deeply cynical—

27

sometimes attractively so. But all the same, their lives are made to seem sterile. Between this cynicism and this mindless circle-dancing you don't seem to offer us much.

Kundera: I'm not a priest. I can't tell people what to believe.

McEwan: You were in paradise yourself once. You danced in a circle after 1948, didn't you, when the communists first came into power in Czechoslovakia? When did you leave the dance? Was it another very slow process or was it decisive?

Kundera: The further away I get from it, the more I have the impression it was a swift process. But that is certainly the optical illusion of somebody who is already very far removed from it: it could not have been very swift.

McEwan: I was interested to find in the last section of your new novel, *The Unbearable Lightness of Being*, a very different attitude to paradise. Your heroine Tereza has retreated to the countryside with her husband Tomas and their dog Karenin. You write: 'Comparing Adam and Karenin leads me to the thought that in Paradise man was not yet man. Or to be more precise, man had not yet been cast out on man's path. Now we are longtime outcasts, flying through the emptiness of time in a straight line.' And just a little later you reflect on the danger of treating animals as soulless machines: 'By doing so man cuts the thread binding him to Paradise and has nothing left to hold or comfort him on his flight through the emptiness of time.' So this is a paradise worth hanging on to. What relationship does it have to that other, mindless paradise you describe so scornfully elsewhere?

Kundera: Tereza longs for paradise. It's a longing, ultimately, not to be man.

McEwan: But the man who dances in your circle, lost in mindless enthusiasm—hasn't he also ceased to be a man?

Kundera: Fanatical people don't cease to be human. Fanaticism is human. Fascism is human. Communism is human. Murder is human. Evil is human. This is why Tereza longs for a state in which man is not man. The paradise of political Utopia is based on the belief in man. This is why it ends in massacres. Tereza's paradise isn't based on the belief in man.

McEwan: Towards the end of *The Unbearable Lightness of Being*, you elaborate on the idea of kitsch. By kitsch, then, you mean more than just bad taste?

Kundera: Oh yes, far more. I use the word, which was first used in Munich in the nineteenth century, in its original sense. Germany and Central Europe were both Romantic in the nineteenth century—more Romantic than realist. And they really produced kitsch in enormous quantities. The nineteenth century is the first century without a style. All kinds of styles were imitated, especially in architecture: renaissance, baroque, gothic, everything all at once. Hermann Broch wrote a very fine essay called 'Comments on Kitsch' in which he asks this: wasn't the nineteenth century really the century not of Romanticism but of kitsch? By which he means a kind of absolute artistic opportunism capable of drawing on anything in order to move people emotionally. It was eclecticism with one imperative: that it must please. The great Romantics were, according to Broch, exceptions in a sea of kitsch. Broch sees Wagner as kitsch, for example, and Tchaikovsky.

McEwan: You have written: 'Kitsch is the aesthetic ideal of all politicians and all political parties and movements.' According to you the function of kitsch is to conceal death. Does this mean there is no conceivable politics without kitsch?

Kundera: In my view, politics—in the sense of political parties, elections, *modern* politics—is unthinkable without kitsch. It is inevitable. The function of the successful politician is to please. He is meant to please the largest number of people humanly possible, and to please so many you must rely on the clichés they want to hear.

29

McEwan: Do the Russians want to please?

Kundera: It's true they don't need to. They have power without being obliged to please people to keep it. Brezhnev didn't need to please anybody. But the party slogans, party demagogy, and all that: that's intended to please. That's kitsch on a grand scale.

McEwan: Ortega y Gasset said that tears and laughter are aesthetically false.

Kundera: Yes, I don't know that quotation, but that's right. I had a letter the other day from a Swedish reader who said: 'But do you realize that, in fact, to accept you, we cover up what disturbs us and turn you into kitsch? When *The Book of Laughter and Forgetting* was published, the reviewers talked only about the character, Tamina. It is an interesting part of the book. It's no worse than the rest. But it also has an emotional, "kitschifiable" motif—the relationship between a woman and her dead husband whom she still loves. Nobody mentioned the last part of your book which has this anti-social, anti-human quality. And the reason they didn't mention it was to kitschify you.'

McEwan: Let's pass on to other things. Do you think the key to all human relations is to be found in sexual relationships? Is what happens between a man and a woman a mirror for all human relationships?

Kundera: I don't know. It is certainly a very revealing situation, but I wouldn't like to say that everything stops there.

McEwan: Your starting point always seems to be a marriage, an affair . . . . There seems to be an obsession with constant love-making.

Kundera: Yes, but it either reveals the essence of a situation or it has no place in the novel. When my characters make love, they grasp, suddenly, the truth of their life or their relationship. For example, in *The Farewell Party*: Jakob and Olga have always been secure in their relationship. All at once they sleep together, and their relationship becomes unbearable. It becomes unbearable because this feeling of pity suddenly materializes during the sexual act and it becomes something absolutely horrible: pity is an impossible foundation for love. In *The Joke*, when Ludwik makes love to Helena, we suddenly see that his sexuality is based on vengeance. The whole book is based on this single act of intercourse. When Sabina makes love with Franz, in *The Unbearable Lightness of Being*, she suddenly becomes aware that he is like a puppy feeding from her breasts, sucking. She sees him as an animal—a small animal who has come to depend on her—and this aspect of him suddenly disgusts her. At a glance, she sees the truth of their relationship.

McEwan: The identity of your characters is revealed through their sexuality . . . .

Kundera: Take Tereza in *The Unbearable Lightness of Being*. Her problem is her identity, the relationship of body and soul; her soul doesn't feel comfortable in her body. It is expressed most clearly in a scene when she is making love with the engineer. She suddenly feels that her soul is completely remote during the act, watching her body making love. She becomes excited by this detachment; you see her problem, the theme on which her character is based, suddenly emerge during that act of love. In that sense, these erotic scenes serve to illuminate characters and situations.

McEwan: You write very well about the desire to be a victim. Being a victim, according to you, is not simply something which happens to someone, it is also something that someone, the victim, dreams.

Kundera: For example?

McEwan: Many of your characters are consumed by sexual jealousy. They inhabit their jealousy; they seem to love it, or need it. They are victims, of course, but they cultivate their own particular hell.

31

Kundera: That's an interesting idea, but to be honest I've never thought about it that way. I've got nothing much to add; you're right.

McEwan: You write a lot about the obsession with sexual conquest. Do you think there is any connection between that and political conquest, the conquest of one country by another?

Kundera: I don't know.

McEwan: For example, sometimes the fate of your characters is very much caught up with the fate of their country. Tamina in *The Book of Laughter and Forgetting* is strongly identified with Czechoslovakia. She is in exile, she is cut off from her own past. Can one talk of countries as victims? Some of your most victimized characters make strong identifications with the oppressors. Ruzena in *The Farewell Party*, for example, is a pathetic figure in some ways, but she sides with the mad old men who go round killing people's dogs, and she is on the side of the fat women at the swimming pool who revel in their nakedness and ugliness. There is a collusion between the oppressors and oppressed, an intimacy that is almost sexual.

Kundera: It is true. You're absolutely right; I was not completely conscious of it. But it is true.

McEwan: It would be better for me to say some things that weren't true: you could deny them eloquently . . . . Novels and films where the private and the political can be resolved inside one situation are always attractive.

Kundera: The same things that happen at the level of high politics happen in private life. George Orwell has written of a world in which the Political Power rewrites history: decides what the truth is, what is to be remembered, what forgotten. As a novelist, though, I have different interests. I am much more interested in the fact that each of us, consciously or unconsciously, rewrites our own history. We are constantly rewriting our own biographies, constantly bringing our own sense—the sense we want—to events. We are selecting and shaping—picking out the things that reassure and flatter us, while deleting anything that might possibly detract. To rewrite history, then—to rewrite history even in Orwell's sense—is not an inhuman activity. On the contrary, it is very human. People always see the political and the personal as different worlds, as if each had its own logic, its own rules. But the very horrors that take place on the big stage of politics resemble, strangely but insistently, the small horrors of our private life.

McEwan: You once said you thought it was the task of the novel to expose 'anthropological scandals'. What did you mean by that?

Kundera: I was talking about the situation in totalitarian states. I said that for a writer everything that was going on there was not a political scandal, but an anthropological one. That is, I didn't look at it in terms of what a political regime could do, but in terms of this question: what is man capable of?

McEwan: But why scandal?

Kundera: A scandal is what shocks us; everybody talks about the shocking ways of this bureaucracy, this communist system, that has given birth to the gulags, political trials, and stalinist purges. They describe it all as a political scandal. But people forget the obvious fact that a political system can do no more than the men in it: if man wasn't capable of killing, no political system could engender a war. A system exists around the limits of what human beings can do. Nobody, for example, can spit four metres into the air, even if the system demands it. You can't do more than half a metre. Or piss that far: even if Stalin orders it, you can't do it. But you can kill. So the anthropological question—the question of what man is capable of—is always there behind the political one.

McEwan: I have the impression you believe the novel is capable of granting us a very special understanding of the world, of permitting insights that no other form of enquiry could equal.

Kundera: Yes, I believe that the novel can say something that can't be said any other way. But just what this specific thing is, it is very difficult to say. You could put it negatively. You could say, for example, that the novel's purpose is not to describe society, because there are certainly better ways of doing that. Nor does it exist to describe history, because that can be done by historiography. Novelists are not here to denounce stalinism because Solzhenitsyn can do that in his proclamations. But the novel is the only way to describe, to show, to analyse, to peel away human existence in all its aspects. I don't see any intellectual activity which could do what the novel accomplishes. Not even existential philosophy. Because the novel has an inbuilt scepticism in relation to all systems of thought. Novels naturally begin by assuming that it is essentially impossible to fit human life into any kind of system. That is why the questions you put to me a moment ago were not easy for me to answer. The questions of paradise, or power, or the relation of power to existence or to eroticism. I examine these questions only as they are expressed in the relations between different fictional characters, and that means that, in the novel, you are always aware of several possible answers to every question. The novel doesn't answer questions: it offers possibilities.

McEwan: A distinctive feature of your fiction is the presence of the author as a kind of chorus, questioning and commenting on the behaviour and motives of his characters. This voice seems to emerge in *The Joke* and its presence has been very strong in the last two novels. Are the techniques of the traditional novel, with its invisible author, insufficient for your purposes?

Kundera: Well, there are three things to say here. First, I'd already used that technique in an earlier book. You'll find this narrator in *Life is Elsewhere*. You'll find it too in my short stories. But it is true that recently I've used this voice more and more. Second, y ou ask if this kind of narration supersedes the traditional novel, which doesn't need any commentary. But it was really only in the nineteenth century that the narrator disappeared completely. He was always there in eighteenth century novels. He is there in Rabelais, in Cervantes, in Sterne. My third point: I said earlier that for me the value of the novel is in the way it can examine the essence of a situation. It doesn't just represent situations— jealousy, say, or tenderness, or the taste for power—it arrests them, comes to a halt by them, looks closely at them, ponders them, interrogates them, asks questions of them, understands them as enigmas. Once you start to understand them as enigmas then you have to start thinking about them. Take jealousy, for example. It is so commonplace as to make any explanation seem unnecessary. But if you begin to pause and think about it, it is different. It's unbearable to see a woman you love making love to another man. Suddenly the commonplace becomes difficult, troubling, enigmatic. I'd even say it is the novelist's ambition to represent the enigmatic, precisely because so much in everyday life has become commonplace and trivialized. I need to hear in the novel the voice that is thinking, but not the voice of a philosopher. What does that mean? You asked me questions about my novels which already contained a great deal of knowledge, even though formulated as questions. That's very much like the novelist's method, which is to go further and further, right to the heart of the problem, without ever offering an answer.

McEwan: You go to great lengths to avoid giving your characters a 'psychology'—in fact your work seems quite opposed to the psychological novel. You often stop to remind us that your characters are pure artifice. And yet, paradoxically, you manage to make them seem very real. I think this is because your intrusive narrator talks about your characters in much the same way as perceptive people might talk about a close friend. Your interventions are a form of higher gossip. And that makes us think these characters really exist.

Kundera: Yes, that's right. I don't claim to know everything about the character. I can't, just as I can't claim to know everything about a friend. I am really writing on the level of hypothesis. It is the same with friends. Even if you are talking of your best friend—and you say everything that can be said—your observation remains a hypothesis.

McEwan: Was it your admiration for Kafka that caused you to write that the novel investigates life in the trap the world has become?

Kundera: Ah yes, the novel of today examines the trap the world has become. The history of the novel is a mirror of man's history, but something happened when Kafka arrived. . . something which is still not properly recognized. Usually Modernism in the novel is represented by the trinity of Joyce, Proust and Kafka. Whereas it has always seemed to me that Proust and Joyce are the fulfillment, the completion of a long process of evolution that goes back to Flaubert. Something quite different begins with Kafka and possibly with Broch and Musil. Until Kafka, the monster that man fought against was the monster inside him—what determined his inner life, his past, his childhood, his complexes. In Kafka, for the first time, the monster comes from the outside: the world is perceived as the trap. In Kafka, man is being determined from outside himself: the power of *The Castle,* from the power of the invisible tribunal of *The Trial.* In my books, it is history which traps the European man. What are the possibilities in a world that has become our trap? What choices do we have? What forms of life are there? Now it makes no difference, ultimately, if K. has an Oedipus complex or a father-fixation: it won't change his fate in the least. But it would change the fate of a Proust character completely. The world of Proust or Flaubert was open. History was invisible. It was something that couldn't be grasped, even. For us, history is concrete, palpable. It is war. It is a political regime. It is the end of Europe. It is absolutely graspable—*grasping*—and we're in it: caught. Hence, the trap.

McEwan: You have a phrase about solitude being violated in Kafka's characters.

Kundera: Yes. You're surrounded by a community—that was Kafka's nightmare—in which your solitude is utterly violated, massacred: it ceases to exist. Everybody can see you; you're never alone. Kafka is still interpreted in the terms of the generation that preceded him. It's like talking about Beethoven in terms of Haydn. Kafka is still seen through the romantic cliché of solitude: that man is threatened by solitude, that solitude is purely negative, that the tragedy of the intellectual is that he has lost his roots among the people. And Kafka himself is thus the author suffering from solitude, looking for community, for brotherhood, wanting to find his place in the world—even though it was precisely this very cliché which Kafka turned upside down. Kafka's world is in fact totally different. The Land Surveyor in *The Castle* is bored and fed up with the world around him. It's not brotherhood he's looking for; it's a job. But instead he's pestered by everybody. He is watched. He sleeps in the same bed as his assistants and can't sleep with Frida because they are always there, with him. In Kafka, those who find their place in society do so by renouncing their solitude and, in the long run, their personalities.

What, ultimately, does brotherhood mean? Kafka turns the notion on its head. It becomes something hateful, terrible, and threatening. Kafka challenges one of the most accepted notions about society. And this is precisely the task of all novelists: to challenge, constantly, the principal notions on which our very existence is based.

Translated from the French by Ian Patterson

New from Faber and Faber

The Unbearable Lightness of Being
MILAN KUNDERA

Milan Kundera's new novel displays to the full his sardonic
sense of humour and playful mastery of the erotic nuances of
life. In it he brings together story and dream and juxtaposes
different states of mind, different geographies, the present
with times past. It is the novel for which Kundera's many
readers have been waiting. £9.50 *May 21st*

Mouroir
BREYTEN BREYTENBACH

Breyten Breytenbach is one of South Africa's finest living
writers and the recipient of all that country's major literary
awards. He is also one of its victims, having been sentenced in
1975 to nine years imprisonment on charges of 'terrorism'.
Mouroir is the product of that time, and it is one of the most
haunting and memorable works of fiction to have appeared in
recent years. £8.50 *April 30th*

They Shoot Writers, Don't They?
Edited by GEORGE THEINER

In the ten years since the first issue appeared of *Index On
Censorship* an increasing number of writers have been banned,
exiled, imprisoned and tortured. For them and persecuted
intellectuals throughout the world the journal has become a
vital mouthpiece and source of hope. This book brings
together many of the powerful, thought-provoking articles it
has published on the role of the writer in societies where
words can cost lives. Faber Paperback £4.00 *June*

faber and faber

MILAN KUNDERA
SOUL AND BODY

1

I have been thinking about Tomas for many years, but not until I saw him in the light of a new perception did I see him clearly. I saw him standing at the window of his flat and looking across the courtyard at the opposite walls, not knowing what to do.

He had first met Tereza about three weeks earlier in a small Czech town. They had spent scarcely an hour together. She had accompanied him to the station and waited with him until he boarded the train. Ten days later she paid him a visit. They made love the day she arrived. That night she came down with a fever, and stayed a whole week in his flat with the flu.

He had come to feel an inexplicable love for this all but complete stranger; she seemed a child to him, a child someone had laid in a bulrush basket daubed with pitch, and sent downstream for Tomas to fetch at the riverbank of his bed.

She stayed with him a week, until she was well again, then went back to her town, some hundred and twenty-five miles from Prague. And then came the moment I have just spoken of and see as the key to his life: standing by the window, he looked out over the courtyard at the walls opposite him and deliberated. Should he call her back to Prague for good? He feared the responsibility. If he invited her to come, she would come, and then offer her life to him.

Or should he resist approaching her? Then she would remain a waitress in the hotel restaurant of the provincial town and he would never see her again.

Did he want her to come or not?

He looked out over the courtyard at the opposite walls seeking an answer.

He kept recalling her lying on his bed; she reminded him of no one in his former life. She wasn't a mistress or a wife; she was a child whom he had taken from a bulrush basket daubed with pitch. She fell asleep. He knelt down next to her. Her feverous breath quickened and she gave out a weak moan. He pressed his face to hers and whispered calming words into her sleep. After a while he felt her breath return to normal and her face rise unconsciously to meet his. He smelled the delicate aroma of her fever and breathed it in, as if trying to glut himself with the intimacy of her body. And all at once he fancied she had been with him for many years and was dying. He had a sudden clear feeling that he would not survive her death. He would lie down beside her and want to die with her. He pressed his face into the pillow beside her head and kept it there for a long time.

Now he was standing at the window trying to call that moment to account. What could it have been if not love declaring itself?

But was it love? The feeling of wanting to die beside her was clearly exaggerated: he had seen her only once before in his life. Wasn't it only the hysteria of a man who, aware deep down of his inaptitude for love, felt the self-deluding need to simulate it? And was his unconscious so cowardly that the best partner it could choose for its little comedy was this miserable provincial waitress with practically no chance at all to enter his life?

Looking out over the courtyard at the dirty walls, he realized he had no idea whether it was hysteria or love.

And he was distressed that in a situation where a real man would have instantly known how to act, he was vacillating and therefore depriving the most beautiful moments he had ever experienced (kneeling at her bed and thinking he would not survive her death) of their meaning.

He remained annoyed with himself until he realized that not knowing what he wanted was actually quite natural: we can never know what to want, because, living only one life, we can neither compare it with our previous lives nor perfect it in our lives to come.

Is it better to be with Tereza or to remain alone?

There is no means of testing which decision is better, because there is no basis for comparison. We live everything as it comes, without warning, like an actor going on cold. And what can life be worth if the first rehearsal for life is life itself? That is why life is always like a sketch. No, sketch is not quite the word, because a sketch is an outline of something, the groundwork for a picture, whereas the sketch that is our life is a sketch for nothing, an outline with no picture.

Einmal ist keinmal, says Tomas to himself. What happens but once, says the German adage, might as well not have happened at all. If we have only one life to live, we might as well not have lived at all.

2

But then one day during a break from surgery, he was called to the telephone by a nurse. He heard Tereza's voice coming from the receiver. She was phoning him from the station. He was overjoyed. Unfortunately he was busy that evening and could not invite her to his place until the next day. The moment he hung up, he reproached himself for not telling her to go straight there. He had time enough to cancel his plans, after all! He tried to imagine what Tereza would do in Prague for the thirty-six long hours before they were to meet, and had half a mind to jump into his car and drive through the streets looking for her.

She arrived the next evening, dangling a handbag over her shoulder and looking more elegant than the last time they met. She had a thick book under her arm. It was Tolstoy's *Anna Karenina*. She seemed in a good mood, even a little boisterous, and tried to make him think she had just happened to drop in, things had just worked out that way: she was in Prague on business, perhaps (at this point she became rather vague) to find a job.

Later, as they lay naked and spent side by side on the bed, he asked her where she was staying. It was night by then, and he offered to drive her there. Embarrassed, she answered that she still had to find a hotel and had left her suitcase at the station.

Only the day before he had feared that if he invited her to Prague she would offer her life to him. When she told him her suitcase was at the station, he realized in an instant that the suitcase contained her life and that she had left it at the station only until she could offer it to him.

The two of them got into his car, which was parked in front of the house, and drove to the station. There he claimed the suitcase (which was large and enormously heavy) and took both it and Tereza home with him.

How had he come to make such a sudden decision when for nearly a fortnight he had wavered so much he could not even bring himself to send a postcard asking her how she was?

He himself was surprised. He was acting against his own principles. Ten years earlier, when he had divorced his first wife, he had celebrated the event the way others celebrate a marriage. He had come to believe that he was not born to live side by side with any woman and could be fully himself only as a bachelor. He tried to design his life in such a way that no woman could move in with a suitcase. That was why his flat had only the one bed. And even though it was quite a wide bed, Tomas would tell his mistresses that he was unable to fall asleep with anyone next to him, and drive them home after midnight. And so, on Tereza's first visit, it was not because of the flu that he avoided sleeping with her. The first night he spent in his large armchair, and the rest of that week he drove every night to the hospital, where he had a cot in his office for night shifts.

But this time he fell asleep by her side. When he woke up the next morning he found Tereza, who was still asleep, holding his hand. Could they have been hand in hand all night? It was hard to believe.

And while she breathed the deep breath of sleep and held his hand (firmly—he was unable to disengage it from her grip), the enormously heavy suitcase stood watch by the bed.

He refrained from loosening his hand from her grip for fear of waking her, and turned carefully on his side to observe her better.

Again it occurred to him that Tereza was a child laid in a pitch-daubed bulrush basket and sent downstream. He couldn't very well let a basket with a child in it float down a stormy river! If the Pharaoh's daughter hadn't snatched the basket carrying little Moses from the waves, there would have been no Old Testamant, no civilization as we know it! How many ancient myths begin with the rescue of an abandoned child! If Polybus hadn't taken in the young Oedipus, Sophocles wouldn't have written his most glorious tragedy!

Tomas did not realize at the time that metaphors are dangerous. Metaphors are not to be trifled with. A single metaphor can give birth to love.

3

He lived a scant two years with his first wife and they had a son. At the divorce proceedings, the judge awarded the child to its mother and ordered Tomas to pay a third of his salary for its support. He also granted him the right to visit the boy every other week.

But each time Tomas was supposed to see him, the boy's mother found an excuse to keep him away. He soon realized that bringing them expensive gifts would make things a good deal easier, that he was expected to bribe the mother for the son's love. He saw himself making quixotic attempts to inculcate his views in the boy, views opposed in every way to the mother's. The very thought of it exhausted him. When, one Sunday, the boy's mother again cancelled a scheduled visit, Tomas decided never to see him again.

Why should he feel more for that child, to whom he was bound by nothing but a single improvident night, than for any other? He would be scrupulous about paying support; he just didn't want anybody making him fight for the boy in the name of paternal sentiments.

Needless to say, he found no sympathizers. His own parents condemned him roundly: if Tomas refused to take an interest in his son, then they, Tomas's parents, would no longer take an interest in theirs. They made a great show of maintaining good relations with their daughter-in-law and trumpeted their exemplary stance and sense of justice.

Thus in practically no time Tomas managed to rid himself of wife, son, mother, and father. The only thing they bequeathed to him was a fear of women. He desired them, but feared them. And feeling the need to fashion a compromise between fear and desire, he invented erotic friendship. As he would tell his mistresses: the only relationship that can make both partners happy is one in which sentimentality has no place and neither partner makes any claim on the life and freedom of the other.

To ensure that erotic friendship never grew into aggressive love, he would meet each of his long-term mistresses only at intervals. He considered this method flawless and propagated it among his friends: 'The important thing is to abide by the rule of threes. Either you see a woman three times in quick succession and then never again, or you maintain your relationship over a number of years, but make sure the rendezvous are at least three weeks apart.'

The rule of threes enabled Tomas to keep intact his liaisons with some women while continuing to engage in short-term affairs with many others. He was not always understood. The woman who understood him best was Sabina. She was a painter.

It was Sabina he turned to when he needed to find a job for Tereza in Prague. Following the unwritten rules of erotic friendship, she promised to do everything in her power, and before long she had located a place for her in the darkroom of an illustrated weekly. Although her new job did not require any particular qualifications, it raised her status from waitress to member of the press. And when Sabina herself then went on to introduce Tereza to everyone on the weekly, Tomas knew he had never had a better friend for a mistress than Sabina.

4

The unwritten contract of erotic friendship stipulated that Tomas exclude all love from his life. The moment he violated that clause of the contract, his other mistresses would assume inferior status and become ripe for insurrection.

Accordingly, he rented a room for Tereza and her heavy suitcase. He wanted to be able to watch over her, protect her, enjoy her presence, but felt no need to change his way of life. He did not want word to get out that Tereza was sleeping at his place: spending the night together was the *corpus delicti* of love.

He never spent the night with the others. After making love he had an uncontrollable craving to be by himself. Waking in the middle of the night at the side of an alien body was distasteful to him, and rising in the morning with an intruder was repellent. He had no desire to be overheard brushing his teeth in the bathroom, nor was he enticed by the thought of an intimate breakfast.

That is why he was so surprised to wake up and find Tereza squeezing his hand so tightly. Lying there looking at her, he could not quite understand what had happened. But as he ran through the previous few hours in his mind, he began to sense an aura of hitherto unknown happiness emanating from them.

From that time on they both looked forward to sleeping together. I might even say that the goal of their love-making was not so much orgasm as the sleep that followed it. She especially was affected. Whenever she stayed overnight in her rented room (which quickly became only an alibi for Tomas) she was unable to fall asleep. In his arms she would fall asleep no matter how wrought up she might have been. He would whisper impromptu fairy tales about her, or gibberish, words he repeated monotonously, words soothing or comical, which turned into vague visions lulling her through the first dreams of the night. He had complete control over her sleep: she dozed off at the second he chose.

While they slept, she held him as on the first night, keeping a firm grip on wrist, finger or ankle. If he wanted to move without waking her, he had to resort to artifice. After freeing his finger (wrist or ankle) from her clutches—a process which never failed to rouse her partially, as she guarded him carefully even in her sleep—he would calm her by slipping an object into her hand (a rolled-up pyjama top, a slipper, a book), which she then gripped as tightly as if it were a part of his body.

Once, when he had just lulled her to sleep but she had gone no farther than dream's antechamber and was therefore still responsive to him, he said to her, 'Goodbye, I'm going now.'

'Where?' she asked, still in her sleep.

'Away,' he answered sternly.

'Then I'm going with you,' she said, sitting up in bed.

'No, you can't. I'm going away for good,' he said, going out into the hall. She stood up and followed him out, squinting. She was naked beneath her short nightdress. Her face was blank, expressionless, but she moved energetically. He walked through the hall of the flat into the hall of the building (the hall shared by all the occupants), closing the door in her face. She flung it open and continued to follow him, convinced in her sleep that he meant to leave her for good and she had to stop him. He walked down the stairs to the first landing and waited for her there. She went down after him, took him by the hand, and led him back to bed.

It was then that Tomas came to the conclusion that making love with a woman and sleeping with a woman are two separate passions, not merely different but near opposites. Love does not make itself felt in the desire for copulation (which desire extends to an infinite number of women) but in the desire for shared sleep (which desire is limited to one woman).

5

In the middle of the night she started moaning in her sleep. Tomas woke her up, but when she saw his face she said, with hatred in her voice, 'Get away from me! Get away from me!' Then she told him her dream: the two of them and Sabina had been in a big room together. There was a bed in the middle of the room. It was like a podium in the theatre. Tomas ordered her to stand in the corner while he made love to Sabina. The sight of it caused Tereza intolerable suffering. Hoping to alleviate the pain in her heart by pains of the flesh, she jabbed needles under her fingernails. 'It hurt so much,' she said, squeezing her hands into fists as if they actually were wounded.

He pressed her to him, and she gradually (trembling violently for a long time) fell asleep in his arms.

Thinking about the dream the next day, he remembered something. He opened a desk drawer and took out a packet of letters Sabina had written to him. He was not long in finding the following passage: 'I want to make love to you in my studio. It will be like a stage surrounded by people. The audience won't be allowed up close, but they won't be able to take their eyes off us....'

The worst of it was that the letter was dated. It was quite recent, written long after Tereza had moved in with Tomas.

'So you've been rummaging in my letters!'

She did not deny it. 'Throw me out then!'

But he did not throw her out. He could picture her pressed against the wall of Sabina's studio jabbing needles up under her nails. He took her fingers between his hands and stroked them, brought them to his lips and kissed them, as if they still had drops of blood on them.

But from that time on everything seemed to conspire against him. Not a day went by without her learning something about his secret love life.

At first he denied it all. Then, when the evidence became too blatant, he argued that his polygamous way of life did not in the least run counter to his love for her. He was inconsistent: first he disavowed his infidelities, then he tried to justify them.

Once he was making a date with a woman on the phone, and as he said goodbye he heard a strange sound in the next room, a sound suggestive of teeth chattering loudly.

Tereza had happened to come home without his realizing it. She was pouring something from a medicine bottle down her throat, and her hand shook so badly the glass bottle clinked against her teeth.

He pounced on her as if trying to save her from drowning. The bottle fell to the ground, spotting the carpet with valerian drops. She put up a good fight, and he had to keep her in a straitjacket-like hold for a quarter of an hour before he could calm her.

He knew he couldn't justify his position, based as it was on complete inequality.

One evening, before she discovered his correspondence with Sabina, they had gone to a bar with some friends to celebrate Tereza's new job. She was still at the weekly but had left the darkroom to become a staff photographer. Because Tomas had never been much for dancing, one of his younger colleagues took over. He and Tereza made a splendid couple on the dance floor, and Tomas found her more beautiful than ever. He looked on in amazement at the precision and deference with which Tereza anticipated her partner's moves. The dance seemed to him a declaration that her devotion, her ardent desire to satisfy his every whim was not necessarily bound to his person, that she was willing to respond to the call of any man she met. He had no difficulty imagining Tereza and his colleague as lovers. And the ease with which he did so wounded his pride. The realization that he could effortlessly visualize Tereza's body coupling with any male body put him in a foul mood. Not until late that night, at home, did he admit to her he was jealous.

This absurd jealousy, grounded as it was in mere hypotheses, proved that he considered her fidelity an unconditional postulate of their relationship. How then could he begrudge her her jealousy of his very real mistresses?

6

During the day she tried (though with only partial success) to believe what Tomas told her and to be as cheerful as she had been before. But her jealousy thus tamed by day burst forth all the more savagely in her dreams, each of which ended in a wail he could silence only by waking her.

Her dreams recurred like themes and variations or television series. For example, she repeatedly dreamed of cats jumping at her face and digging their claws into her skin. We need not look far for an interpretation: in Czech slang the word 'cat' means a pretty woman. Tereza saw herself threatened by women, all women. All women were potential mistresses for Tomas, and she feared them all.

In another cycle she was being sent to her death. Once when he woke her screaming in terror in the dead of night she told him about it. 'I was at a large indoor swimming-pool. There were about twenty of us. All women. We were naked and had to march around the pool. There was a basket hanging from the ceiling and a man standing in the basket. The man wore a broad-brimmed hat shading his face, but I could see it was you. You kept giving orders. Shouting at us. We had to sing as we marched, sing and do kneebends. If one of us did a bad kneebend, you would shoot her with a pistol and she would fall dead into the pool. Which made everybody laugh and sing even louder. You never took your eyes off us, and the minute we did something wrong, you would shoot. The pool was full of corpses floating just below the surface. And I knew I lacked the strength to do the next kneebend and you were going to shoot me!'

In a third cycle she was dead. Lying in a hearse as big as a furniture van, she was surrounded by dead women. There were so many of them that the back door would not close and several legs dangled out.

'But I'm not dead!' Tereza cried. 'I can still feel!'

'So can we,' the corpses laughed.

They laughed the same laugh as the living women who used to tell her cheerfully that it was perfectly normal that one day she would have bad teeth, faulty ovaries, and wrinkles, because all women had bad teeth, faulty ovaries, and wrinkles. Laughing the same laugh, they told her that she was dead and it was perfectly all right!

Suddenly she felt a need to urinate. 'You see,' she cried. 'I need to pee. That's proof positive I'm not dead!'

But all they did was laugh again. 'Needing to pee is perfectly normal! You'll go on feeling that kind of thing for a long time yet. Like a person who has an arm cut off and keeps feeling it's there. We may not have a drop of pee left in us, but we keep needing to pee.'

Tereza huddled up against Tomas in bed. 'And the way they talked to me! Like old friends, people who'd known me for ever. I was appalled at the thought of having to stay with *them* for ever.'

7

To assuage Tereza's sufferings, he married her (they could finally give up the room, which she had not lived in for quite some time) and gave her a puppy. It was born to a Saint Bernard owned by a colleague. The sire was a neighbour's German shepherd.

They tried to come up with a name for it. Tomas wanted the name to be a clear indication that the dog was Tereza's, and he thought of the book she was clutching under her arm when she arrived unannounced in Prague. He suggested they call the puppy Tolstoy.

'It can't be Tolstoy,' Tereza objected. 'It's a girl. How about Anna Karenina?'

'It can't be Anna Karenina,' said Tomas. 'No woman could possibly have so funny a face. It's much more like Karenin. Yes, Anna's husband. That's just how I've always pictured him.'

'But won't calling her Karenin affect her sexuality?'

'It is entirely possible,' said Tomas, 'that a female dog addressed continually by a male name will develop lesbian tendencies.'

Strangely enough, Tomas's prediction came true. Karenin decided he was in love with Tereza. Tomas was grateful to him for it. He would stroke his head and say, 'Well done, Karenin! That's just what I want you for. Since I can't cope with her by myself, you must help me.'

But even with Karenin's help he failed to make Tereza happy. He became aware of his failure on approximately the tenth day after his country was occupied by Russian tanks. It was August 1968, and Tomas was receiving daily phone calls from a hospital in Zurich. The director there, a physician who had struck up a friendship with Tomas at an international conference, was worried about him and kept offering him a job.

8

If Tomas rejected the Swiss doctor's offer without a second thought, it was for Tereza's sake. He assumed she would not want to leave. She had spent the whole first week of the occupation in a kind of trance almost resembling happiness. After roaming the streets with her camera, she would hand the rolls of film to foreign journalists, who actually fought to get them. Once, when she went too far and took a close-up of an officer pointing his revolver at a crowd of people, they arrested her and kept her overnight at Russian military headquarters. There they threatened to shoot her, but no sooner did they let her go than she was back in the streets with her camera.

That is why Tomas was surprised when on the tenth day of the occupation she said to him, 'Why is it you don't want to go to Switzerland?'

'Why should I?'

'They could make it hard for you here.'

'They can make it hard for anybody,' replied Tomas with a wave of the hand. 'What about you? Could you live abroad?'

'Why not?'

'You've been out there risking your life for this country. How can you be so nonchalant about leaving it?'

'Now that Dubcek is back, things have changed.'

It was true: the general euphoria lasted no longer than the first week. A number of official Czech representatives had been dragged away by the Russian army like criminals; no one knew where they were; everyone feared for the men's lives, and hatred for the Russians drugged the populace like alcohol. It was a drunken carnival of hate.

Czech towns were decorated with thousands of handpainted posters bearing ironic texts, epigrams, poems, and cartoons of Brezhnev and his soldiers—jeered at by one and all as a circus of illiterates. But no carnival can go on for ever. In the meantime the Russians had forced the Czech representatives to sign a compromise agreement in Moscow. When Dubcek returned with them to Prague, he gave a speech over the radio. He was so devastated after his six-day imprisonment he could hardly talk; he kept stuttering and gasping for breath, making long pauses between sentences, pauses lasting nearly thirty seconds.

The compromise saved the country from the worst: the executions and mass deportations to Siberia that had everyone terrified. But one thing was clear: the country would have to bow to the conqueror, stutter, stammer, gasp for air like Alexander Dubcek. The carnival was over. In its wake came workaday humiliation.

Even though Tereza had lived through the events with Tomas and he knew her reaction to be valid, he also knew beneath that reaction was another, more basic reason why she wanted to leave Prague: she had never really been happy before.

The days she walked through the streets of Prague taking pictures of Russian soldiers and looking danger in the face were the best days of her life. They were the only days when the television series of her dreams had been interrupted and she had enjoyed a few happy nights. The Russians had brought equilibrium in their tanks, and now that the carnival was over, she feared her nights again and wanted to escape them. She now knew there were conditions under which she could feel strong and fulfilled, and she longed to go off into the world and seek those conditions somewhere else.

'It doesn't bother you that Sabina has emigrated to Switzerland, too?' Tomas asked.

'Geneva isn't Zurich,' said Tereza. 'She'll be much less of a difficulty there than she was in Prague.'

A person who longs to leave the place where he lives is an unhappy person. That is why Tomas accepted Tereza's desire to emigrate as the culprit accepts his sentence, and why one day, as part of that sentence, he and Tereza and Karenin found themselves in the largest city of Switzerland.

9

He bought a bed for their empty flat (they had no money yet for other furniture) and threw himself into his work with the frenzy of a man of forty beginning a new life.

He made several telephone calls to Geneva. A show of Sabina's work had opened by chance eight days after the Russian invasion, and in a wave of sympathy for her tiny country, Geneva's patrons of the arts bought up all her paintings. 'Thanks to the Russians I'm a rich woman,' she laughed into the telephone. She invited Tomas to come and see her new studio, and assured him it did not differ greatly from the one he had known in Prague.

He would have been only too glad to visit her, but was unable to find an excuse to explain his absence to Tereza. And so Sabina came to Zurich. She stayed at a hotel. Tomas went to see her after work. He phoned first from the reception desk, then went upstairs. When she opened the door, she stood before him on her beautiful long legs wearing nothing but panties and bra. And a black bowler hat. She stood there staring at him, mute and motionless. Tomas did the same. Suddenly he realized how touched he was. He removed the bowler from her head and placed it on the bedside table. Then they made love without saying a word.

Leaving the hotel for his Zurich abode (which had long since acquired table, chairs, couch, and carpet), he thought happily that he carried his way of living with him as a snail carries his house. Tereza and Sabina represented the two poles of his life, distant and irreconcilable, yet equally vital to it. But the fact that he carried like a part of his body everything he felt was vital to his life meant that Tereza's dreams continued.

They had been in Zurich for six or seven months when he came home late one evening to find a letter on the table. It told him she had left for Prague. She had left because she lacked the strength to live abroad. She knew she was supposed to bolster him up, but did not know how to go about it. She had been silly enough to think that going abroad would change her. She thought that after what she had been through during the invasion she would stop being petty and grow up, grow wise and strong, but she had overestimated herself. She was weighing him down and would do so no longer. She had drawn the necessary conclusions before it was too late. And she apologized for taking Karenin with her.

He took some sleeping pills but did not close his eyes until morning. Luckily it was Saturday and he could stay at home. For the hundred and fiftieth time he went over the facts: the borders between his country and the rest of the world were no longer open. No telegrams or telephone calls could bring her back. The authorities would never let her travel abroad. Her departure was staggeringly definitive.

10

The realization that he was utterly powerless was like the blow of a sledge-hammer, yet it was curiously calming as well. No one was forcing him into a decision. He felt no need to stare at the walls of the houses across the courtyard and ponder whether to live with her or not. Tereza had made the decision herself.

He went to a restaurant to have lunch. He was depressed, but as he ate, his original sense of desperation began to dissipate, lose its edge, and soon all that was left was melancholy. Looking back on the years he had spent with her, he came to feel that their story could have had no better ending. If someone had invented the story, this is how he would have had to end it. One day Tereza came to him uninvited. One day she left the same way. She came with a heavy suitcase. She left with a heavy suitcase.

He paid the bill, left the restaurant, and started walking through the streets, his melancholy growing more and more beautiful. The seven years he had lived with Tereza were, he realized, more attractive in retrospect than in reality.

His love for Tereza was beautiful, but it was also tiring: he had constantly had to hide things from her, sham, dissemble, make amends, buck her up, calm her down, give her evidence of his feelings, play the defendant to her jealousy, her suffering, and her dreams, feel guilty, make excuses and apologies. Now what had been so exhausting had disappeared and only the beauty remained.

Saturday found him for the first time strolling alone through Zurich, breathing in the heady smell of freedom. New adventures hid round each corner. The future was a secret again. He was on his way back to the bachelor life, the life he had once felt destined for, the life that would let him be what he actually was.

For seven years he had lived bound to her, his every step subject to her scrutiny. She might as well have chained iron balls to his ankles. Suddenly his step was much lighter. He soared. He was enjoying the sweet lightness of being.

(Did he feel like phoning Sabina in Geneva? Contacting one or another of the women he had met during his several months in Zurich? No, not in the least. Perhaps he sensed that any woman would make his memory of Tereza unbearably painful.)

11

This curious melancholic fascination lasted until Sunday evening. On Monday everything changed. Tereza forced her way into his thoughts: he imagined her sitting there writing her farewell letter; he felt her hands trembling; he saw her lugging her heavy suitcase in one hand and leading Karenin on his leash with the other; he pictured her unlocking their Prague flat, suffered the utter sense of abandonment breathing her in the face as she opened the door.

During those two beautiful days of melancholy his compassion had taken a holiday. It had slept the sound Sunday sleep of a miner who, after a hard week's work, needed to gather strength for his Monday shift.

On Saturday and Sunday he felt the sweet lightness of being. On Monday he was hit by a weight the like of which he had never known. The tons of steel in the Russian tanks were nothing compared to it. For there is nothing heavier than compassion. Not even one's own pain weighs so heavy as the pain one suffers with someone and for someone—a pain intensifed by the imagination and prolonged by a hundred echoes.

He kept warning himself not to give in to compassion, and compassion listened with bowed head and a seemingly guilty conscience. Compassion knew it was being presumptuous, yet it quietly stood its ground, and on the fifth day after her departure Tomas informed the director of his hospital (the man who had phoned him daily in Prague after the Russian invasion) that he had to return at once. He was ashamed. He knew that the move would appear irresponsible, inexcusable to the man. He had a good mind to unbosom himself and tell him the story of Tereza and the letter she had left on the table for him. But in the end he did not.

The head of the hospital was in fact offended.

Tomas shrugged his shoulders and said, *'Es muss sein. Es muss sein.'*

It was an allusion. The last movement of Beethoven's last quartet is based on the following two motifs: *'muss es sein? es muss sein! Es muss sein!'*

To make the meaning of the words absolutely clear, Beethoven introduced the movement with the phrase *'Der schwer gefasste Entschluss,'* which is commonly translated as 'the difficult resolution.'

This allusion to Beethoven was actually Tomas's first step back to Tereza, because she was the one who had induced him to buy records of the Beethoven quartets and sonatas.

The allusion was even more pertinent than he had thought, because the Swiss doctor was a great music lover. Smiling serenely, he asked, in the melody of Beethoven's motif, *'Muss es sein?'*

'Ja, es muss sein,' Tomas said again.

12

I can just picture Tomas approaching the Swiss border and a sullen, shock-headed Beethoven conducting the local fire brigade in a rousing farewell-to-emigration brass-band arrangement of the *Es Muss Sein March.*

But then Tomas crossed the Czech border and was welcomed by columns of Russian tanks. He had to stop his car and wait a half hour before they passed. A ghastly soldier in black, the leader of the tank brigade, stood at the cross-roads directing traffic as if every road in the country belonged to him and him alone.

'*Es muss sein!*' was Tomas's first reaction, but then he began to doubt. Did it really have to be?

Yes, it was unbearable for him to stay in Zurich imagining Tereza living on her own in Prague.

But how long would he have been tortured by compassion? All his life? Or all year? Or a month? Or only a week?

How could he have known? How could he have gauged it?

Any schoolboy can do experiments in the physics laboratory to test the validity of one or another scientific hypothesis. But man, because he has only one life to live, cannot verify a hypothesis by experiment and so can never know for sure whether to follow his passion (compassion) or not.

It was with these thoughts in mind that he opened the door to his flat. Karenin made the homecoming easier by jumping up on him and licking his face. The desire to fall into Tereza's arms (he could still feel it getting into his car in Zurich) had completely disintegrated. He fancied himself standing opposite her in the midst of a snowy plain, the two of them shivering from the cold.

13

From the very beginning of the occupation Russian military planes flew over Prague all night long. No longer accustomed to the noise, Tomas was unable to fall asleep.

Twisting and turning beside the slumbering Tereza, he recalled something she had once told him a long time before in the course of an insignificant conversation. They had been talking about his friend Z. when she announced, 'If I hadn't met you, I'd certainly have fallen in love with him.'

Even then her words had left Tomas in a strange state of melancholy, and now he realized it was only a matter of chance that Tereza loved him and not his friend Z. Apart from her consummated love for Tomas, there was an infinite number of unconsummated loves for other men in the realm of possibility.

We all reject out of hand the idea that the love of our life may be something light, weightless; we presume our love was meant to be, that without it our life would no longer be the same; we feel that Beethoven himself, gloomy and awe-inspiring, is playing the *'Es muss sein!'* to our own great love.

Tomas often thought of Tereza's remark about his friend Z. and came to the conclusion that the love story of his life exemplified not *'Es muss sein!'*, it must be so, but rather *'Es könnte auch anders sein'*: it could as well be otherwise.

Seven years earlier, a complex neurological case *happened* to have been discovered at the hospital in Tereza's town. They called in the chief surgeon of Tomas's hospital in Prague for consultation, but the chief surgeon of Tomas's hospital *happened* to be suffering from sciatica, and since he was unable to travel he sent Tomas to the provincial hospital instead. The town had several hotels, but Tomas *happened* to be given a room in the one where Tereza was employed. He *happened* to have had enough free time before his train left to stop at the hotel restaurant. Tereza *happened* to be on duty, and *happened* to be serving Tomas's table. It had taken six chance happenings to push Tomas towards Tereza, as if he had little inclination to go to her on his own.

He had gone back to Prague because of her. So fateful a decision resting on so fortuitous a love, a love that would not even have existed had it not been for his boss's sciatica seven years earlier. And that woman, that personification of absolute fortuity, now again lay asleep beside him, breathing deeply.

It was late at night. His stomach started acting up as it tended to do in times of psychic stress.

Once or twice her breath turned into mild snores. Tomas felt no compassion. All he felt was the pressure in his stomach and the despair of having returned.

14

After Tomas had returned to Prague from Zurich, he began to feel uneasy at the thought that his acquaintance with Tereza was the result of six improbable fortuities.

But is not an event in fact more significant and noteworthy the greater the number of fortuities necessary to bring it about?

Chance and chance alone has a message for us. Everything that occurs out of necessity, everything expected, repeated day in and day out, is mute. Only chance can speak to us. We read its message much as gypsies read the images made by tea leaves in the bottom of a cup.

Tomas appeared to Tereza in her restaurant as chance in the absolute. There he sat, poring over an open book, when suddenly he raised his eyes to her, smiled, and said, 'A cognac, please.'

At that moment, the radio happened to be playing music. On her way back to the counter to pour the cognac, Tereza turned the volume up. She recognized Beethoven. She had known his music from the time a string quartet from Prague had visited their town. Tereza (who, as we know, yearned for 'something higher') went to the concert. The hall was nearly empty. The only other people in the audience were the local chemist and his wife. And although the quartet of musicians on stage faced only a trio of spectators down below, they were kind enough not to cancel the concert, giving them a private performance of the last three Beethoven quartets.

Then the chemist invited the musicians to dinner and asked the girl in the audience to go along with them. From then on, Beethoven became her image of the world on the other side, the world she yearned for. Rounding the counter with Tomas's cognac, she tried to read chance's message: How was it possible that at the very moment she was taking an order of cognac to a stranger she found attractive, at that very moment she heard Beethoven?

Necessity knows no magic formulae; they are all left to chance. If a love is to be unforgettable, fortuities must immediately start fluttering down to it like birds to Francis of Assisi's shoulder.

15

He called her back to pay for the cognac. He closed his book (the emblem of the secret brotherhood), and she thought of asking him what he was reading.

'Can you have it charged to my room?' he asked.

'Yes,' she said. 'What number are you in?'

He showed her his key, which was attached to a piece of wood with a red six drawn on it.

'That's odd,' she said. 'Six.'

'What's so odd about that?' he asked.

She had remembered that the house in Prague they had lived in before her parents were divorced was number six. But she answered something else (which we may credit to her wiles): 'You're in room six and my shift ends at six.'

'Well, my train leaves at seven,' said the stranger.

She did not know how to respond, so she gave him the bill for his signature and took it over to the reception desk. When she finished work, the stranger was no longer at his table. Had he understood her discreet message? She left the restaurant in a state of excitement.

Opposite the hotel was a barren little park, as wretched as only the park of a dirty little town can be, but for Tereza it had always been an island of beauty: it had grass, four poplars, benches, a weeping willow, and a few forsythia bushes.

He was sitting on a yellow bench that afforded a clear view of the restaurant entrance. The very same bench she had sat on the day before with a book in her lap! She knew then (the birds of fortuity had begun alighting on her shoulders) that this stranger was her fate. He called out to her, invited her to sit next to him. (The crew of her soul rushed up to the deck of her body.) Then she walked him to the station, and he gave her his card as a farewell gesture. 'If ever you should happen to come to Prague...'

16

Much more than the card he slipped her at the last minute, it was the implication of all those fortuities (the book, Beethoven, the number six, the park bench) that gave her the courage to leave home and take her fate into her own hands. It may well be those few fortuities (quite modest, by the way, even drab, just what one would expect from so lack-lustre a town) that set her love in motion and provided her with a source of energy she had not yet exhausted at the end of her days.

Our day-to-day life is bombarded with fortuities or, to be more precise, with the accidental meetings of people and events we call coincidences. 'Coincidence' means that two events unexpectedly happen at the same time; they meet: Tomas appears in the hotel restaurant at the same time as the radio is playing Beethoven. We do not even notice the great majority of such coincidences. If the seat Tomas occupied had been occupied instead by the local butcher, Tereza never would have noticed that the radio was playing Beethoven (though the meeting of Beethoven and the butcher would also have been an interesting coincidence). But her nascent love inflamed her sense of beauty, and she would never forget that music. Whenever she heard it, she would be touched. Everything going on around her at that moment would bask in the glow of the music and take on its beauty.

Early in the novel that Tereza clutched under her arm when she went to visit Tomas, Anna meets Vronsky in curious circumstances: they are at the railway station when someone is run over by a train. At the end of the novel, Anna throws herself under a train. This symmetrical composition—the same motif appears at the beginning and at the end—may seem quite 'novelistic' to you, and I am willing to agree, but only on condition that you refrain from reading such notions as 'fictive,' 'fabricated,' and 'untrue to life' into the word 'novelistic.' Because human lives are composed in precisely such a fashion.

They are composed like music. Guided by his sense of beauty, an individual transforms a chance occurrence (Beethoven's music, a suicide at the railway station) into a motif, which then assumes a permanent place in the composition of the individual's life. Anna could have chosen another way to take her life. But the motif of death and the railway station, unforgettably bound to the birth of love, enticed her in her hour of despair with its dark beauty. Without realizing it, the individual composes her life according to the laws of beauty even in times of greatest distress.

It is wrong, then, to chide the novel for being fascinated by mysterious coincidences (like the meeting of Anna, Vronsky, the railway station, and death or the meeting of Beethoven, Tomas, Tereza, and the cognac), but it is right to chide man for being blind to such coincidences in his daily life. For he thereby deprives his life of a dimension of beauty.

17

Impelled by the birds of fortuity fluttering down on her shoulders, she took a week's leave and, without a word to her mother, boarded the train to Prague. During the journey, she made frequent trips to the toilet to look in the mirror and beg her soul not to abandon for a moment the deck of her body on this most crucial day of her life. Scrutinizing herself on one such trip, she had a sudden scare: she felt a scratch in her throat. Could she be coming down with something on this most crucial day of her life?

But there was no turning back. So she phoned him from the station, and the moment he opened the door, her stomach started rumbling terribly. She was mortified. She felt as though she were carrying her mother in her stomach and her mother had guffawed to spoil her meeting with Tomas.

For the first few seconds she was afraid he would throw her out on account of the crude noices she was making, but then he put his arms around her. She was grateful to him for ignoring her rumbles, and kissed him passionately, her eyes misting. Before the first minute was up, they were making love. She screamed while making love. She had a fever by then. She had come down with the flu.

When she travelled to Prague a second time, it was with a heavy suitcase. She had packed all her things, determined never again to return to the small town. He had invited her to come to his place the following evening. That night, she had slept in a cheap hotel. In the morning, she carried her heavy suitcase to the station, left it there, and roamed the streets of Prague the whole day with *Anna Karenina* under her arm. Not even after she rang the doorbell and he opened the door would she part with it. It was like a ticket into Tomas's world. She realized she had nothing but that miserable ticket and the thought brought her nearly to tears. To keep from crying, she talked non-stop in a raucous voice; and she laughed. And again he took her in his arms almost at once and they made love. She had entered a mist in which nothing could be seen and only her scream could be heard.

18

It was no sigh, no moan; it was a real scream. She screamed so hard that Tomas had to turn his head away from her face, afraid that her voice so close to his ear would rupture his eardrum. The scream was not an expression of sensuality. Sensuality is the total mobilization of the senses: an individual observes his or her partner intently, straining to catch every sound. But her scream aimed at crippling the senses, preventing all seeing and hearing. What was screaming in fact was the naive idealism of her love trying to banish all contradictions, banish the duality of body and soul, banish perhaps even time.

Were her eyes closed? No, but they were not looking anywhere. She kept them fixed on the void of the ceiling. At times she twisted her head violently from side to side.

When the scream died down, she fell asleep at his side, clutching his hand. She held his hand all night.

Even at the age of eight she would fall asleep by pressing one hand into the other and making believe she was holding the hand of the man whom she loved, the man of her life. So if in her sleep she pressed Tomas's hand with tenacity, we can understand why: she had been training for it since childhood.

19

'I want to make love to you in my studio. It will be like a stage surrounded by people. The audience won't be allowed up close, but they won't be able to take their eyes off us...'

As time passed, the image lost some of its original cruelty and began to excite Tereza. She started whispering the details to him while they made love.

Then it occurred to her that there might be a way to avoid the condemnation she saw in Tomas's infidelities: all he had to do was take her along, take her with him when he went to see his mistresses!

Maybe then her body would again become the first and only among all the others. Her body would become his second, his assistant, his alter ego. 'I'll undress them for you, give them a bath, bring them in to you,' she would whisper to him as they pressed together. She yearned for the two of them to merge into a hermaphrodite. Then the other women's bodies would be their play-things.

20

Oh, to be the alter ego of his polygamous life! Tomas refused to understand, but she could not get it out of her head, and tried to cultivate her friendship with Sabina. Tereza began by offering to do a series of photographs of her, portraits.

Sabina invited her to her studio, and at last she saw the spacious room and its centrepiece: the large, square, platform-like bed.

'I feel awful you've never been here before', said Sabina, as she showed her the pictures leaning against the wall. She even pulled out an old canvas, an ironworks under construction, which she had done during her schooldays, a period when the strictest realism had been required of all students (art that was not realistic was said to sap the foundations of socialism). In the spirit of the wager she had tried to be stricter than her teachers and had painted in a style concealing the brush strokes and closely resembling colour photography.

Next to the bed stood a small table, and on the table the model of a human head, the kind hairdressers put wigs on. Sabina's wig-stand sported a bowler hat rather than a wig. 'It used to belong to my grandfather,' she said with a smile.

It was the kind of hat—black, hard, round—that Tereza had seen only on the screen, the kind of hat Chaplin wore. She smiled back, picked it up, and after studying it for a time, said, 'Would you like me to take your picture in it?'

Sabina laughed for a long time at the idea. Tereza put down the bowler hat, picked up her camera, and starting taking pictures.

When she had been at it for almost an hour, she suddenly said, 'What would you say to some nude shots?'

'Nude shots?' Sabina laughed.

'Yes', said Tereza, repeating her proposal more boldly, 'nude shots.'

'That calls for a drink', said Sabina, and opened a bottle of wine.

Tereza felt her body going weak; she was suddenly tongue-tied. Sabina, meanwhile, strode back and forth, wine in hand, going on about her grandfather, who'd been the mayor of a small town; Sabina had never known him; all he'd left behind was this bowler hat and a picture showing a raised platform with several small-town dignitaries on it; one of them was Grandfather; it wasn't at all clear what they were doing up there on the platform; maybe they were officiating at some ceremony, unveiling a monument to a fellow dignitary who had also once worn a bowler hat at public ceremonies.

Sabina went on and on about the bowler hat and her grandfather until, emptying her third glass, she said, 'I'll be right back' and disappeared into the bathroom.

She came out in her bathrobe. Tereza picked up her camera and put it to her eye. Sabina threw open the robe.

21

The camera served Tereza as both a mechanical eye through which to observe Tomas's mistress and a veil by which to conceal her face from her.

It took Sabina some time before she could bring herself to slip out of the robe entirely. The situation she found herself in was proving a bit more difficult than she had expected. After several minutes of posing, she went up to Tereza and said, 'Now it's my turn to take your picture. Strip.'

Sabina had heard the command 'Strip!' so many times from Tomas that it was engraved in her memory. And so, Tomas's mistress had just given Tomas's command to Tomas's wife. The two women were joined by the same magic word. That was Tomas's way of unexpectedly turning an innocent conversation with a woman into an erotic situation. Instead of stroking, flattering, pleading, he would issue a command, issue it abruptly, unexpectedly, softly yet firmly and authoritatively, and at a distance: at such moments he never touched the woman he was addressing. He often used it on Tereza as well, and even though he said it softly, even though he whispered it, it was a command, and obeying never failed to arouse her. Hearing the word now made her desire to obey even stronger, because doing a stranger's bidding is a special madness, a madness all the more heady in this case because the command came not from a man but from a woman.

Sabina took the camera away from her, and Tereza took off her clothes. There she stood before Sabina naked and disarmed. Literally *disarmed:* deprived of the apparatus she had been using to cover her face, and aim at Sabina like a weapon. She was completely at the mercy of Tomas's mistress. This beautiful submission intoxicated Tereza. She wished that the moments she stood naked opposite Sabina would never end.

I imagine that Sabina, too, felt the strange enchantment of the situation: her lover's wife standing oddly compliant and timorous before her. But after clicking the shutter two or three times, almost frightened by the enchantment and eager to dispel it, she burst into loud laughter.

Tereza followed suit, and the two of them got dressed.

22

All previous crimes of the Russian empire had been committed under the cover of a discreet shadow. The deportation of a million Lithuanians, the murder of hundreds of thousands of Poles, the liquidation of the Crimean Tatars remain in our memory, but no photographic documentation exists; sooner or later they will therefore be proclaimed as mystifications. Not so the 1968 invasion of Czechoslovakia, of which both stills and motion pictures are kept in archives throughout the world.

Czech photographers and cameramen were acutely aware that they were the ones who could best do the only thing left to do: preserve the face of violence for the distant future. Seven days in a row, Tereza roamed the streets, photographing Russian soldiers and officers in compromising situations. The Russians did not know what to do. They had been carefully briefed about how to behave if someone fired at them or threw stones, but they had received no directives about what to do when someone aimed a lens.

She shot roll after roll and handed about half of them, undeveloped, to foreign journalists (the borders were still open, and reporters passing through were grateful for any kind of document). Many of her photographs turned up in the Western press. They were pictures of tanks, of threatening fists, of houses destroyed, of corpses covered with bloodstained red-white-and-blue Czech flags, of young men on motorcycles racing full speed around the tanks and waving Czech flags on long staffs, of young girls in unbelievably short skirts provoking the miserable sexually-famished Russian soldiers by kissing random passers-by before their eyes. As I have said, the Russian invasion was not only a tragedy; it was a carnival of hate filled with a curious (and no longer explicable) euphoria.

23

She took some fifty prints with her to Switzerland, prints she had made herself with all the care and skill she could muster. She offered them to a high-circulation illustrated magazine. The editor gave her a kind reception (all Czechs still wore the halo of their misfortune, and the good Swiss were touched); he offered her a seat, looked through the prints, praised them, and explained that because a certain time had elapsed since the events, they hadn't the slightest chance ('not that they aren't very beautiful!') of being published.

'But it's not over yet in Prague!' she protested, and tried to explain to him in her bad German that at this very moment, even with the country occupied, with everything against them, workers' councils were forming in the factories, the students were going out on strike demanding the departure of the Russians, and the whole country was saying aloud what it thought. 'That's what's so unbelievable! And nobody here cares anymore.'

The editor was glad when an energetic woman came into the office, and interrupted the conversation. The woman handed him a folder and said, 'Here's the nudist beach article.'

The editor was delicate enough to fear that a Czech who photographed tanks would find pictures of naked people on a beach frivolous. He laid the folder at the far end of the desk and quickly said to the woman, 'How would you like to meet a Czech colleague of yours? She's brought me some marvellous pictures.'

The woman shook Tereza's hand and picked up her photographs. 'Have a look at mine in the meantime,' she said.

Tereza leaned over to the folder and took out the pictures.

Almost apologetically, the editor said to Tereza, 'Of course they're completely different from your pictures.'

'Not at all,' said Tereza. 'They're the same.'

Neither the editor nor the photographer understood her, and even I find it difficult to explain what she had in mind when she compared a nude beach to the Russian invasion. Looking through the pictures, she stopped for a time at one that showed a family of four standing in a circle: a naked mother leaning over her children, her giant tits hanging low like a goat's or cow's, and the husband leaning the same way on the other side, his penis and scrotum also looking very much like an udder, in miniature.

'You don't like them, do you?' asked the editor.

'They're good photographs.'

'She's shocked by the subject matter,' said the woman. 'I can tell just by looking at you that you've never set foot on a nude beach.'

'No,' said Tereza.

The editor smiled. 'You see how easy it is to guess where you're from? The Communist countries are awfully puritanical.'

'There's nothing wrong with the naked body,' the woman said, with maternal affection. 'It's normal. And everything normal is beautiful!'

24

The woman photographer invited Tereza to the magazine's cafeteria for a cup of coffee. 'Those pictures of yours, they're very interesting. I couldn't help noticing what a terrific sense of the female body you have. You know what I mean. The girls with the provocative poses!'

'The ones kissing passers-by in front of the Russian tanks?'

'Yes. You'd be a top-notch fashion photographer, you know? You'd have to get yourself a model first, someone like you who's looking for a break. Then you could make a portfolio of photographs and show them to the agencies. It would take some time before you made a name for yourself, naturally, but I can do one thing for you here and now: introduce you to the editor in charge of our garden section. He might need some shots of cactuses and roses and things.'

'Thank you very much,' Tereza said sincerely, because it was clear that the woman sitting opposite her was full of good will.

But then she said to herself, Why take pictures of cactuses? She had no desire to go through in Zurich what she'd been through in Prague: battles over job and career, over every picture published. She had never been ambitious out of vanity. All she had ever wanted was to escape from her mother's world. Yes, she saw it with absolute clarity: no matter how enthusiastic she was about taking pictures, she could just as easily have turned her enthusiasm to any other endeavour. Photography was nothing but a way of getting at 'something higher' and living beside Tomas.

She said, 'My husband is a doctor. He can support me. I don't need to take pictures.'

The woman photographer replied, 'I don't see how you can give it up after the beautiful work you've done.'

Yes, the pictures of the invasion were something else again. She had not done them for Thomas. She had done them out of passion. But not passion for photography. She had done them out of passionate hatred. The situation would never recur. And these photographs, which she had made out of passion, were the ones nobody wanted because they were out of date. Only cactuses had perennial appeal. And cactuses were of no interest to her.

She said, 'You're too kind, really, but I'd rather stay at home. I don't need a job.'

The woman said, 'But will you be fulfilled sitting at home?'

Tereza said, 'More fulfilled than by taking pictures of cactuses.'

The woman said, 'Even if you take pictures of cactuses, you're leading *your* life. If you live only for your husband, you have no life of your own.'

All of a sudden Tereza felt annoyed: 'My husband is my life, not cactuses.'

70

The woman photographer responded in kind: 'You mean you think of yourself as happy?'

Tereza, still annoyed, said, 'Of course I'm happy!'

The woman said, 'The only kind of woman who can say that is very...' She stopped short.

Tereza finished it for her: '...limited. That's what you mean, isn't it?'

The woman regained control of herself and said, 'Not limited. Anachronistic.'

'You're right,' said Tereza wistfully. 'That's just what my husband says about me.'

25

She was at home alone. Tomas spent days on end at the hospital. At least she had Karenin and could take him on long walks. Home again, she would pore over her German and French grammars. But she felt sad and had trouble concentrating. She kept coming back to the speech Dubcek had given over the radio after his return from Moscow. Although she had completely forgotten what he said, she could still hear his quivering voice. She thought about how foreign soldiers had arrested him, the head of an independent state, in his own country, held him for four days somewhere in the Ukrainian mountains, informed him he was to be shot—as, twelve years before, they had shot his Hungarian predecessor Imre Nagy—then packed him off to Moscow, ordered him to have a bath and shave, to change his clothes and put on a tie, apprised him of the decision to commute his execution, instructed him to consider himself head of state once more, sat him at a table opposite Brezhnev, and forced him to act.

He returned, humiliated, to address his humiliated nation. He was so humiliated he could not even speak. Tereza would never forget those awful pauses in the middle of his sentences. Was he that exhausted? Ill? Had they drugged him? Or was it only despair? If nothing was to remain of Dubcek, then at least those awful long pauses when he seemed unable to breathe, gasping for air before a whole nation glued to its radios, at least those pauses would remain. Those pauses contained all the horror that had descended on their country.

It was the seventh day of the invasion. She heard the speech in the editorial offices of a newspaper that had been transformed overnight into an organ of the resistance. Everyone present hated Dubcek at that moment. They reproached him for compromising; they felt humiliated by his humiliation; his weakness offended them.

Thinking back to those days, she no longer felt any aversion to the man. The word 'weak' no longer sounded like a verdict. Any man confronted with superior strength is weak, even a man of Dubcek's athletic build. The very weakness that had seemed unbearable, repulsive, to them at the time, the weakness that had driven Tereza and Tomas from the country, suddenly attracted her. She realized that she too belonged among the weak, in the camp of the weak, in the country of the weak, and that because they were weak and gasped for air in the middle of a sentence she owed them her allegiance.

She felt attracted by this weakness as by vertigo. She felt attracted by it because she felt weak herself. Again she began to feel jealous and again her hands shook. When Tomas noticed it, he did what he usually did: he took her hands in his and tried to calm them by pressing hard. She tore them away from him.

'What's the matter?' he asked.

'Nothing.'

'What do you want me to do for you?'

'I want you to be old. Ten years older. Twenty years older!'

What she meant was: I want you to be weak. As weak as I am.

26

Karenin was not overjoyed by the move to Switzerland. Karenin hated change. Dog time cannot be plotted along a straight line; it does not move on and on, from one thing to the next. It moves in a circle like the hands of a clock, turning round and round day in and day out following the same path. In Prague, when Tomas and Tereza bought a new chair or moved a flower pot, Karenin would look on in displeasure. It disturbed his sense of time. It was as though they were trying to dupe the hands of the clock by changing the numbers on its face.

He was the time-piece of their lives. One day when they came back from a walk, the phone was ringing. She picked up the receiver.

It was a woman's voice speaking German and asking for Tomas. It was an impatient voice, and Tereza felt it had a ring of derision to it. When she said that Tomas wasn't there and she didn't know when he'd be back, the woman on the other end of the line started laughing. Then she hung up without saying good-bye.

Tereza knew it did not mean a thing. It could have been a nurse from the hospital, a patient, a secretary, anyone. But still she was upset and was unable to concentrate on anything. It was then she realized she had lost the last bit of strength she had had at home: she was absolutely incapable of tolerating this absolutely insignificant incident.

Being in a foreign country means walking a tightrope high above the ground without the net you have in your homeland—the net of family, colleagues, friends and where you can easily say what you have to say in a language you have known from childhoood. In Prague she was dependent on Tomas only when it came to the heart; here she was dependent on him for everything. What would happen to her here if he abandoned her? Would she have to live her whole life in fear of losing him?

She told herself: their acquaintance had been based on a fallacy from the start. The copy of *Anna Karenina* under her arm amounted to false papers; it had given Tomas the wrong idea. In spite of their love, they had made each other's life a hell. The fact that they loved each other was merely proof that the fault lay not in themselves, in their behaviour or any inconstancy of feeling, but rather in their incompatibility, because he was strong and she was weak. She was like Dubcek, who made a thirty-second pause in the middle of a sentence; she was like her country, which stuttered, gasped for breath, could not speak.

But when the strong were too weak to hurt the weak, the weak had to be strong enough to leave.

And having told herself all this, she pressed her face against Karenin's furry head and said, 'Sorry, Karenin. It looks as though you're going to have to move again.'

27

Sitting crushed into a corner of the train compartment with her heavy suitcase above her head and Karenin squeezed against her legs, she kept thinking about the cook at the hotel restaurant where she had worked when she lived with her mother. The cook would take every opportunity to give her a slap on the behind, and never tired of asking her in front of everyone when she would give in and go to bed with him. It was odd that he was the one who came to mind. He had always been the prime example of everything she loathed. And now all she could think of was looking him up and telling him, 'You used to say you wanted to sleep with me. Well, here I am.'

She longed to do something drastic, burn her boats. She longed to enact the brutal destruction of the past seven years of her life. It was vertigo. A heady, insuperable longing to fall.

We might also call vertigo the intoxication of the weak. Aware of his weakness, a man decides to give in rather than stand up to it. He is drunk with weakness, wishes to grow even weaker, wishes to fall down in the middle of the main square, in front of everybody, wishes to be down, lower than down.

She tried to talk herself into settling outside Prague and giving up her profession as a photographer. She would go back to the small town from which Tomas's voice had once lured her.

But once in Prague, she found she had to spend some time taking care of various practical matters, and began putting off her departure.

On the fifth day, Tomas suddenly turned up. Karenin jumped all over him, so it was a while before they had to make any overtures to each other.

They felt they were standing on a snow-covered plain, shivering with cold.

Then they moved together like lovers who had never kissed before.

'Has everything been all right?' he asked.

'Yes,' she answered.

'Have you been to the magazine?'
'I've given them a call.'
'Well?'
'Nothing yet. I've been waiting.'
'For what?'
She made no response. She could not tell him she had been waiting for him.

28

Now we return to a moment we already know about. Tomas was desperately unhappy and had a bad stomach-ache. He did not fall asleep until very late at night.

Soon thereafter Tereza awoke. (There were Russian airplanes circling over Prague, and it was impossible to sleep for the noise.) Her first thought was that he had come back because of her. Because of her, he had changed his destiny. Now he would no longer be responsible for her: now she was responsible for him.

The responsibility, she felt, seemed to require more strength than she could muster.

But all at once she recalled that just before he had appeared at the door of their flat the day before, the church bells had chimed six o'clock. On the day they first met, her shift had ended at six. She saw him sitting there in front of her on the yellow bench and heard the bells in the belfry chime six.

No, it was not superstition. It was a sense of beauty that cured her of her depression and imbued her with a new will to live. The birds of fortuity had alighted once more on her shoulders. There were tears in her eyes, and she was unutterably happy to hear him breathing at her side.

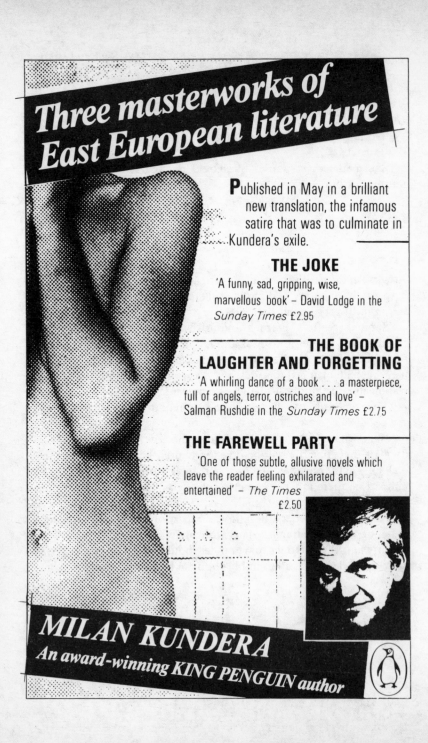

MILAN KUNDERA

SOMEWHERE BEHIND

> Poets don't invent poems
> The poem is somewhere behind
> It's been there for a long long time
> The poet discovers it only
>
> Jan Skacel

1

In one of his books, my friend Josef Skvorecky tells a true story. Several years ago, an engineer from Prague was invited to a conference in London. So he went, took part in the proceedings, and returned to Prague. Some hours after his return, sitting in his office, he picked up *Rude Pravo*—the official daily paper of the Czech Party—and read the following: 'A Czech engineer, attending a conference in London, has made a statement to the Western press which is slanderous to his socialist homeland, and he has decided to stay in the West.'

Illegal emigration combined with a statement of that kind is no trifle. It would be worth about twenty years in gaol. Our engineer can't believe his eyes. But there's no doubt about it, the article refers to him. His secretary, coming into his office, is horrified to see him: 'My God, you've come back! I can't understand—have you seen what's been written about you?'

Our engineer has seen fear in his secretary's eyes. What can he do? He rushes to the *Rude Pravo* office. He finds the journalist concerned, who offers his excuses, saying that, yes, it is a really awkward business, but that he, the journalist, has nothing to do with it—he got the text of the article direct from the Ministry for the Interior.

So the engineer goes off to the Ministry. There they say yes, of course, it's all a mistake, but that they, the Ministry, have nothing to do with it: they got the report on the engineer from their intelligence service at the London embassy. The engineer asks for a retraction. No, he's told, retractions aren't ever made, but he should rest assured that nothing can happen to him; he need have no worries.

But our engineer *is* worried. He soon realizes that all of a sudden he's being closely watched, that his telephone is being tapped and that he's being followed in the street. He can't sleep. He has nightmares until, unable to bear the pressure any longer, he takes a lot of real risks to leave the country illegally. And that's how he became a real émigré.

2

The story I've just told (an almost banal story for anyone in Prague today) is one that we could immediately call 'Kafkaesque'. This term, drawn from a work of art and based on a novelist's images, stands out as the only common denominator of (real and fictional) situations that no other word allows us to apprehend and to which neither political nor social nor psychological science give us any key.

But what is 'Kafkaesque'? Let's try to describe some aspects of the phenomenon.

One: Our engineer is confronted by an authority characterized by an *unending labyrinth*. He can never get to the end of its interminable corridors and will never succeed in finding out who issued the fatal sentence. He is therefore in the same situation as Joseph K. in front of the court, or the surveyor K. before the castle. All three are in a world which is nothing other than a single, huge, labyrinthine institution which they cannot escape and which they cannot understand.

Novelists before Kafka often unmasked institutions as arenas where conflicts between different personal and public interests were played out. In Kafka, however, the institution is a mechanism obeying its own laws. No one knows now who set up those laws, nor when they were set up; they have nothing to do with human interests and are thus unintelligible.

Two: In chapter V of *The Castle*, the village mayor explains in detail to K. the long history of his file. In short: about ten years before, a village representative proposed that the castle should call in a surveyor. The request was soon found to be groundless and a second petition was sent from the village to the castle to cancel the earlier proposal. Unfortunately, the second file was lost somewhere between the offices and was only found again many years later, just at the time K. received his invitation. So he arrived in the village by mistake. More than that: given that within the logic of the novel the castle and village constitute the only significant universe, K.'s whole existence is a mistake.

In the Kafkaesque world, the file has the role of a platonic ideal. It represents true reality, while man's physical existence is only a shadow thrown on to the screen of illusions. And in fact the surveyor K. and our engineer from Prague are but the shadows of their filing cards; and they are still much less than that: they are the shadows of a mistake in the file, shadows without even the right to exist as shadows.

But if man's life is only a shadow and if true reality lies elsewhere, in the realm of the inaccessible, or the inhuman or the superhuman, then we enter directly the domain of theology. Indeed, Kafka's first interpreters explained his novels as religious parables.

This kind of interpretation seems to me to be wrong (because it sees allegory where Kafka grasped the concrete situations of human life) but also revealing: wherever authority renders itself god-like, it automatically produces its own theology; wherever it behaves like God, it arouses religious feelings towards itself; such a world can be described in theological terms.

Kafka did not write religious allegories, but the Kafkaesque (in reality, in fiction) is inseparable from its theological (or rather: *pseudo-theological*) dimension.

Three: Dostoevsky's Raskolnikov cannot bear the weight of his guilt and, to find peace, consents of his own free will to his punishment. It's the well-known situation of *the fault seeking the punishment.*

In Kafka, the logic is reversed. The punished does not know the reason for the punishment. The absurdity of the punishment is so unbearable that to find peace the person accused needs to find a justification for his penalty: *punishment seeks the fault.*

Our engineer from Prague is punished by intensive police surveillance. This punishment calls out for a crime that was not committed, and the engineer accused of emigrating ends up emigrating in fact. *The punishment finds the fault in the end.*

Not knowing what the charges against him are, K., in chapter VII of *The Trial*, decides to examine his whole life, his entire past 'down to the smallest details'. The mechanism of 'self-accusation'—the psychological mechanism that implants a feeling of guilt in an innocent person—has been put into motion. I would call this mechanism 'culpabilization'. *The accused seeks his crime.*

One day, Amalia in *The Castle* receives an obscene letter from a castle official. She tears it up in outrage. The castle doesn't even need to criticize Amalia's rash behaviour. Fear (the same fear our engineer saw in his secretary's eyes) acts all by itself. Without any order or noticeable signal from the castle, everyone avoids Amalia's family as if it were infected with the plague.

Amalia's father tries to defend his family. But there is a problem: not only is the maker of the judgement unfindable, but the judgement itself does not exist! To appeal, to request a pardon, you have to be convicted first! The father begs the castle to proclaim the crime. It's an understatement to say that the punishment seeks the crime. In this pseudo-theological world, *the punished beseech recognition of their guilt!*

It often happens in Prague nowadays that a disgraced person cannot find even the smallest job. He asks in vain for certification of the fact that he has committed a crime and that his employment is forbidden. The judgement is nowhere to be found. And since in Prague work is a duty laid down by law, he ends up being charged with 'scrounging'; that means he is guilty of avoiding work. *The punishment finds the crime.*

Four: The story of our engineer from Prague is like a humorous story, a joke: it provokes laughter.

Two gentlemen, perfectly ordinary chaps (not 'inspectors' as some translations would have us believe) surprise Joseph K. in bed one morning, tell him he is arrested, and eat his breakfast for him. K. is a well-disciplined civil servant: instead of throwing the men out of his flat, he stands in his nightgown and gives a lengthy self-defence. When Kafka read the first chapter of *The Trial* to his friends, everyone, including the author, laughed.

Philip Roth imagined a film version of *The Castle:* he saw Groucho Marx playing the surveyor K., with Chico and Harpo as his two assistants. Yes, he was quite correct: comedy is inseparable from the very essence of the Kafkaesque.

But it's small comfort to the engineer to know that his story is funny. He is trapped in the joke of his own life like a fish in a bowl, and he doesn't find it funny. Of course a joke is only a joke if you're outside the bowl; the Kafkaesque takes us inside, into the innards of a joke, into the *horror of comedy*.

In the world of the Kafkaesque, comedy is not a counterpoint to tragedy as in Shakespeare; it's not there to make the tragic more bearable by lightening the tone; it doesn't *accompany* the tragic, not at all: rather it *destroys it in the egg* and deprives the victims of the only consolation they could hope for—the consolation deriving from the (real or supposed) grandeur of tragedy. The engineer loses his homeland, and everyone laughs.

3

There are periods of modern history when life resembles the novels of Kafka.

As soon as the philosopher Karel Kosik was accused of counter-revolutionary activities and expelled from Charles University, crowds of admiring young women besieged his small flat in Castle Square. Kosik ('Professor K.K.' to his friends) had never been a playboy or a ladies' man; and the complete change in his sex life after the Russian invasion prompted me to question a hairdresser in love with him. Half-joking, half-serious, she told me: 'All defendants are handsome'.

That was a direct and conscious allusion to Leni, in *The Trial*, who uses those words to explain her erotic interest in the clients of the lawyer Huld, for whom she works. Max Brod cites this passage in support of the religious interpretation of Kafka: K. becomes more handsome because he begins to understand his fault; penitence gives him beauty. The hairdresser would have laughed if she'd had this theory put to her. 'Professor K.K.' was beautiful without the slightest penitence.

I mention my dearest friend only to demonstrate the extent to which the images, situations and even the individual sentences of Kafka's novels are part of life in Prague.

Having said that, one might be tempted to think that Kafka's images are alive in Prague because they are anticipations of totalitarian society.

However, that claim requires correction: the notion of the Kafkaesque is not a sociological or a political one. Attempts have been made to explain Kafka's work as a critique of industrial society, of exploitation, alienation, of bourgeois morality—of capitalism, in a word. But there is almost nothing of what constitutes capitalism in Kafka's universe: money is absent, as is the power of money, together with trade, wage-employment, property, owners, and the class-struggle.

The Kafkaesque does not correspond to a definition of totalitarianism either. The party, ideology and its jargon, politics, the police and the army are all equally missing from Kafka's works.

We should rather say that the Kafkaesque represents one elementary potentiality of man and his world, a potentiality that is not historically determined and which accompanies man more or less eternally.

But these corrections have not dealt with the questions how it is possible that in Prague Kafka's novels merge with real life and why young hairdressers quote lines from *The Trial* to make sense of their desire. And how is it possible for the same novels to be read in Paris as the hermetic expression of an author's entirely subjective world-view? Does this mean that the potentiality of man and his world that is called Kafkaesque is more easily realized in concrete terms in Prague than in Paris?

There are tendencies in modern history which produce the Kafkaesque in the broader dimensions of society: the progressive concentration of power, increasing its propensity to self-deification; the bureaucratization of social activity, transforming all institutions into *unending labyrinths;* and, resulting from this, a growing dehumanization of the individual.

Totalitarian states, as extreme concentrations of these tendencies, have brought out the close relationship between Kafka's novels and real life. But if this relationship cannot easily be seen in the West, it's not only because democratic societies are less Kafkaesque than Prague today. It is also, it seems to me, because over here, inevitably, the sense of the real has been lost.

In fact democratic societies are also familiar with the processes of dehumanization and bureaucratization; the entire planet has become the theatre of such processes. Kafka's novels represent them in an imaginary, dreamlike hyperbole; a totalitarian state represents them in a prosaic and concrete hyperbole.

But why was Kafka the first novelist to grasp these trends, which impinged, explicitly and brutally, on the course of History, however, only after the novelist's death?

4

There are no essential traces of Franz Kafka's political interests. In that sense, he is a case apart from all his Prague friends, from Max Brod, Frans Werfel, Egon Erwin, and from all the avant-garde movements which, claiming to know the meaning of History, indulge in conjuring up the face of the future.

So how is it that it is not their works, but those of their solitary, introverted companion, preoccupied with his own life and his art, which can be received today as a socio-political prophecy, and are banned for that very reason in large parts of the world?

I thought of this mystery one day after I had witnessed a domestic scene in the family of an old friend of mine. The woman friend in question had been arrested in 1951 during the Stalinist trials in Prague, and convicted of crimes she hadn't committed. Hundreds of communists were in the same situation at that time. All their life they had identified themselves entirely with their Party. When it suddenly became their prosecutor, they agreed like Joseph K. 'to examine their whole life, their entire past, down to the smallest details' to find the hidden fault and, in the end, to confess to imaginary crimes. My friend managed to save her own life because she had the extraordinary courage to refuse to undertake (as her comrades undertook) the 'search for her fault'. Refusing to assist her persecutors, she became unusable for the final show trial.

So instead of hanging she got away with life imprisonment. After fifteen years she was completely rehabilitated, and released.

This woman had a one-year old child when she was arrested. On release from prison she thus found a sixteen-year-old son, and had the joy of sharing her lonely, modest life with him from then on. That she became passionately attached to the boy is entirely comprehensible. When I went to see them one day, her son was already twenty-six. The mother, hurt and angry, was crying. The cause was utterly trivial—the son had overslept, or something like that. I asked the mother: 'Why get so upset over such nonsense? Is it worth crying over? Aren't you overdoing it?'

It was the son who answered for his mother: 'No, my mother's not overdoing it. My mother is a splendid, brave woman. She resisted when everyone else cracked. She wants me to become a real man. It's true, I overslept, but what my mother reproaches me for is something much deeper. It's my attitude. My selfish attitude. I want to become what my mother wants me to be. And with you as witness, I promise her I will.'

What the party never managed to do with the mother, the mother had managed to do to her son. She had forced him to identify himself with an absurd accusation, 'to seek his fault', to make a public confession. I looked on, dumbfounded, at this scene from a Stalinist mini-trial, and I understood all at once that the psychological mechanisms engaged in great (apparently incredible and inhuman) historical events are the same as those which regulate (quite ordinary and human) domestic situations.

5

The celebrated letter that Kafka wrote and never sent to his father shows very well that he derived his knowledge of the *guilt-inducing techniques*, which became a major theme of his fiction, from the family, from the relationship between the child and the deified power of the parents. In 'The Judgement', a short story intimately bound up with the author's experience of his family, the father accuses the son and commands him to drown himself. The son accepts his fictitious guilt and throws himself into the river as submissively as, in a later work, his successor Joseph K., convicted by a mysterious organization, has his own throat cut. The similarity between the two charges, the two inducements of guilt and the two executions, reveals the link which runs unbroken from Kafka's domestic, familial 'totalitarianism' to his great social visions.

Totalitarian society, especially in its more extreme versions, tends to abolish the boundary between public and private domains. Authority, as it grows ever more opaque, requires the lives of citizens to be entirely transparent. The ideal of *life without secrets* corresponds to the ideal of the exemplary family: a citizen does not have the right to hide anything at all from the Party, or the State, just as a child has no right to keep a secret from his father or his mother. Totalitarian societies project an idyllic smile in their propaganda: they want to be seen as 'one big family'.

It's often been said that Kafka's novels express a passionate desire for community and human contact; it seems that the rootless being who is K. has a single goal—to overcome the curse of solitude. This interpretation is not only facile and reductive, it also turns sense on its head.

The surveyor K. is not in the least out to win people over, does not seek warmth and does not want to become 'a man among men', like Sartre's Orestes. He wants acceptance not from a community but from an institution. To have it, he must pay a high price: he must renounce his solitude. This then is his hell: he is never alone, the two assistants sent by the castle follow him always. When he first makes love with Frida, the two men are there, sitting on the café counter over the lovers, and from then on are never absent from the lovers' bed.

Not the curse of solitude, but the violation of solitude, is Kafka's obsession!

Karl Rossemann is for ever disturbed by everyone else. His clothes are sold; his only snapshot of his parents is taken away; in the dormitory, beside his bed, boys fight and now and again fall on top of him; two hooligans, Robinson and Delaroche, force him to live with them, so that big Brunelda's sighs thunder through his sleep.

Joseph K.'s story also begins with the raping of privacy: two unknown men come to arrest him in bed. From that day on, he never feels alone: the court follows him, watches him, talks to him; his private life disappears bit by bit, swallowed up by the mysterious organization on his heels.

Lyrical souls who like to preach the abolition of secrets and the transparency of private life do not realize what is the nature of the process they are unleashing. The starting-point of totalitarianism resembles the beginning of *The Trial*: you'll be taken unawares in your bed. They'll come just like your father and mother used to.

People often wonder whether Kafka's novels are projections of the author's most personal and private conflicts, or descriptions of an objective 'social machine'. What is Kafkaesque is not restricted either to the private or to the public domain: it encompasses both. The public is the mirror of the private, the private reflects the public.

6

When I refer to microsocial practices which generate the Kafkaesque, I think not only of family life but also of the organization in which Kafka spent all his adult life: the office.

Kafka's heroes are often seen as allegorical projections of the intellectual, but there's nothing intellectual about Gregor Samsa. When he wakes up metamorphosed into a beetle, his one worry is: in this new state, how to get to the office on time. In his head he has nothing but the obedience and discipline to which his profession has accustomed him. He's a functionary, a clerk, an *employee* as are all Kafka's characters, an employee not just in the sense of a sociological type (as in the manner of a writer like Zola), but as a human potentiality, as an attitude, as a way of grasping the world.

In this bureaucratic world there is no initiative, no invention, no freedom of action, there are only orders and rules: *it is the world of obedience.*

Also, the bureaucratic clerk carries out a small part of a larger administrative action whose aim and horizons he cannot see: *it is the world where gestures have become mechanical* and where people do not know the meaning of what they do.

Finally, the bureaucratic clerk deals only with nameless persons and with files: *it is the world of the abstract*.

To place a novel in this world of obedience, of the mechanical and the abstract, where the only human adventure is to move from one office to another, seems to run counter to the very essence of epic poetry. Thus the question: how has Kafka managed to metamorphose such dull, grey and anti-poetical material into entrancing fictions?

The answer can be found in a letter the novelist wrote to Milena: 'The office is not a stupid institution; it's more in the realm of the fantastic than the stupid.' The sentence conceals one of Kafka's greatest secrets. He saw what no one could see: not only the capital importance of the bureaucratic phenomenon for man, for his condition and for his future, but also (even more surprisingly) the poetic potential contained in the fantastic aspect of the office organization.

But what does it mean: bureaucracy belongs to the realm of the fantastic?

Our engineer from Prague would understand. A mistake in his file propelled him to London; so he wandered around Prague as a veritable *phantom*, seeking his *lost body*, while the offices he visited seemed like an *interminable labyrinth* from some unknown *mythology*.

Thanks to the fantastic he saw in the bureaucratic world, Kafka succeeded in doing what had seemed unimaginable before: he transformed the profoundly anti-poetic material of a highly bureaucratized society into the great poetry of the novel; he transformed a very ordinary story of a man who cannot obtain a promised job (which is, in fact, all the story of *The Castle*) into myth, into epic, into unknown beauty.

By his expansion of a bureaucratic setting to the gigantic dimensions of a universe, Kafka succeeded, without suspecting it for a moment, in creating an image which fascinates by its resemblance to a society that the novelist never knew and that is Prague today.

A totalitarian State is in fact a single, immense administration; and since all work in it is nationalized, everyone in every trade is an *employee*. A worker is not a worker, a judge is not a judge, a shopkeeper is not a shopkeeper, a priest is not a priest, but all are functionaries of the State. 'I belong to the court,' the priest says to Joseph, in the cathedral. Kafka's lawyers also work for the court. No one in Prague today is surprised by that. No one would get a better defence counsel than K. because, over there, lawyers do not work for defendants, but for the court.

7

In a cycle of one hundred quatrains which explore the gravest and most complex areas with an almost child-like simplicity, the great Czech poet Jan Skacel writes:

> Poets don't invent poems
> The poem is somewhere behind
> It's been there for a long long time
> The poet discovers it only.

For the poet, writing thus means breaking down a wall behind which something immutable (the 'poem') lies hidden in darkness. That's why, with this sudden unveiling, the 'poem' strikes us first as *blinding light*.

I read *The Castle* for the first time when I was fifteen and the book will never envelop me as fully again, even though all the vast understanding it contains (all the real import of the Kafkaesque) was not comprehensible to me at that time: but I was *blinded by light*.

Later on, my eyes adjusted to the light of the poem and I began to see my own lived experience in what had dazzled me; but the light hasn't disappeared.

'The poem,' says Jan Skacel, has been waiting for us, immutable, 'for a long long time.' However, in a world of perpetual change, is the immutable not a mere illusion?

No, it isn't. Any situation that is of man's doing can only contain what is contained in man; thus one can imagine that the situation (and all its metaphysical implications) has existed as a human potentiality 'for a long long time'.

But in that case, what does History (the non-immutable) represent for the poet?

In the eyes of the poet, strange as it may seem, History is in a position similar to the poet's own: History *invents* nothing, it *discovers*. In new situations, History reveals what man is, what has been in him 'for a long long time', what his potentialities are.

If the poem is already there, then it would be illogical to grant the poet the gift of *foresight:* no, he 'only discovers' a human potentiality (the 'poem' that has been there 'a long long time') that History will in its turn discover one day.

Kafka made no prophecies. All he did was to see what was 'somewhere behind'. He did not know that his seeing was also fore-seeing. He had no intention of unmasking a social system. He illuminated the mechanisms he knew from private and microsocial human practice, not suspecting that later developments would put those mechanisms into action in the great theatre of History.

The hypnotic eye of authority, the desperate search for one's own fault, exclusion and the anguish of being excluded, being condemned to conform, the ghostliness of reality and the magical reality of the bureaucratic file, the perpetual violation of private life, etc.—all these experiments which History has performed with man in its great laboratory, Kafka performed (some years earlier) in his novels.

There will always be something mysterious about the confluence of the real world of totalitarian states and Kafka's poems, and it will always bear witness to the poet's act being, in its very essence, incalculable—and paradoxical: the enormous social, political and 'prophetic' import of Kafka's novels lies precisely in their 'uncommittedness', that is to say in their total autonomy from all political programmes, ideological concepts and futurological prognoses.

Indeed, if instead of seeking 'the poem' hidden 'somewhere behind', the poet 'commits' himself to the service of a truth known from the outset (which offers itself as truth and lies 'before us'), then he has renounced the mission proper to poetry. And it matters little whether the preconceived truth is called revolution or dissidence,

Christian faith or atheism, whether it is more correct or less correct; a poet who serves any truth other than the truth *to be discovered* (which is *blinding light*) is a false poet.

If I hold so firmly to the inheritance of Kafka, if I defend it as my personal inheritance, it is not because I think it useful to imitate the inimitable (and to discover again the Kafkaesque) but because it is such a formidable example of the *radical autonomy* of the novel (of the poetry that is the novel). Thanks to that autonomy, Franz Kafka (or the great, forgotten Hermann Broch) has told us things about our human condition (as it reveals itself in our age) which no sociological or political reflection will ever be able to tell.

Translated from the French by David Bellos

MILAN KUNDERA
A KIDNAPPED WEST
OR
CULTURE BOWS OUT

1

In November 1956, the director of the Hungarian News Agency, shortly before his office was flattened by artillery fire, sent a telex to the entire world with a desperate message announcing that the Russian attack against Budapest had begun. The despatch ended with these words: 'We are going to die for Hungary and for Europe.'

What did this sentence mean? It certainly meant that the Russian tanks were endangering Hungary and with it all of Europe. But in what sense was Europe in danger? Were the Russian tanks also about to push past the Hungarian borders and into the West? No. The director of the Hungarian News Agency meant that the Russians, in attacking Hungary, were attacking Europe itself. He was ready to die so that Hungary might remain Hungary and European.

Even if the sense of the sentence seems clear, it continues to intrigue us. Actually, in France, in America, one is accustomed to thinking that what was at stake during the invasion was neither Hungary nor Europe but a political regime. One would never have said that Hungary as such had been threatened; still less would one ever understand why a Hungarian, faced with his own death, addressed Europe. When Solzhenitsyn denounces communist oppression, does he invoke Europe as a fundamental value worth dying for?

No. 'To die for one's country *and* for Europe'—that is a phrase that could not be thought in Moscow or Leningrad; it is precisely the phrase that could be thought in Budapest or Warsaw.

2

In fact, what does Europe mean to a Hungarian, a Czech, a Pole? Their nations have always belonged to the part of Europe rooted in Roman Christianity. They have participated in every period of its history. For them, the word 'Europe' does not represent a phenomenon of geography but a spiritual notion synonymous with the word 'West'. The moment Hungary is no longer European—

that is, no longer Western—it is driven from its own destiny, beyond its own history: it loses the essence of its identity.

'Geographic Europe' (extending from the Atlantic to the Ural Mountains) was always divided into two halves which evolved separately: one tied to ancient Rome and the Catholic Church; the other anchored in Byzantium and the Orthodox Church. After 1945, the border between the two Europes shifted several hundred kilometres to the west, and several nations that had always considered themselves to be Western woke up to discover that they were now in the East.[1]

As a result, three fundamental situations developed in Europe after the war: that of Western Europe; that of Eastern Europe; and, most complicated, that of that part of Europe situated geographically in the centre—culturally in the West and politically in the East.

The contradictions of the Europe I call Central help us to understand why during the last thirty-five years the drama of Europe has been concentrated there: the great Hungarian revolt in 1956 and the bloody massacre that followed; the Prague Spring and the occupation of Czechoslovakia in 1968; the Polish revolts of 1956, 1968, 1970 and of recent years. In terms of dramatic content and historical impact, nothing that has occurred in 'Geographic Europe', in the West or the East, can be compared with the succession of revolts in Central Europe. Every single one involved almost the entire population. And, in every case, each regime could not have defended itself for more than three hours, if it had not been backed by Russia. That said, we can no longer consider what took place in Prague or Warsaw in its essence as a drama of Eastern

---

[1] The responsibility of Central European communists who, after the war, did so much to set up totalitarian regimes in their countries, is enormous. But they would never have succeeded without the initiative, the violent pressure and the international power of Russia. Just after their victory, Central European communists understood that not they but the USSR was the master of their countries; from that point began the slow splitting up of Central European regimes and parties.

Europe, of the Soviet Bloc, of communism; it is a drama of the West—a West that, kidnapped, displaced, and brainwashed, nevertheless insists on defending its identity.

The identity of a people or civilization is always reflected and concentrated in what has been created by the mind—in what is known as 'culture'. If this identity is threatened with extinction, cultural life grows correspondingly more intense, more important, until culture itself becomes the living value around which all people rally. That's why, in each of the revolts in Central Europe—in which the actual extinction of a people was feared—the collective cultural memory and the contemporary creative output assumed roles so great and so decisive—far greater and far more decisive than they have been in any other mass-European revolt.[2]

It was a number of Hungarian writers, in a group named after the Romantic poet Petöfi, who undertook the massive critique that led the way to the explosion of 1956. It was the theatre, the films, the books and the texts of philosophy that, circulated in the years before 1968, led ultimately to the emancipation of the Prague Spring. And it was the banning of a play by Mickiewicz, the greatest Polish Romantic poet, that triggered the famous revolt of Polish students in 1968. This happy marriage of culture and life, of creative achievement and the people, has marked the revolts of central Europe with a beauty so inimitable that it will always cast a spell over those who lived through those times.

---

[2] For the outside observer this paradox is hard to understand; the period after 1945 is at once the most tragic for Central Europe and also one of the greatest in its cultural history. Whether in exile (Gombrowicz, Milosz), or under the form of clandestine creative activity (Czechoslovakia after 1968) or as an activity tolerated by the authorities under the pressure of public opinion—no matter under which of these circumstances—the films, the novels, the plays and the works of philosophy born in Central Europe during this period often reach the summits of European culture.

3

One could say: We'll admit that Central European countries are defending their threatened cultural traditions, but their situation is not unique. Russia is in a similar situation. It, too, is about to lose its identity. In fact, it's not Russia but communism that deprives nations of their essence, which, moreover, made the Russian people its first victim. True, the Russian language is suffocating the languages of the other nations in the Soviet Empire, but it's not because the Russians themselves want to 'Russianize' the others; it's because the Soviet bureaucracy—deeply a-national, anti-national, supra-national—needs a tool to unify its State.

I understand the logic. I also understand the predicament of the Russians who fear that their beloved homeland will be confused with detested communism.

But it is also necessary to understand the Pole, whose homeland, except for a brief period between the two world wars, has been subjugated by Russia for two centuries and has been, throughout, subjected to a 'Russianization'—the pressure to conform to being Russian—as patient as it has been implacable.

In Central Europe, the eastern border of the West, everyone has always been particularly sensitive to the dangers of the Russian might. And it's not just the Poles. Frantisek Palacky, the great historian and the figure most representative of Czech politics in the nineteenth century, wrote in 1848 a famous letter to the revolutionary parliament of Frankfurt in which he justified the continued existence of the Habsburg Empire as the only possible rampart against Russia, against 'this power which, having already reached an enormous size today, is now augmenting its force beyond the reach of any Western country.' Palacky warned of Russia's imperial ambitions; it aspired to become a 'universal monarchy', which means it sought world domination. 'A Russian universal monarchy,' Palacky wrote, 'would be an immense and indescribable disaster, an immeasurable and limitless disaster.'

Central Europe, according to Palacky, ought to be a family of equal nations, each of which—treating the others with mutual

respect and secure in the protection of a strong, unified state—
would also cultivate its own individuality. And this dream, although
never fully realized, would remain powerful and influential. Central
Europe longed to be a condensed version of Europe itself in all its
cultural variety, a small arch-European Europe, a reduced model of
Europe made up of nations conceived according to one rule: the
greatest variety within the smallest space. How could Central
Europe not be horrified facing a Russia founded on the opposite
principle: the smallest variety within the greatest space?

Indeed, nothing could be more foreign to Central Europe and
its passion for variety than Russia: uniform, standardizing,
centralizing, determined to transform every nation of its empire
(the Ukrainians, the Belorussians, the Armenians, the Latvians,
the Lithuanians, and others) into a single Russian people (or, as is
more commonly expressed in this age of generalized verbal
mystification, into a 'single Soviet people').[3]

And so, again: is communism the negation of Russian history or
its fulfillment?

Certainly it is both its negation (the negation, for example, of its
religiosity) *and* its fulfillment (the fulfillment of its centralizing
tendencies and its imperial dreams).

Seen from within Russia, this first aspect—the aspect of its
discontinuity—is the more striking. From the point of view of the
enslaved countries, the second aspect—that of its continuity—is
what is felt more powerfully.[4]

---

[3] One of the great European nations (there are nearly forty
million Ukrainians) is slowly disappearing. And this enormous
event, which is almost unbelievable, is something Europe doesn't
realize!

[4] Leszek Kolakowski writes (*Zeszyty literacke*, No. 2, Paris,
1983): 'Although I believe, as does Solzhenitsyn, that the Soviet
system has surpassed Czarism in its oppressive character . . . I will
not go so far as to idealize the system against which my ancestors
fought under terrible conditions and under which they died or were
tortured or suffered humiliations . . . . I believe that Solzhenitsyn
has a tendency to idealize Czarism, a tendency that neither I nor,
I'm sure, any other Pole can accept.'

4

But am I being too absolute in contrasting Russia and Western civilization? Isn't Europe, though divided into East and West, still a single entity anchored in ancient Greece and Judeo-Christian thought?

Of course. Moreover, during the entire nineteenth century, Russia, attracted to Europe, drew closer to it. And the fascination was reciprocated. Rilke claimed that Russia was his spiritual homeland, and no one has escaped the impact of the great Russian novels, which remain an integral part of the common European cultural legacy.

Yes, all this is true; the cultural betrothal between the two Europes remains a great and unforgettable memory.[5] But it is no less true that Russian communism vigorously reawakened Russia's old anti-Western obsessions and turned it brutally against Europe.

But Russia isn't my subject and I don't want to wander into its immense complexities, about which I'm not specially knowledgeable. I want simply to make this point once more: on the Eastern border of the West—more than anywhere else—Russia is seen not just as one more European power but as a singular civilization, an *other* civilization.

---

[5] The most beautiful union between Russia and the West is the work of Stravinsky that summarizes the whole thousand-year history of Western music and at the same time remains in its musical imagination deeply Russian. Another excellent marriage was celebrated in Central Europe in two magnificent operas of that great Russophile, Leos Janacek: one of them based on Ostrovski (*Katya Kabanova*, 1924), and the other, which I admire infinitely, based on Dostoevsky (*From the House of the Dead*, 1928). But it is symptomatic that these operas have never been staged in Russia and their very existence is unknown there. Communist Russia repudiates misalliances with the West.

In his book *The Native Realm*, Czesław Milosz speaks of the phenomenon: in the sixteenth and seventeenth centuries, the Poles waged war against the Russians 'along distant borders. No one was especially interested in the Russians . . . . It was this experience, when the Poles found only a big void to the east, that engendered the Polish concept of a Russia situated "out there"—outside the world.'[6]

Kasimierz Brandys, in his *Warsaw Diary*, recalls this interesting story: a Polish writer's meeting with the Russian poet Anna Akhmatova.

The Pole was complaining: his works—all of them—had been banned.

She interrupted: 'Have you been imprisoned?'

'No,' the Pole said.

'Have you at least been expelled from the Writers' Union?'

'No,' the Pole said.

'Then what exactly are you complaining about?' Akhmatova was genuinely puzzled.

And Brandys observes:

Those are typical Russian consolations. Nothing seems horrible to them, compared to the fate of Russia. But these consolations make no sense to us. The fate of Russia is not part of our consciousness; it's foreign to us; we're not responsible for it. It weighs on us, but it's not our heritage. That was also my response to Russian literature. It scared me. Even today I'm still horrified by certain stories by Gogol and by everything Saltykov-Shchedrin wrote. I would have preferred not to have known their world, not to have known it even existed.

---

[6] Czeslaw Milosz's books *The Captive Mind* (1953) and *The Native Realm* (1959) are basic: the first close analyses that are not Manichaean of Russian communism and its *Drang nach West*.

Brandy's remarks on Gogol do not, of course, deny the value of his work as art; rather they express the horror of the *world* this art evokes. It is a world that—provided we are removed from it—intrigues and attracts us; the moment it closes around us, though, it reveals its terrifying foreignness. I don't know if it is worse than ours, but I do know it is different: Russia knows another (greater) dimension of disaster, another image of space (a space so immense entire nations are swallowed up in it), another sense of time (slow and patient), another way of laughing, living and dying.

This is why the countries in Central Europe feel that the change in their destiny that occurred after 1945 is not merely a political catastrophe: it is also an attack on their civilization. And the deep meaning of their resistance is the struggle to preserve their identity—or, put another way, to preserve their Westernness.[7]

5

There are no longer any illusions about the regimes of Russia's satellite-countries. But what we forget is their essential tragedy: these countries have vanished from the map of the West.

Why has this disappearance remained invisible?

We can locate the cause in Central Europe itself.

---

[7] The word 'central' contains a danger: it evokes the idea of a bridge between Russia and the West. T. G. Masaryk, the founding president of Czechoslovakia, had already spoken of this idea by 1895: 'It's often said that Czechs have as our mission to serve as a mediator between the West and the East. This idea is meaningless. The Czechs are not next to the East (they are surrounded by Germans and Poles, that is, the West), but also there is no need whatsoever for a mediator. The Russians have always had much closer and more direct contacts with the Germans and the French than we have, and everything the Western nations have learned about the Russians they have learned directly, without mediators.'

The history of the Poles, the Czechs, the Slovaks, the Hungarians has been turbulent and fragmented. Their traditions of statehood have been weaker and less continuous than those of the larger European nations. Boxed in by the Germans on the one side and the Russians on the other, the nations of Central Europe have used up their strength in the struggle to survive and to preserve their languages. As they have never been entirely integrated into the consciousness of Europe, they have remained the least known and the most fragile part of the West—hidden, even further, by the curtain of their strange and scarcely accessible languages.

The Austrian Empire had the great opportunity of making Central Europe into a strong, unified state. But the Austrians, alas, were divided between an arrogant Pan-German nationalism and their own Central-European mission. They did not succeed in building a federation of equal nations, and their failure has been the misfortune of the whole of Europe. Dissatisfied, the other nations of Central Europe blew apart their Empire in 1918, without realizing that, in spite of its inadequacies, it was irreplaceable. After the First World War, Central Europe was therefore transformed into a region of small, weak states, whose vulnerability ensured first Hitler's conquest and ultimately Stalin's triumph. Perhaps it is for this reason that, in the European memory, these countries always seem to be the source of dangerous troubles.

And, to be frank, I feel that the error made by Central Europe was because of what I call the 'ideology of the Slavic world'. I say 'ideology' advisedly, for it is only a piece of political mystification invented in the nineteenth century. The Czechs (in spite of the severe warnings of their most respected leaders) loved to brandish naively their 'Slavic ideology' as a defence against German aggressiveness. The Russians, on the other hand, enjoyed making use of it to justify their own imperial ambitions. 'The Russians like to label everything Russian as Slavic, so that later they can label everthing Slavic as Russian,' the great Czech writer Karel Havlicek declared in 1844, trying to warn his compatriots against their silly and ignorant enthusiasm for Russia. It was ignorant because the Czechs, throughout their entire thousand-year history, have never had any direct contact with Russia. In spite of their linguistic kinship, the Czechs and the Russians have never shared a common

103

world: neither a common history nor a common culture. The relationship between the Poles and the Russians, though, has never been anything less than a struggle of life and death.

Joseph Conrad was always irritated by the label of 'Slavic soul' that people loved to slap on him and his books because of his Polish origins, and, about sixty years ago, he wrote that, 'nothing could be more alien to the "Slavic spirit"—as it's described in the literary world—than the Polish temperament with its chivalric devotion to moral constraints and its exaggerated respect for individual rights.' (And how well I understand him! I, too, know of nothing more ridiculous than this cult of obscure depths, this noisy and empty sentimentality of the 'Slavic soul' that is attributed to me from time to time!)[8]

Nevertheless, the idea of a Slavic world is a commonplace of world historiography. The division of Europe after 1945—which united this supposed Slavic world (including the poor Hungarians and Rumanians whose language is not, of course, Slavic—but why bother over trifles?)—has therefore been able to seem almost like a natural solution.

---

[8] There is an amusing little book named *How to be an Alien* in which the author, in a chapter titled 'Soul and Understatement', speaks of the Slavic soul: 'The worst kind of soul is the great Slav soul. People who suffer from it are usually very deep thinkers. They may say things like this: "Sometimes I am so merry and sometimes I am so sad. Can you explain why?" (You cannot, do not try). Or they may say: "I am so mysterious . . . . I sometimes wish I were somewhere else than where I am." Or "When I am alone in a forest at night and jump from one tree to another, I often think that life is so strange."' Who would dare to make fun of the great Slavic soul? Of course the author is George Mikes, of Hungarian origin. Only in Central Europe does the Slavic soul appear ridiculous.

6

So, is it the fault of Central Europe that the West hasn't even noticed its disappearance?

Not entirely. At the beginning of our century, Central Europe was, despite its political weakness, a great cultural centre, perhaps the greatest. And, admittedly, while the importance of Vienna, the city of Freud and Mahler, is readily acknowledged today, its importance and originality make little sense unless they are seen against the background of the other countries and cities that together participated in, and contributed creatively to, the culture of Central Europe. If the school of Schoenberg founded the twelve-tone system, the Hungarian Béla Bartók, one of the greatest musicians of the twentieth century, knew how to discover the last original possibility in music based on the tonal principle. With the work of Kafka and Hasek, Prague created the great counterpart in the novel to the work of the Viennese Musil and Broch. The cultural dynamism of the non-German-speaking countries was intensified even more when after 1918 Prague offered the world the innovations of structuralism and the Prague Linguistic Circle.[9] And

---

[9] Structuralist thinking started toward the end of the 1920s in the Prague Linguistic Circle. It was made up of Czech, Russian, German and Polish scholars. During the 1930s, in this very cosmopolitan environment, Mukarovsky worked out his structuralist aesthetics. Prague structuralism was organically rooted in Czech formalism of the nineteenth century. (Formalist tendencies were stronger in Prague than elsewhere, in my opinion, thanks to the dominant position of music and, therefore, of musicology which is 'formalist' by its very nature.) Inspired by recent developments in Russian formalism, Mukarovsky went beyond its one-sided nature. The structuralists were the allies of Prague avant-garde poets and painters (thereby anticipating a similar alliance that was created in France thirty years later). Through their influence the structuralists protected avant-garde art against the narrowly ideological interpretation that has dogged modern art everywhere.

in Poland the great trinity of Gombrowicz, Schulz and Witkiewicz anticipated the European modernism of the 1950s, notably the so-called theatre of the absurd.

A question arises: was this entire creative explosion just a coincidence of geography? Or was it rooted in a long tradition, a shared past? Or, phrased another way: does Central Europe constitute a true cultural configuration with its own history? And if such a configuration exists, can it be defined geographically? What are its borders?

It would be senseless to try to draw its borders exactly. Central Europe is not a state: it's a culture or a fate. Its borders are imaginary and must be drawn and redrawn with each new historical situation.

For example, by the middle of the fourteenth century, Charles University in Prague had already brought together intellectuals (professors and students) who were Czech, Austrian, Bavarian, Saxon, Polish, Lithuanian, Hungarian and Rumanian with the germ of the idea of a multinational community in which each nation would have the right of its own language: indeed, it was under the indirect influence of this University (at which the religious reformer Jan Huss was once Rector) that the first Hungarian and Rumanian translations of the Bible were undertaken.

Other situations followed: the Hussite revolution; the Hungarian Renaissance during the time of Mathias Korvin with its international influence; the advent of the Habsburg Empire as the union of three independent states—Bohemia, Hungary and Austria; the wars against the Turks; the Counter-Reformation of the seventeenth century. At this time the specific nature of Central European culture appeared suddenly in an extraordinary explosion of baroque art, a phenomenon that unified this vast region, from Salzburg to Wilno. On the map of Europe, baroque Central Europe (characterized by the predominance of the irrational and the dominant role of the visual arts and especially of music) became the opposite pole of classical France (characterized by the predominance of the rational and the dominant role of literature and philosophy). It is in the baroque period that one finds the origins of the extraordinary development of Central European music, which, from Haydn to Schoenberg, from Liszt to Bartók, condensed within itself the evolution of all European music.

In the nineteenth century, the national struggles (of the Poles, the Hungarians, the Czechs, the Slovaks, the Croats, the Slovenes, the Rumanians, the Jews) brought into opposition nations that, insulated, egotistic, closed-off—had nevertheless lived through the same great existential experience: the experience of a nation that chooses between its existence and its non-existence; or, put another way, between retaining its authentic national life and being assimilated into a larger nation. Not even the Austrians, though belonging to the dominant nation of the Empire, avoided the necessity of facing this choice: they had to choose between their Austrian identity and being submerged by the larger German one. Nor could the Jews escape this question. By refusing assimilation, Zionism, also born in Central Europe, chose the same path as the other Central-European nations.

The twentieth century has witnessed other situations: the collapse of the Austrian Empire, Russian annexation and the long period of Central-European revolts, which are only an *immense* bet staked on an unknown solution.

Central Europe therefore cannot be defined and determined by political frontiers (which are inauthentic, always imposed by invasions, conquests, and occupations), but by the great *common situations* that reassemble peoples, regroup them in ever new ways along the imaginary and ever-changing boundaries that mark a realm inhabited by the same memories, the same problems and conflicts, the same common tradition.

7

Sigmund Freud's parents came from Poland, but young Sigmund spent his childhood in Moravia, in present-day Czechoslovakia. Edmund Husserl and Gustav Mahler also spent their childhood there. The Viennese novelist Joseph Roth had his roots in Poland. The great Czech poet Julius Zeyer was born in Prague to a German-speaking family: it was his own choice to speak Czech. The mother tongue of Hermann Kafka, on the other hand, was Czech, while his son Franz took up German. The key figure in the Hungarian revolt of 1956, the writer Tibor Déry, came from a German-Hungarian family, and my dear Danilo Kis, the excellent novelist, is Hungario-Yugoslav. What a tangle of national destinies among even the most representative figures of each country!

And all of these names I've just mentioned are Jews. Indeed, no part of the world has been as deeply marked by the influence of Jewish genius. Aliens everywhere and everywhere at home, lifted above national quarrels, the Jews in the twentieth century were the principal cosmopolitan, integrating element in Central Europe: they were its intellectual cement, a condensed version of its spirit, creators of its spiritual unity. That's why I love Jews and cling to their heritage with as much passion and nostalgia as though it were my own.

Another thing makes the Jewish people so precious to me: in their destiny the fate of Central Europe seems to be concentrated, reflected and to have found its symbolic image. What is Central Europe? An uncertain zone of small nations between Russia and Germany. I underline the words: *small nation*. Indeed, what are the Jews if not a small nation, *the* small nation *par excellence*? The only one of all the small nations of all time which has survived empires and the devastating march of History.

But what is a small nation? I offer you my definition: the small nation is one whose very existence may be put in question at any moment; a small nation can disappear and it knows it. A French, a Russian, or an English man is not used to asking questions about the very survival of his nation. His anthems speak only of grandeur and eternity. The Polish anthem, however, starts with the verse: 'Poland has not yet perished . . . .'

Central Europe as a family of small nations has its own vision of the world, a vision based on a deep distrust of History. History, that goddess of Hegel and Marx, that incarnation of Reason that judges us and arbitrates our fate—that is the History of conquerors. The people of Central Europe are not conquerors. They cannot be separated from European History; they cannot exist outside it; they represent the wrong side of this History: its victims and outsiders. It's this disabused view of history that is the source of their culture, of their wisdom, of the 'non-serious spirit' that mocks grandeur and glory. 'Never forget that only in opposing History itself can we resist the history of our own day.' I would love to engrave this sentence by Witold Gombrowicz above the entry gate to Central Europe.

Thus it was in this region of small nations who have 'not yet perished' that Europe's vulnerability, all of Europe's vulnerability, was more clearly visible before anywhere else. Actually, in our modern world where power has a tendency to become more and more concentrated in the hands of a few big countries, *all* European nations run the risk of becoming small nations and of sharing their fate. In this sense the destiny of Central Europe anticipates the destiny of Europe in general, and its culture assumes an enormous relevance.[10]

It's enough to read the greatest Central European novels: in Hermann Broch's *The Sleepwalkers*, History appears as a process of gradual degradation of values; Musil's *The Man without Qualities* paints a euphoric society that doesn't realize that tomorrow it will disappear; in Hasek's *The Good Soldier Schweik*, pretending to be an idiot becomes the last possible method for preserving one's freedom; the novelistic visions of Kafka speak to us of a world without memory, of a world that comes after historic time.[11] All of this century's great Central European works of art, even up to our own day, can be understood as long meditations on the possible end of European humanity.

---

[10] The problem of Central-European culture is examined in a very important periodical published by the University of Michigan: *Cross Currents: a Yearbook of Central European Culture.*

[11] With this great circle of Central European writers, with Kafka, Hasek, Broch and Musil, a new post-Proustian, post-Joycean aesthetic of the novel, it seems to me, arises in Europe. Broch is the one I personally care for the most. It's high time this Viennese novelist, one of the greatest of this century, were rediscovered.

8

Today, all of Central Europe has been subjugated by Russia with the exception of little Austria, which, more by chance than necessity, has retained its independence. But ripped out of its Central European setting, it has lost most of its individual character and all of its importance. The disappearance of the cultural home of Central Europe was certainly one of the greatest events of the century for all of Western civilization. So, I repeat my question: how could it possibly have gone unnoticed and unnamed?

My answer is simple: Europe hasn't noticed the disappearance of its cultural home because Europe no longer perceives its unity as a cultural unity.

In fact, what is European unity based on?

In the middle ages, it was based on a shared religion.

In the modern era, in which the medieval God has been changed into a *Deus absconditus*, religion has bowed out, giving way to culture, which has become the expression of the supreme values by which European humanity understands itself, defines itself, identifies itself as European.[12]

---

[12] America was born at about the same time as the Europe of the modern era; America is the 'child' of the modern era. Nevertheless, the definition of the modern era as the period when culture becomes the embodiment of the supreme values by which Europeans understand themselves, define themselves, identify themselves as European, does not seem to me to apply entirely to America.

There are no such figures as Descartes or Cervantes, Pascal or Rembrandt in the very foundations of America. For a long time its culture remained provincial and, most important, without any *representativeness*. Mozart embodied the very spirit of Austria, just as Dvorak symbolized the Czech homeland. Victor Hugo or Paul Valéry are representatives of France, as Goethe and Thomas Mann speak for Germany, if not all of Europe. Faulkner, as a great an artist as he might be, could never claim such a 'representativeness' for himself.

That's why America cannot respond as Europe does with 'a strong sense of distress' to the passage from the age of culture to another era in which 'culture bows out.'

Now it seems that another change is taking place in our century, as important as the one that divided the middle ages from the modern era. Just as God long ago gave way to culture, culture in turn is giving way.

But to what and to whom? What realm of supreme values will be capable of uniting Europe? Technical feats? The marketplace? The mass media? (Will the great poet be replaced by the great journalist?)[13] Or by politics? But by which politics? The right or the left? Is there a discernible shared ideal that still exists above this Manichaeanism of the left and the right that is as stupid as it is insurmountable? Will it be the principle of tolerance, respect for the beliefs and ideas of other people? But won't this tolerance become empty and useless if it no longer protects a rich creativity or a strong set of ideas? Or should we understand the abdication of culture as a sort of deliverance, to which we should ecstatically abandon ourselves? Or will the *Deus absconditus* return to fill the empty space and reveal himself? I don't know, I know nothing about it. I think I know only that culture has bowed out.

Hermann Broch was obsessed by this in the 1930s. He said: 'Painting has become a totally esoteric matter relevant only to the world of museums; there is no longer a general interest in it or its problems; it is virtually a relic of the past.'

---

[13] To oppose the writer to the journalist is a very European way of thinking: the writer creates work with enduring value that takes part in the evolution of European literature (its poetry, fiction and drama) and is thereby the guardian of its memory and continuity; the journalist is not a creator of a work of art but a commentator on current events, on what is going on at the present moment.

If journalism at one time seemed to be an appendix to culture, today, by contrast, culture finds it is at the mercy of journalism, that it is part of a world dominated by journalism. The mass-media decide who will be known and to what degree and according to which interpretation. The writer no longer addresses the public directly; he must communicate with it through the semi-transparent barrier of the mass media.

A European is more sensitive to this change than an American.

Broch, the great innovator of the novel, the defender of Picasso and Joyce, did not wish to attack modern painting for its modernity. He had merely (with a distinct sense of melancholy) defined its situation. His words were surprising at the time; they are no longer surprising. In the past few years I've conducted a little poll and innocently asked people I meet who is their favourite contemporary painter. I've noticed that no one has a favourite contemporary painter and that most people can't even name one.

Such a situation would have been unthinkable thirty years ago at the time of Matisse and Picasso.[14] Since then painting has lost the weight of its authority; it has become a marginal activity. Is it because it's no longer any good? Or because we've lost the taste or the feeling for it? In every case it now seems that the art that forged the style of each era, accompanying Europe through the centuries, is abandoning us—or, we are abandoning it.

And poetry, music, architecture, philosophy? They, too, have lost the capacity of forging European unity, of being its foundation. This is a change as important for European humanity as the decolonization of Africa.

---

[14] The generation of Matisse and Picasso was the last which had the power to unify Geographic Europe, from the Atlantic to the Ural Mountains, and I can only seize this occasion to bow deeply before Russian, Ukrainian and Baltic modernism, which later was wiped out in the cruellest possible fashion by Stalin.

In the years I spent in Czechoslovakia I found even in the most modest apartments reproductions of modern art on the walls: works by Picasso, Matisse, Modigliani, Mondrian and, of course, by the Fauves and the Impressionists. Why would a village-school teacher and a hairdresser decorate their bedrooms with these pictures? Partly because of personal taste, and partly to show that they belonged to a West whose art had been forbidden in Prague, placed in the cellars of museums and denounced by the communist mass-media.

9

Franz Werfel spent the first third of his life in Prague, the second third in Vienna and the last third as an emigrant, first in France, then in America—there you have a typically Central European biography. In 1937 he was in Paris with his wife, the famous Alma, Mahler's widow; he'd been invited there by the Organization for Intellectual Cooperation within the League of Nations to a conference on 'The Future of Literature.' During the conference Werfel took a stand not only against Hitlerism but also against the totalitarian threat in general, the ideological and the journalistic mindlessness of our times that was on the verge of destroying culture. He ended his speech with a proposal he thought might arrest this demonic process: to found a World Academy of Poets and Thinkers (*Weltakademie der Dichter und Denker*).[15] In no instance should the members be named by their states. The selection of members should be dependent only on the value of their work. The number of members, made up of the greatest writers in the world, should be between twenty-four and forty. The task of this

---

[15] Werfel's speech was not at all naive and it has not lost its relevance. It reminds me of another speech, one that Robert Musil read in 1935 to the Congress for the Defence of Culture in Paris. Like Werfel, Musil saw a danger not only in fascism but also in communism. The defence of culture for him did not mean the commitment of culture to a political struggle (as everyone else thought at the time) but on the contrary it meant the protection of culture from the mindlessness of politicization. Both writers realized that in the modern world of technology and mass media, the prospects for culture were not bright. Musil's and Werfel's opinions were very coolly received in Paris. However, in all the political and cultural discussions I hear around me, I would have almost nothing to add to what they have said, and I feel, in such moments, very close to them—I feel, in those moments, irreparably Central European.

academy, free of politics and propaganda, would be to 'confront the politicization and barbarization of the world.'

Not only was this proposal rejected, it was openly ridiculed. Of course, it was naive. Terribly naive. In a world absolutely politicized, in which artists and thinkers were already irremediably 'committed', already politically *engagé*, how could such an independent academy possibly be created? Wouldn't it have the rather comic edge of an assembly of noble souls?

However, this naive proposal strikes me as moving, because it reveals the desperate need to find once again a moral authority in a world stripped of values. It reveals the anguished desire to hear the inaudible voice of culture, the voice of the *Dichter und Denker*.

This story is mixed up in my mind with the memory of a morning when the police, after making a mess of the apartment of one of my friends, a famous Czech philosopher, confiscated a thousand pages of philosophic manuscript. Shortly after we were walking through the streets of Prague. We walked down from the Castle hill, where he lived, toward the peninsula of Kampa; we crossed the Manes Bridge. He was trying to make a joke of it all: how were the police going to decipher his philosophical lingo, which was rather hermetic? But no joke could soothe his anguish, could make up for the loss of ten years' work that this manuscript represented—for he did not have another copy.

We talked about the possibility of sending an open letter abroad in order to turn this confiscation into an international scandal. It was perfectly clear to us that we shouldn't address the letter to an institution or a statesman but only to some figure above politics, someone who stood for an unquestionable moral value, someone universally acknowledged in Europe. In other words, a great cultural figure. But who was this person?

Suddenly we understood that this figure did not exist. To be sure, there were great painters, playwrights and musicians, but they no longer held a privileged place in society as moral authorities that Europe would acknowledge as its spiritual representatives. Culture no longer existed as a realm in which supreme values were enacted.

We walked towards the square in the old city near which I was then living, and we felt an immense loneliness, a void, the void in the European space from which culture was slowly withdrawing.[16]

10

The last direct personal experience of the West that Central European countries remember is the period from 1918 to 1938. Their picture of the West, then, is of the West in the past, of a West in which culture had not yet bowed out.

With this in mind, I want to stress a significant circumstance: the Central European revolts were not nourished by the newspapers, radio or television—that is, by the media. They were prepared, shaped, realized by novels, poetry, theatre, cinema, historiography, literary journals (*revues*), popular comedy and cabaret, philosophical discussions—that is, by culture.[17] The mass media— that, for the French and Americans, are indistinguishable from whatever the West today is meant to be—played no part in these revolts (since the media were completely under state control).

---

[16] At last, after a long period of hesitation, he sent the letter after all—to Jean-Paul Sartre. Yes, he was the last great world cultural figure: on the other hand, he is the very person who, with his theory of 'engagement', provided, in my opinion, the theoretical basis for the abdication of culture as an autonomous force, specific and irreducible. Despite what he might have been, he did respond promptly to my friend's letter with a statement published in *Le Monde*. Without this intervention, I doubt whether the police would have finally returned (nearly a year later) the manuscript to the philosopher. On the day Sartre was buried, the memory of my Prague friend came back to my mind: now his letter would no longer find a recipient.

[17] We have had a bit of a problem translating the word '*revue*'. A *revue* is a periodical (monthly, fortnightly or weekly) run not by journalists but by people of culture (writers, art critics, scholars, philosophers, musicians); it deals with cultural questions and

That's why, when the Russians occupied Czechoslovakia, they did everything possible to destroy Czech culture.[18] This destruction had three consequences: first, it destroyed the centre of the opposition; second, it undermined the identity of the nation, enabling it to be more easily swallowed up by Russian civilization; third, it put a violent end to the modern era, the era in which culture still represented the realization of supreme values.

This third consequence seems to me the most important. In effect, totalitarian Russian civilization is the radical negation of the modern West, the West created four centuries ago at the dawn of the modern era: the era founded on the authority of the thinking, doubting individual, and on an artistic creation which expressed his uniqueness. The Russian invasion has thrown Czechoslovakia into

comments on social events from the cultural point of view. In the nineteenth and twentieth centuries in Europe and Russia, all of the important intellectual movements formed around such reviews. The German Romantic musicians clustered around the *Neue Zeitschrift für Musik* founded by Robert Schumann. Russian literature is unthinkable without such reviews as *Sovremennik* or *Viesy*, just as French literature depended on the *Nouvelle Revue Française* or *Les Temps Modernes*. All of Viennese cultural activity was concentrated around *Die Fackel* directed by Karl Kraus. Gombrowicz's entire journal was published in the Polish review *Kultura*. Etc., etc. The disappearance of these *revues* or their complete marginalization is, in my opinion, the sign that 'culture is bowing out.'

[18] 500,000 people (especially intellectuals) were pushed out of their jobs. 120,000 emigrated. Around two hundred Czech and Slovak writers have been forbidden to publish. Their books have been banned from every public library and their names have been erased from history textbooks. One hundred and forty-five Czech historians have been fired. From a single faculty of arts in Prague, fifty teachers were dismissed. (At the darkest moment of the Austro-Hungarian empire, after the revolution of 1848, two Czech professors were driven out of the University—what a scandal at the time!). Every literary and cultural journal has been liquidated. The great Czech cinema, the great Czech theatre no longer exist.

a 'post-cultural' era and left it defenceless and naked before the Russian army and the omnipresent State television.

While still shaken by this triply tragic event that the invasion of Prague represented, I arrived in France and tried to explain to French friends the massacre of culture that had taken place after the invasion: 'Try to imagine! All of the literary and cultural *revues* were liquidated! Every one, without exception! That never happened before in Czech history, not even under the Nazi occupation during the war!'

Then my friends would look at me indulgently with an embarrassment that I understood only later. When all the *revues* in Czechoslovakia were liquidated, the entire nation knew it, and was in a state of anguish because of the immense impact of the event.[19] If all the *revues* in France or England disappeared, no one would notice it, not even their editors. In Paris, even in a completely cultivated milieu, during dinner parties people discuss television programmes, not *revues*. For culture has already bowed out. Its disappearance, which we experienced in Prague as a catastrophe, a shock, a tragedy, is perceived in Paris as something banal and insignificant, scarcely visible, a non-event.

---

[19] The weekly publication, *Literarni noviny (Literary Journal)*, which published 300,000 copies (in a land of ten million people), was produced by the Czech Writers' Union. It was this publication that over the years led the way to the Prague Spring and was afterwards a platform for it. Its format did not resemble such weeklies as *Time* which have spread all over Europe and America. No, it was truly literary: in it could be found long art chronicles, analyses of books. The articles devoted to history, sociology and politics were not written by journalists but by writers, historians and philosophers. I don't know of a single European weekly in our century that has played as important a historical role nor played it so well. The circulation for Czech literary monthlies varied between ten thousand and forty thousand copies, and their level was remarkably high, in spite of censorship. In Poland *revues* have a comparable importance; today there are hundreds of underground journals there!

11

After the destruction of the Austrian empire, Central Europe lost its ramparts. Didn't it lose its soul after Auschwitz, which swept the Jewish nation off its map? And after having been torn away from Europe in 1945, does Central Europe still exist?

Yes, its creativity and its revolts suggest that it has 'not yet perished.' But if to live means to exist in the eyes of those we love, then Central Europe no longer exists. More precisely: in the eyes of its beloved Europe, Central Europe is just a part of the Soviet Empire and nothing more, nothing more.

And why should this surprise us? By virtue of its political system, Central Europe is the East; by virtue of its cultural history, it is the West. But since Europe itself is in the process of losing its own cultural identity, it perceives in Central Europe nothing but a political regime; put another way, it sees in Central Europe only Eastern Europe.

Central Europe, therefore, should fight against not only its big oppressive neighbour but also the subtle, relentless pressure of time, which is leaving the era of culture in its wake. That's why in Central European revolts there is something conservative, nearly anachronistic: they are desperately trying to restore the past, the past of culture, the past of the modern era. It is only in that period, only in a world that maintains a cultural dimension, that Central Europe can still defend its identity, still be seen for what it is.

The real tragedy for Central Europe, then, is not Russia but Europe: this Europe that represented a value so great that the director of the Hungarian News Agency was ready to die for it, and for which he did indeed die. Behind the Iron Curtain, he did not suspect that the times had changed and that in Europe itself Europe was no longer experienced as a value. He did not suspect that the sentence he was sending by telex beyond the borders of his flat country would seem outmoded and would never be understood.

Translated from the French by Edmund White

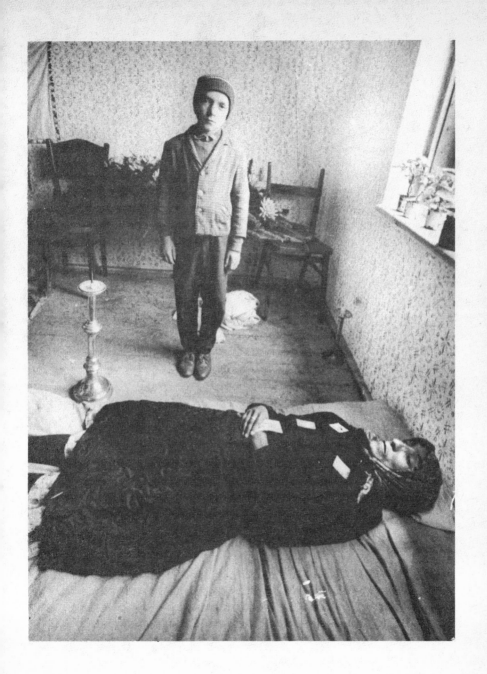

SALMAN RUSHDIE
OUTSIDE THE WHALE

Anyone who has switched on the television set, been to the cinema or entered a bookshop in the last few months will be aware that the British Raj, after three and half decades in retirement, has been making a sort of comeback. After the big-budget fantasy double-bill of *Gandhi* and *Octopussy*, we have had the blackface minstrel-show of *The Far Pavilions* in its TV serial incarnation, and immediately afterwards the grotesquely overpraised *Jewel in the Crown*. I should also include the alleged 'documentary' about Subhas Chandra Bose, Granada Television's *War of the Springing Tiger*, which, in the finest traditions of journalistic impartiality, described India's second-most-revered Independence leader as a 'clown'. And lest we begin to console ourselves that the painful experiences are coming to an end, we are reminded that David Lean's film of *A Passage to India* is in the offing. I remember seeing an interview with Mr Lean in *The Times*, in which he explained his reasons for wishing to make a film of Forster's novel. 'I haven't seen Dickie Attenborough's *Gandhi* yet,' he said, 'but as far as I'm aware, nobody has yet succeeded in putting India on the screen.' The Indian film industry, from Satyajit Ray to Mr N.T. Rama Rao, will no doubt feel suitably humbled by the great man's opinion.

These are dark days. Having expressed my reservations about the *Gandhi* film elsewhere, I have no wish to renew my quarrel with Mahatma Dickie. As for *Octopussy*, one can only say that its portrait of modern India was as grittily and uncompromisingly realistic as its depiction of the skill, integrity and sophistication of the British secret services.

In defence of the Mahattenborough, he did allow a few Indians to be played by Indians. (One is becoming grateful for the smallest of mercies.) Those responsible for transferring *The Far Pavilions* to the screen would have no truck with such tomfoolery. True, Indian actors were allowed to play the villains (Saeed Jaffrey, who has turned the Raj revival into a personal cottage industry, with parts in *Gandhi* and *The Jewel in the Crown* as well, did his hissing and hand-rubbing party piece; and Sneh Gupta played the selfish princess, but unluckily for her, her entire part consisted of the interminably repeated line, 'Ram Ram'). Meanwhile, the good-guy roles were firmly commandeered by Ben Cross, Christopher Lee, Omar Sharif, and, most memorably, Amy Irving as the good princess, whose makeup person obviously believed that Indian princesses dip their eyes in black ink and get sun-tans on their lips.

Now of course *The Far Pavilions* is the purest bilge. The great processing machines of TV-soap opera have taken the somewhat more fibrous garbage of the M.M. Kaye book and puréed it into easy-swallow, no-chewing-necessary drivel. Thus, the two central characters, both supposedly raised as Indians, have been lobotomized to the point of being incapable of pronouncing their own names. The man calls himself 'A Shock', and the woman 'An Jooly'. Around and about them there is branding of human flesh and snakery and widow-burning by the natives. There are Pathans who cannot speak Pushto. And, to avoid offending the Christian market, we are asked to believe that the child 'A Shock', while being raised by Hindus and Muslims, somehow knew that neither 'way' was for him, and instinctively, when he wished to raise his voice in prayer, 'prayed to the mountains'. It would be easy to conclude that such material could not possibly be taken seriously by anyone, and that it is therefore unnecessary to get worked up about it. Should we not simply rise above the twaddle, switch off our sets and not care?

I should be happier about this, the quietist option—and I shall have more to say about quietism later on—if I did not believe that it matters, it always matters, to name rubbish as rubbish; that to do otherwise is to legitimize it. I should also mind less were it not for the fact that *The Far Pavilions,* book as well as TV serial, is only the latest in a very long line of fake portraits inflicted by the West on the East. The creation of a false Orient of cruel-lipped princes and dusky slim-hipped maidens, of ungodliness, fire and the sword, has been brilliantly described by Edward Said in his classic study *Orientalism,* in which he makes clear that the purpose of such false portraits was to provide moral, cultural and artistic justification for imperialism and for its underpinning ideology, that of the racial superiority of the Caucasian over the Asiatic. Let me add only that stereotypes are easier to shrug off if yours is not the culture being stereotyped; or, at the very least, if your culture has the power to counterpunch against the stereotype. If the TV screens of the West were regularly filled by equally-hyped, big-budget productions depicting the realities of India, one could stomach the odd M.M. Kaye. When praying to the mountains is the norm, the stomach begins to heave.

Paul Scott was M.M. Kaye's agent, and it has always seemed to me a damning indictment of his literary judgement that he believed *The Far Pavilions* to be a good book. Even stranger is the fact that *The Raj Quartet* and the Kaye novel are founded on identical strategies of what, to be polite, one must call borrowing. In both cases, the central plot-motifs are lifted from earlier and much finer novels. In *The Far Pavilions,* the hero Ash ('A Shock')—raised an Indian, discovered to be a sahib, and ever afterwards torn between his two selves—will be instantly recognizable as the cardboard cut-out version of Kipling's Kim. And the rape of Daphne Manners in the Bibighar Gardens derives just as plainly from Forster's *Passage to India.* But because Kaye and Scott are vastly inferior to the writers they follow, they turn what they touch to pure lead. Where Forster's scene in the Marabar caves retains its ambiguity and mystery, Scott gives us not one rape but a gang assault, and one perpetrated, what is more, by peasants. Smelly persons of the worst sort. So class as well as sex is violated; Daphne gets the works. It is useless, I'm sure, to suggest that if a rape must be used as the metaphor of the Indo-British connection, then surely, in the interests of accuracy, it should be the rape of an Indian woman by one or more Englishmen of whatever class...not even Forster dared to write about such a crime. So much more evocative to conjure up white society's fear of the darkie, of big brown cocks.

You will say I am being unfair; Scott is a writer of a different calibre from M.M. Kaye. What's more, very few of the British characters come at all well out of the *Quartet*—Barbie, Sarah, Daphne, none of the men. (Kaye, reviewing the TV adaptation, found it excessively rude about the British.)

In point of fact, I am not sure that Scott is so much finer an artist. Like Kaye, he has an instinct for the cliché. Sadistic, bottom-flogging policeman Merrick turns out to be (surprise!) a closet homosexual. His grammar-school origins give him (what else?) a chip on the shoulder. And all around him is a galaxy of chinless wonders, regimental *grandes dames,* lushes, empty-headed blondes, silly-asses, plucky young things, good sorts, bad eggs and Russian counts with eyepatches. The overall effect is rather like a literary version of Mulligatawny soup. It tries to taste Indian, but ends up being ultra-parochially British, only with too much pepper.

And yes, Scott is harsh in his portraits of many British characters; but I want to try and make a rather more difficult point, a point about *form*. The *Quartet*'s form tells us, in effect, that the history of the end of the Raj was largely composed of the doings of the officer class and its wife. Indians get walk-ons, but remain, for the most part, bit-players in their own history. Once this form has been set, it scarcely matters that individual, fictional Brits get unsympathetic treatment from their author. The form insists that *they are the ones whose stories matter,* and that is so much less than the whole truth that it must be called a falsehood. It will not do to argue that Scott was attempting only to portray the British in India, and that such was the nature of imperialist society that the Indians *would* only have had bit parts. It is no defence to say that a work adopts, in its structure, the very ethic which, in its content and tone, it pretends to dislike. It is, in fact, the case for the prosecution.

I cannot end this brief account of the Raj revival without returning to David Lean, a film director whose mere interviews merit reviews. I have already quoted his masterpiece in *The Times*; here now are three passages from his conversation with Derek Malcolm in *The Guardian* of January 23 1984:

> Forster was a bit anti-English, anti-Raj and so on. I suppose it's a tricky thing to say, but I'm not so much. I intend to keep the balance more. I don't believe all the English were a lot of idiots. Forster rather made them so. He came down hard against them. I've cut out that bit at the trial where they try to take over the court. Richard [Goodwin, the producer] wanted me to leave it in. But I said no, it just wasn't right. They wouldn't have done that.

> As for Aziz, there's a hell of a lot of Indian in him. They're marvellous people but maddening sometimes, you know .... He's a goose. But he's warm and you like him awfully. I don't mean that in a derogatory way—things just happen to him. He can't help it. And Miss Quested ... well, she's a bit of a prig and a bore in the book, you know. I've changed her, made her more sympathetic. Forster wasn't always very good with women.

One other thing. I've got rid of that 'Not yet, not yet' bit. You know, when the Quit India stuff comes up, and we have the passage about driving us into the sea? Forster experts have always said it was important, but the Fielding-Aziz friendship was not sustained by those sorts of things. At least I don't think so. The book came out at the time of the trial of General Dyer and had a tremendous success in America for that reason. But I thought that bit rather tacked on. Anyway, I see it as a personal not a political story.

Forster's life-long refusal to permit his novel to be filmed begins to look rather sensible. But once a revisionist enterprise gets under way, the mere wishes of a dead novelist provide no obstacle. And there can be little doubt that in Britain today the refurbishment of the Empire's tarnished image is under way. The continuing decline, the growing poverty and the meanness of spirit of much of Thatcherite Britain encourages many Britons to turn their eyes nostalgically to the lost hour of their precedence. The recrudescence of imperialist ideology and the popularity of Raj fictions put one in mind of the phantom twitchings of an amputated limb. Britain is in danger of entering a condition of cultural psychosis, in which it begins once again to strut and posture like a great power while in fact its power diminishes every year. The jewel in the crown is made, these days, of paste.

Anthony Barnett has cogently argued, in his television-essay 'Let's Take the "Great" out of Britain', that the idea of a *great* Britain (originally just a collective term for the countries of the British Isles, but repeatedly used to bolster the myth of national grandeur) has bedevilled the actions of all post-war governments. But it was Margaret Thatcher who, in the euphoria of the Falklands victory, most plainly nailed her colours to the old colonial mast, claiming that the success in the South Atlantic proved that the British were still the people 'who had ruled a quarter of the world.' Shortly afterwards she called for a return to Victorian values, thus demonstrating that she had embarked upon a heroic battle against the linear passage of Time.

I am trying to say something which is not easily heard above the clamour of praise for the present spate of British-Indian fictions: that works of art, even works of entertainment, do not come into being in a social and political vacuum; and that the way they operate in a society cannot be separated from politics, from history. For every text, a context; and the rise of Raj revisionism, exemplified by the huge success of these fictions, is the artistic counterpart to the rise of conservative ideologies in modern Britain. And no matter how innocently the writers and film-makers work, no matter how skilfully the actors act (and nobody would deny the brilliance of, for example, the performances of Susan Wooldridge as Daphne and Peggy Ashcroft as Barbie in the TV *Jewel*), they run the grave risk of helping to shore up that conservatism, by offering it the fictional glamour which its reality so grievously lacks.

The title of this essay derives, obviously, from that of an earlier piece (1940) by the year's other literary phenomenon, Mr Orwell. And as I'm going to dispute its assertions about the relationship between politics and literature, I must of necessity begin by offering a summary of that essay, 'Inside the Whale'.

It opens with a largely admiring analysis of the writing of Henry Miller:

> On the face of it, no material could be less promising. When *Tropic of Cancer* was published the Italians were marching into Abyssinia and Hitler's concentration camps were already bulging....It did not seem to be a moment at which a novel of outstanding value was likely to be written about American dead-beats cadging drinks in the Latin Quarter. Of course a novelist is not obliged to write directly about contemporary history, but a novelist who simply disregards the major public events of the day is generally either a footler or a plain idiot. From a mere account of the subject matter of *Tropic of Cancer,* most people would probably assume it to be no more than a bit of naughty-naughty left over from the twenties. Actually, nearly everyone who read it saw at once that it was ... a very remarkable book. How or why remarkable?

His attempt to answer that question takes Orwell down more and more tortuous roads. He ascribes to Miller the gift of opening up a new world 'not by revealing what is strange, but by revealing what is familiar.' He praises him for using English 'as a spoken language, but spoken *without fear,* i.e. without fear of rhetoric or of the unusual or poetic word. It is a flowing, swelling prose, a prose with rhythms in it.' And most crucially he likens Miller to Whitman, 'for what he is saying, after all, is "I accept".'

Around here things begin to get a little bizarre. Orwell quite fairly points out that to say 'I accept' to life in the thirties 'is to say that you accept concentration camps, rubber truncheons, Hitler, Stalin, bombs, aeroplanes, tinned food, machine guns, putsches, purges, slogans, Bedaux belts, gas masks, submarines, spies, provocateurs, press censorship, secret prisons, aspirins, Hollywood films and political murders.' (No, I don't know what a Bedaux belt is, either.) But in the very next paragraph he tells us that 'precisely because, in one sense, he is passive to experience, Miller is able to get nearer to the ordinary man than is possible to more purposive writers. For the ordinary man is also passive.' Characterizing the ordinary man as a victim, he then claims that only the Miller type of victim-books, 'non-political ... non-ethical ... non-literary ... non-contemporary,' can speak with the people's voice. So to accept concentration camps and Bedaux belts turns out to be pretty worthwhile, after all.

There follows an attack on literary fashion. Orwell, a thirty-seven-year-old patriarch, tells us that 'when one says that a writer is fashionable one practically always means that he is admired by people under thirty.' At first he picks easy targets—A.E. Housman's 'roselipt maidens' and Rupert Brooke's 'Grantchester' ('a sort of accumulated vomit from a stomach stuffed with place-names'). But then the polemic is widened to include 'the movement', the politically-committed generation of Auden and Spender and MacNeice. 'On the whole,' Orwell says, 'the literary history of the thirties seems to justify the opinion that a writer does well to keep out of politics.' It is true he scores some points, as when he indicates the bourgeois, boarding-school origins of just about all these literary radicals, or when he connects the popularity of Communism among British intellectuals to the general middle-class disillusion with all traditional values: 'Patriotism, religion, the Empire, the family, the sanctity of marriage, the Old School Tie, birth, breeding, honour, discipline—anyone of ordinary education could turn the whole lot of them inside out in three minutes.' In this vacuum of ideology, he suggests, there was still 'the need for something to believe in,' and Stalinist Communism 'filled the void.'

But he distorts, too. For instance, he flays Auden for one line in the poem 'Spain', the one about 'the conscious acceptance of guilt in the necessary murder....It could only be written,' Orwell writes, 'by a person to whom murder is at most a word. Personally, I would not speak so lightly of murder.'

Orwell's accusation is that the line reveals Auden's casual-ness—a politically-motivated casualness—towards human life. Actually, it does nothing of the sort. The deaths referred to are those of people in war. The dying of soldiers is all too often spoken of in euphemisms: 'sacrifice', 'martyrdom', 'fall', and so forth. Auden has the courage to say that these killings are *murders*; and that if you are a combatant in a war, you accept the necessity of murders in the service of your cause. His willingness to grasp this nettle is not inhuman, but humanizing. Orwell, trying to prove the theory that political commitment distorts an artist's vision, has lost his own habitual clear-sightedness instead.*

Returning to Henry Miller, Orwell takes up and extends Miller's comparison of Anaïs Nin to Jonah in the whale's belly. 'The whale's belly is simply a womb big enough for an adult ... a storm that would sink all the battleships in the world would hardly reach you as an echo...Miller himself is inside the whale...a willing Jonah....He feels no impulse to alter or control the process that he is undergoing. He has performed the essential Jonah act of allowing himself to be swallowed, remaining passive, *accepting*. It will be seen what this amounts to. It is a species of quietism.'

---

*I owe this observation to remarks made by Stephen Spender at a group discussion involving Angela Carter, Angus Wilson, and myself, which was part of The Royal Shakespeare Company's two-week series 'Thoughtcrimes' held at the Barbican. I should note that this essay results, in part, from the ideas generated by our exchange.

And at the end of this curious essay, Orwell—who began by describing writers who ignored contemporary reality as 'usually footlers or plain idiots'—embraces and espouses this quietist philosophy, this cetacean version of Pangloss's exhortation to *cultiver notre jardin*. 'Progress and reaction,' Orwell concludes, 'have both turned out to be swindles. Seemingly there is nothing left but quietism—robbing reality of its terrors by simply submitting to it. Get inside the whale—or rather, admit you are inside the whale (for you *are,* of course). Give yourself over to the world-process ... simply accept it, endure it, record it. That seems to be the formula that any sensitive novelist is now likely to adopt.'

The sensitive novelist's reasons are to be found in the essay's last sentence, in which Orwell speaks of 'the *impossibility* of any major literature until the world has shaken itself into its new shape.'

And we are told that fatalism is a quality of Indian thought.

It is impossible not to include in any response to 'Inside the Whale' the suggestion that Orwell's argument is much impaired by his choice, for a quietist model, of Henry Miller. In the forty-four years since the essay was first published, Miller's reputation has more or less completely evaporated, and he now looks to be very little more than the happy pornographer beneath whose scatological surface Orwell saw such improbable depths. If we, in 1984, are asked to choose between, on the one hand, the Miller of *Tropic of Cancer* and 'the first hundred pages of *Black Spring*' and, on the other, the collected works of Auden, MacNeice and Spender, I doubt that many of us would go for old Henry. So it would appear that politically-committed art can actually prove more durable than messages from the stomach of the fish.

It would also be wrong to go any further without discussing the senses in which Orwell uses the term 'politics'. Six years after 'Inside the Whale', in the essay 'Politics and the English Language' (1946), he wrote: 'In our age there is no such thing as "keeping out of politics". All issues are political issues, and politics itself is a mass of lies, evasions, folly, hatred and schizophrenia.'

For a man as truthful, direct, intelligent, passionate and sane as Orwell, 'politics' had come to represent the antithesis of his own world-view. It was an underworld-become-overworld Hell on earth.

'Politics' was a portmanteau term which included everything he hated; no wonder he wanted to keep it out of literature.

I cannot resist the idea that Orwell's intellect and finally his spirit, too, were broken by the horrors of the age in which he lived, the age of Hitler and Stalin (and, to be fair, by the ill health of his later years). Faced with the overwhelming evils of exterminations and purges and fire-bombings, and all the appalling manifestations of politics-gone-wild, he turned his talents to the business of constructing and also of justifying an escape-route. Hence his notion of the ordinary man as victim, and therefore of passivity as the literary stance closest to that of the ordinary man. He is using this type of logic as a means of building a path back to the womb, into the whale and away from the thunder of war. This looks very like the plan of a man who has given up the struggle. Even though he knows that 'there is no such thing as "keeping out of politics",' he attempts the construction of a mechanism with just that purpose. Sit it out, he recommends; we writers will be safe inside the whale, until the storm dies down. I do not presume to blame him for adopting this position. He lived in the worst of times. But it is important to dispute his conclusions, because a philosophy built on an intellectual defeat must always be rebuilt at a later point. And undoubtedly Orwell did give way to a kind of defeatism and despair. By the time he wrote *Nineteen Eighty-Four,* sick and cloistered on Jura, he had plainly come to think that resistance was useless. Winston Smith considers himself a dead man from the moment he rebels. The secret book of the dissidents turns out to have been written by the Thought Police. All protest must end in Room 101. In an age when it often appears that we have all agreed to believe in entropy, in the proposition that things fall apart, that history is the irreversible process by which everything gradually gets worse, the unrelieved pessimism of *Nineteen Eighty-Four* goes some way towards explaining the book's status as a true myth of our times.

What is more (and this connects the year's parallel phenomena of Empire-revivalism and Orwellmania), the quietist option, the exhortation to submit to events, is an intrinsically conservative one. When intellectuals and artists withdraw from the fray, politicians feel safer. Once, the right and left in Britain used to argue about which of them 'owned' Orwell. In those days both sides wanted him; and, as Raymond Williams has said, the tug-of-war did his memory little honour. I have no wish to re-open these old hostilities; but the truth cannot be avoided, and the truth is that passivity always serves the interests of the status quo, of the people already at the top of the heap, and the Orwell of 'Inside the Whale' and *Nineteen Eighty-Four* is advocating ideas that can only be of service to our masters. If resistance is useless, those whom one might otherwise resist become omnipotent.

It is much easier to find common ground with Orwell when he comes to discuss the relationship between politics and language. The discoverer of Newspeak was aware that 'when the general (political) atmosphere is bad, language must suffer.' In 'Politics and the English Language' he gives us a series of telling examples of the perversion of meaning for political purposes. 'Statements like *Marshal Pétain was a true patriot, The Soviet Press is the freest in the world, The Catholic Church is opposed to persecution* are almost always made with intent to deceive,' he writes. He also provides beautiful parodies of politicians' metaphor-mixing: 'The Fascist octopus has sung its swan song, the jackboot is thrown into the melting pot.' Recently, I came across a worthy descendant of these grand old howlers: *The Times,* reporting the smuggling of classified documents out of Civil Service departments, referred to the increased frequency of 'leaks' from 'a high-level mole'.

It's odd, though, that the author of *Animal Farm,* the creator of so much of the vocabulary through which we now comprehend these distortions—doublethink, thoughtcrime, and the rest—should have been unwilling to concede that literature was best able to defend language, to do battle with the twisters, *precisely by entering the political arena.* The writers of Group 47 in postwar Germany—Grass, Böll and the rest, with their 'rubble literature', whose purpose and great achievement was to rebuild the German language from the rubble of Nazism—are prime instances of this power. So, in quite another way, is a writer like Joseph Heller. In *Good as Gold* the character of the Presidential aide Ralph provides Heller with some superb satire at the expense of Washingtonspeak. Ralph speaks in sentences that usually conclude by contradicting their beginnings: 'This Administration will back you all the way until it has to.' 'This President doesn't want yes-men. What we want are independent men of integrity who will agree with all our decisions after we make them.'

135

Every time Ralph opens his oxymoronic mouth he reveals the limitations of Orwell's view of the interaction between literature and politics. It is a view which excludes comedy, satire, deflation; because of course the writer need not always be the servant of some beetle-browed ideology. He can also be its critic, its antagonist, its scourge. From Swift to Solzhenitsyn, writers have discharged this role with honour. And remember Napoleon the Pig.

Just as it is untrue that politics ruins literature (even among 'ideological' political writers, Orwell's case would founder on the great rock of Pablo Neruda), so it is by no means axiomatic that the 'ordinary man', *l'homme moyen sensuel,* is politically passive. We have seen that the myth of this inert commoner was a part of Orwell's logic of retreat; but it is nevertheless worth reminding ourselves of just a few instances in which the 'ordinary man'—not to mention the 'ordinary woman'—has been anything but inactive. We may not approve of Khomeini's Iran, but the revolution there was a genuine mass movement. So is the revolution in Nicaragua. And so, let us not forget, was the Indian revolution. I wonder if independence would have arrived in 1947 if the masses, ignoring Congress and Muslim League, had remained seated inside what would have had to be a very large whale indeed.

The truth is that there is no whale. We live in a world without hiding places; the missiles have made sure of that. However much we may wish to return to the womb, we cannot be un-born. So we are left with a fairly straightforward choice. Either we agree to delude ourselves, to lose ourselves in the fantasy of the great fish—for which a second metaphor is that of Pangloss's garden and for which a third would be the position adopted by the ostrich in time of danger; or we can do what all human beings do instinctively when they realize that the womb has been lost for ever: we can make the very devil of a racket. Certainly, when we cry, we cry partly for the safety we have lost; but we also cry to affirm ourselves, to say, here I am, I matter, too—you're going to have to reckon with me. So, in place of Jonah's womb, I am recommending the ancient tradition of making as big a fuss, as noisy a complaint about the world as is humanly possible. Where Orwell wished quietism, let there be rowdyism; in place of the whale, the protesting wail. If we can cease envisaging ourselves as metaphorical foetuses, and substitute the image of a new-born child, then that will be at least a small intellectual advance. In time, perhaps, we may even learn to toddle.

I must make one thing plain. I am not saying that all literature must now be of this protesting, noisy type. Perish the thought; now that we are babies fresh from the womb, we must find it possible to laugh and wonder as well as rage and weep. I have no wish to nail myself, let alone anyone else, to the tree of political literature for the rest of my writing life. Lewis Carroll and Italo Calvino are as important to literature as Swift or Brecht. What I am saying is that politics and literature, like sport and politics, do mix, are inextricably mixed, and that that mixture has consequences.

The modern world lacks not only hiding places, but certainties. There is no consensus about reality between, for example, the nations of the North and of the South. What President Reagan says is happening in Central America differs so radically from, say, the Sandinista version that there is almost no common ground. It becomes necessary to take sides, to say whether or not one thinks of Nicaragua as the United States' 'front yard'. (Vietnam, you will recall, was the 'back yard'.) It seems to me imperative that literature enter such arguments, because what is being disputed is nothing less than *what is the case,* what is truth and what untruth. If writers leave the business of making pictures of the world to politicians, it will be one of history's great and most abject abdications.

Outside the whale is the unceasing storm, the continual quarrel, the dialectic of history. Outside the whale there is a genuine need for political fiction, for books that draw new and better maps of reality, and make new languages with which we can understand the world. Outside the whale we see that we are all irradiated by history, we are radioactive with history and politics; we see that it can be as false to create a politics-free fictional universe as to create one in which nobody needs to work or eat or hate or love or sleep. Outside the whale it becomes necessary, and even exhilarating, to grapple with the special problems created by the incorporation of political material, because politics is by turns farce and tragedy, and sometimes (e.g. Zia's Pakistan) both at once. Outside the whale the writer is obliged to accept that he (or she) is part of the crowd, part of the ocean, part of the storm, so that objectivity becomes a great dream, like perfection, an unattainable goal for which one must struggle in spite of the impossibility of success. Outside the whale is the world of Samuel Beckett's famous formula: *I can't go on, I'll go on.*

This is why (to end where I began) it really is necessary to make a fuss about Raj fiction and the zombie-like revival of the defunct Empire. The various films and TV shows and books I discussed earlier propagate a number of notions about history which must be quarrelled with, as loudly and as embarrassingly as possible.

These include: the idea that non-violence makes successful revolutions; the peculiar notion that Kasturba Gandhi could have confided the secrets of her sex-life to Margaret Bourke-White; the bizarre implication that any Indians could look or speak like Amy Irving or Christopher Lee; the view (which underlies many of these works) that the British and Indians actually understood each other jolly well, and that the end of the Empire was a sort of gentlemen's agreement between old pals at the club; the revisionist theory—see David Lean's interviews—that *we, the British, weren't as bad as people make out*; the calumny, to which the use of rape-plots lends credence, that frail English roses were in constant sexual danger from lust-crazed wogs (just such a fear lay behind General Dyer's Amritsar massacre); and, above all, the fantasy that the British Empire represented something 'noble' or 'great' about Britain; that it was, in spite of all its flaws and meannesses and bigotries, fundamentally glamorous.

If books and films could be made and consumed in the belly of the whale, it might be possible to consider them merely as entertainment, or even, on occasion, as art. But in our whaleless world, in this world without quiet corners, there can be no easy escapes from history, from hullabaloo, from terrible, unquiet fuss.

"The most influential, readable and far-ranging magazine now existing in the Western World"

So one of Britain's leading political commentators, **Peregrine Worsthorne**, wrote of ENCOUNTER in 1983, shortly before the magazine's 30th anniversary. He was echoing the opinion of the **International Herald Tribune** ("Encounter ... one of the few great beacons of English-language journalism"), **John Wain** in the **Times Educational Supplement** ("An invaluable forum for the discussion of general ideas") ... and many others.

As if to demonstrate its continuing vitality, ENCOUNTER celebrated its 30th anniversary with a radical redesign. Larger format ... colourful eye-catching covers ... better paper and clearer type.

The contents, however, have not changed. The new-look ENCOUNTER continues its established tradition of first-class journalism, its unique blend of current affairs, literature and the arts. If you are not already a regular reader, why not become one now? We will enrol you as a subscriber for one year (ten issues) for the special rate of £14.40 (USA $29.00) — **a saving of 20% on the normal rate.** Please return the coupon below (or a letter in similar terms).

Martha Gellhorn
Testimonial

The following document was given to me in San Salvador, in the dusty yard behind the offices of the Archdiocese. There are a few shade trees in the yard, a couple of wooden benches, and a green corrugated tin shack, the headquarters of the Commission of Human Rights of El Salvador. The shack is filled with shelves of box files, odd-lot tables for desks, chairs, an old typewriter, an old mimeograph machine and people. Wherever power resides in San Salvador, it is protected by armed guards, high walls and steel doors. This place is open; nobody is afraid to talk; the air is different. In that diseased city, the yard and the shack are beautiful.

The Commission of Human Rights is a company of volunteers determined to record for the world, if the world will listen, ceaseless violations of human rights by Salvadoran Security Forces. The volunteers are young, probably not long ago students at the university which is now closed, looted and occupied by soldiers. They are a band of heroes, nothing less, and their life expectancy is uncertain. Human rights in El Salvador are reduced to one: the right to live. Two people, who originally set up the commission, are dead in their thirties: a woman lawyer, assassinated, which means her body was found; a gifted doctor, universally loved, disappeared, which means his body will never be found. Everyone working for the commission is marked. The witnesses themselves are in danger; it is 'subversive' to testify to the crimes of the state. The Security Forces can do what they like to anyone they choose: none of them has ever been punished for kidnapping, torture and murder. They are invulnerable against the defenceless.

In 1982, the Human Rights Commission recorded the fate of 6,952 Salvadorans, men, women, boys, girls, who were seized (*capturados)*, disappeared or assassinated. Torture is not recorded as a separate violation of human rights because it is automatic. The Security Forces and the Death Squads, their unofficial colleagues, do not even kill cleanly with a bullet as proved by the mutilated bodies found at random anywhere in El Salvador. Of 6,952 human beings, only 325 survived to be sent, after torture, to the political prisons.

One of these was the young man whose testimony is printed here. It is a unique document, not because his anguish was exceptional, but because he lived to tell the story from beginning to end. Had it not been for a fluke rescue, he would have died

143

and disappeared, like thousands before and since. 'Torture in El Salvador,' the Human Rights Commission explains, 'has become routine, as a method of work, considered natural and necessary by those who practise it.' For twelve days, this young man was tortured as routine and for his torturers' pleasure. Diseased imaginations invented these tortures, designed to unhinge the mind while ruining the body. They are an abominable advance on Gestapo techniques. After twelve days, he was interrogated briefly and absurdly. Knowing nothing, he confessed nothing. He was tortured again. Near death, he was revived by doctors. After nineteen days he was taken to court, charged by the Security Forces with concocted 'subversion'. He still had the unbroken nerve and clarity of mind to deny the charges, denounce his torturers and insist that the International Red Cross hear his testimony and examine the marks on his body.

Torture has spread from the Gestapo, the disease carrier, world-wide—increasing in virulence over the years. Before the Second World War, for the first time in modern history, torture was integral state policy in Nazi Germany. It was less systematic but no less vicious in Fascist Italy. The Lubianka was a synonym for torture in stalinist Russia. Torture returned to Spain, like a memory of the Inquisition, in Franco's prisons. If torture was practised elsewhere in the world, then, it was sporadic and secret, not part of the state bureaucracy. Now, Amnesty has evidence of the practice of torture in ninety countries: it is updating its list this year. The earth is covered by one hundred and sixty-four nations, including such miniatures as Andorra and St Lucia. In more than half the nations of our world, torture certifies that the form of government is tyranny. Only tyranny, no matter how camouflaged, needs and employs torturers. Torture has no ideology.

Once we thought that Germany was peculiarly diseased since it produced an abundance of torturers. Now we know that torturers appear wherever they're wanted. Shortage of labour is not a problem. Previous experience is helpful but unnecessary, learn on the job, regular eight-hour shifts, good wages from a grateful government. In ninety countries, torturers are on the state pay-roll, like postmen. What is their work; how do they talk; where do they operate; who are they? It is all here to read, not a fictional horror but a fact of barbarity now. And though the machinery and manner may vary according to nationality—variations from Chile to South Africa to Russia, for instance—the purpose is the same: the purpose is to silence those who disagree.

All member states of the United Nations are obligated to honour the Universal Declaration of Human Rights. El Salvador is a member of the United Nations; so are eighty-five other countries where torture is practised. The majority of the torturers' regimes belong in the Free World, friendly clients or allies. I don't know exactly what 'Free World' means except as a politician's phrase. If it means the total of nations not under communist control, it is a misnomer; we should speak of the Partially Free World, or the Free Enterprise World. Our leaders, especially the present leaders of the two great English-speaking democracies, denounce the Soviet Union for its abuse of human rights. The abuse of human rights, culminating in torture as the final and worst abuse, should always be denounced everywhere. But our freedom-loving leaders condone or—unforgivably—assist the torturers' regimes on our side. El Salvador is only one example. There are too many. Lop-sided morality is not morality at all; it is fraud.

Mr Henry Kissinger is widely regarded by decision-makers and governments as a champion geopolitical thinker. Mr Kissinger believes in power and is believed by the powerful. He talks their language, telling them what they like to hear. He was the natural choice for chairman of President Reagan's advisory committee on Central America. Concluding that task, he said: 'If we cannot manage Central America, it will be impossible to convince threatened nations in the Persian Gulf and other places that we know how to manage the Global Equilibrium.'

The arrogance is matched by the moral idiocy. The people of Central America do not count; they have no individual existence, let alone rights. Nor do the people around the Persian Gulf matter; the oil matters. The Global Equilibrium to which Mr Kissinger refers is a world-wide dread of insane nuclear war coming closer and closer. To balance on a tightrope over an abyss is not the ordinary man's idea of equilibrium.

Geopolitics tend to fail, after causing immeasurable misery. You might say that Hitler was the top geopolitical failure. The bombing of Laos and Cambodia, a geopolitical action guided by Mr Kissinger, did not give the planned results but destroyed two countries and millions of lives. Never mind, if it doesn't work in Southeast Asia, try again in Central America. There must be a Kissinger clone in the Kremlin offices, advising that 'If we cannot manage Afghanistan, it will be impossible to convince threatened nations in Eastern Europe and other places that we know how to manage the Global Equilibrium.'

Governments think big; they think geopolitically. Human rights are irrelevant to geopolitics. This may kill us all in the end.

On 4 April 1982 at around 4.30 in the afternoon, I was waiting at a bus-stop, just opposite the petrol station on San Antonio Abad Street. A military convoy passed, followed by a white Ford truck which stopped in front of me, from which eight policemen—each in military uniform and each carrying an M-16 rifle—stepped out and surrounded me. Two National Police radio cars and two military jeeps arrived, and, in a short time, the entire area was surrounded, holding up traffic. Nobody spoke. Several of the policemen took hold of me and began tying me up. There were people around—whom I regarded as potential witnesses—and I demanded an explanation. There was no reply. An army officer appeared: 'Do you really think,' he asked, 'that I don't know who you are?' He hit me full in the stomach with his rifle butt, and a number of soldiers began beating me. I was bundled into one of the patrol cars.

We arrived at the barracks of the National Police and I was taken through the back entrance and left in a cold room. I was there about fifteen minutes. Some men appeared and one of them—I had assumed it was the officer in charge—put his hand on my shoulder in a friendly way. 'I think I know you,' he said. 'You're from San Miguel, aren't you?'

'Yes,' I said.

'Do you know why you're here or haven't they told you yet?'

'No,' I said.

He turned to one of the soldiers: 'Take him away and give him a bed and some decent food.'

The soldier hesitated: 'The police are expecting him. They've been looking for him, you know.'

'That's no problem. If he doesn't cooperate, we'll hand him over.'

But someone else protested: 'It's not only the police who want him. I've seen his record.' Someone else starting shouting—'Take him away!'—and I was grabbed by the hair and dragged off to a pitch-black room. My clothes were taken from me. I was blindfolded. And suddenly I was alone. The floor was wet and slippery, covered in excrement and urine.

Three or four hours passed before a man appeared. My blindfold was tightened and a cord was tied firmly around my testicles by which he led me to another room in which loud music was being played.

Someone said: 'Do you like the Bee Gees or would you prefer something by a Latin-American band—by Mejia Godoy, say?' I was slow in replying and he became angry. He tied my hands and feet together, and began beating me. He was joined by others. They beat me with rubber truncheons until I fell down. They beat me on the back of the neck, on the ankles, and round the head. Another began beating me around the ears with his hands. Someone else started punching me just under the rib cage and in the thorax. They finished and pulled me to my feet by the cord attached to my testicles. I was upset and complained, and one of them replied by hooking the corners of my mouth with his fingers and stretching it open so that he could insert—well, I don't know what it was, but it filled by entire mouth, forcing my cheeks out. Someone else straddled me across my shoulders and inserted two fingers into each of my nostrils, pulling up until I felt I was going to choke. My nose began to bleed, profusely, and I wanted to speak but couldn't. Someone then mentioned the 'hood': it turned out to be a rubber mask specially made so that it clings to your nostrils whenever you try to breathe through it. They put it on, and at once I panicked—I couldn't breathe and my heartbeat went wild. Someone said 'Now'—which, I soon realized, was the command to remove the mask. They gave me just enough time to gasp some air and then put it back on. Off. On. Off. On. This went on a number times, when—was it the ninth time?—my whole body suddenly went weak and I remember trying to think, trying to account for who I was. I passed out.

My memory is then rather hazy. I seem to recall trying to get up, but couldn't and fell backwards knocking my head sharply on the concrete floor. A bucket of icy water was thrown over me, and, as I lay on my stomach, they put two metal discs on the sole of my left foot. I was rolled onto my back and, after a sticky ointment was rubbed into my forehead, two more discs were fixed there. From just underneath my blindfold, I could make out that the discs were connected by wires to a shiny black industrial box, on top of which there was a row of coloured buttons: red, yellow and green. An electric shock suddenly passed through my whole body—straight down the length of it and back again. I felt my eyes roll uncontrollably into my head. I noticed other things. My hands, for instance, went numb, and my head was flung back—snapped back involuntarily. I did not pass out, but I remember wishing that I had. I also remember wishing that they would interrogate me—what could they possibly be waiting for? I can't hide the fact I was terrified. I was terrified of the next shock. Once again, they rolled me on to my back, and, once again, just beneath my blindfold, I could see a man holding his finger poised over the yellow button as if waiting for the order to press it. He did. This time I passed out.

Some time elapsed. I don't know how much—ten minutes? I heard a voice.
'Get up,' it said. 'Do you want to have a bath?'
'Yes,' I said.
He took me out of the room. 'I want to help you,' he said. 'Have you eaten?'
'No,' I said. 'I'm not hungry.'
'I'll run the bath for you. And just to prove that I mean to help you, I'll take off the blindfold. No one ever does that here.'
The bathroom in which I found myself was spacious and had one fairly large mirror. It was clean and painted the same colours as the National Police uniform, the lower part a dark coffee-brown and the upper a pale yellow. The policeman left, and I began my bath.
Very little time passed before two men entered. They were both tall and heavily built and had Afro-hairstyles. One had a full beard. The other was shaven but with a heavy blue-green shadow on his chin. They were surprised to find me without my blindfold, and they

immediately put it back on, very tightly. They did not look like they were from El Salvador, and they spoke with Argentine accents.

'Put the bolt on the door,' one of them said.

'What do you say,' I heard next, 'shall we screw him?'

The other began to fondle me and I pushed his hand away. He put his hand over my mouth and asked: 'Haven't you ever sucked cock?' I didn't answer, and I was slapped and made to kneel. One grabbed me by the hair from behind, while the other forced his erect penis into my mouth.

When I left the bathroom, I heard the sounds of dawn. I was taken to a clean, newly-painted room where I was to spend quite a bit of time. For three days, I was left entirely on my own. I was given water and, two or three times a day, a corn-flour tortilla to eat. There were other prisoners in this part of building: it was the first time I had been aware of them. I was not allowed out, even to go to the toilet, but I noticed that the others were taken there. I asked, but was rebuffed. Several days later, I asked again. 'I'll take care of your need to pee,' the guard on duty replied.

Ten minutes later, he returned in the company of a number of other men. I was stripped, and a strong—impossibly strong—adhesive was taped over my penis, making it impossible to urinate. The pain was bad and it soon grew worse. At nine o'clock the next morning they returned. I was forced to drink water, and water was splashed on my stomach. I wanted to urinate—I ached to urinate—but I was unable to. At some point during the morning of my tenth day, I was finally taken to the toilet. When I urinated, it was painful, and I bled. I was returned to my room and remained there for three days. During that time I was still not interrogated, but my injuries were taken care of and I was fed well.

On the twelfth day, my interrogation did in fact begin. I was moved to another room, also dry and reasonably well-lit. I was allowed to remove the blindfold. The interrogation was conducted by the 'good' man. He reminded me throughout of the values of cooperation.

'Our ideology is not to kill,' he said. 'We simply want to make you into a new man. It's what society wants. But to become a new man, you must cooperate.'

He asked many questions: the name of my mother, my sister, where they were living, how they were living—while frantically writing my replies in his notebook. The questions were interminable, and he admitted that he was under orders to fill up seventy pages. Then I was asked to account for my travels. I had been—he knew from my passport—to Panama, Costa Rica, Colombia, Venezuela, and, most important to him, Nicaragua. He believed I was a member of the Communist Party and asked me a number of questions about it. But I had nothing to say.

He then put on my blindfold. He hit me on the back of the neck and I fell. He told me to get up, and then hit me in the stomach. He pointed out that he was the kindest officer I was going to meet. He said this squatting on top of me. He then pulled me up by my hair and smashed my head on the ground. My interrogation was completed.

Things then starting getting rough. At the end of my interrogation, a number of men entered my room—I think that made five all together. I was told that I had a bad attitude and that people with bad attitudes were always trussed up. My clothes were removed, my ankles were bound and my hands were tied behind my back. Then, bending my legs backwards, my ankles and hands were bound together in one big knot: it was exactly like a trussed-up fowl. The pain was very great.

I was picked up—by the knot—and was carried, suspended in the air, to another room. I heard the groans of someone else there who, like me, was also trussed up. I shuffled closer to him and we managed to work loose our blindfolds. The man was a peasant, about forty-eight or fifty. He had white hair and a bushy beard, and worked at the Suchitoto hospital. He was still wearing his pale green hospital uniform. 'I am here,' I remember him saying, 'because I stole some mangoes from a tree. And because I broke a street lamp which blacked out the whole block.' Leonidas had been there since eleven o'clock in the morning and they were trying to make him say that the hospital staff was made up of communists. But they weren't—they were good people—and even if they were, Leonidas knew nothing about it.

Some soldiers entered: 'Leonidas,' one of them said, 'you're a good man. You don't want to spend your last days like this. We'll very happily send you abroad: but you must cooperate.'

Leonidas's reply filled me with courage: 'Don't talk to me. I don't even know who you are. You say you want me to cooperate, but you've done nothing but beat me since I got here.' I was so pleased I laughed out loud and the soldier turned to me and kicked me in the rib-cage. 'I have nothing to say,' Leonidas said. 'I don't know anything. My only comrades are Christ and his Apostles.' But then Leonidas added: 'But I know you're a good person at heart. Can't you untie me for a while? I can't take any more.'

The soldier replied: 'Here, we only treat kindly those people who cooperate. We'll untie you if you'll cooperate.'

'Okay,' Leonidas said at last. 'I will cooperate.' He was then untied, but he was unable to walk and another soldier was asked to help.

I was left alone for two days, when, in the early evening, eight men came into my room. They were angry: somehow the Red Cross had learned that I was being held. There must be an informer, they assumed, and, suspending me by my wrists from the ceiling, they beat me with truncheons. Who was the informer, they wanted to know, who was the informer?

Everything was now accelerated. I was taken to the officer's recreation room: red plastic sofas, billiard tables, a television set, a record player, extremely loud music. Every now and then the soldiers would laugh and clap. I learned why later: they were pretending to have a party because they expected a visit from the Red Cross: no representative from it would either want—or be allowed—to visit an officers' private party. During this time I was given electric shocks.

At the end, I was given an injection and made to take a pill which revitalized me and gave me a feeling of euphoria. I was removed to the room in which I had been left on my first day: the floor of which had been covered with urine and shit. Another interrogation: this was extremely intense.

Two soldiers, each wearing rubber gloves, held me by the hair and the scruff of the neck. They would ask me a question and then thrust my head into a toilet already overflowing with human excrement. Question. Thrust. 'Who are your companions?' Thrust. 'Where do you train?' Thrust. It was endless: 'Where is your brother? Where are the safe houses? What countries protect you? Who sends you arms?

What do you know about guns? Who are the subversives in the military? How can you account for the seizure of the Santa Ana barracks? Where is your wife? In what riots have you participated? How many have you executed? How many buses have you blown up? Where are your camps? Where are your collection points? What journalists are your friends? What diplomats? What are the names of the doctors who treat you?' There were many, many questions—far more than I can remember—and it went on until dawn. My answers were always the same: 'None.' 'Don't know.' 'No.'

In the morning, I was taken to a bathroom and had a shower. I was given clean khaki combat trousers and a t-shirt and vaseline with which to tidy my hair. Two fourteen-year-old boys took photographs of me. They were, I realized later, in the event of my being released: the photographs would be distributed around the country among the security forces.

After the photographs, I was taken out of the building and put into a van. The driver was from Panama. There were three other soldiers in the back, and I was put on the floor. We drove off. I didn't know where we were going or why I was suddenly being taken somewhere. One of the soldiers put the barrel of his gun in my mouth. 'Such a pity,' he said, 'to die so young for nothing.' And then he pulled the trigger. He took the gun out of my mouth, and I heard him loading it. Again, he put the barrel in my mouth, and there was a click of the trigger: but nothing happened. He did this several times. I began to cry. I was returned to the barracks.

Back inside I was given another injection. There was someone else in the room with me, another prisoner. We talked for a short while. The prisoner was Mexican. I had asked him why he had been arrested. 'Because I'm Mexican,' he replied. I suggested we sleep. We tried.

But I was not allowed to. Twenty minutes later, I was given something to drink—a thick viscous liquid that tasted of vanilla. I was taken to another cell. My blindfold was removed and there were four men, each wearing a mask, a black balaclava, with openings only for the eyes, nose and mouth. I recognized the voices of two of the men—one with hairy arms—whom I remembered from my first day there when I was locked in the bathroom.

One was wearing nail varnish, and he had a case full of magazines with pictures of naked men. I said I wasn't interested, and he produced a copy of *Playboy*. He took off his clothes, as did his friend; the one with nail varnish seemed to be wearing women's knickers. I was told to masturbate, but I couldn't. My blindfold was put back on, and, shortly after, I heard someone masturbating and felt semen ejaculated into my face. I spat and was then hit ten or fifteen times on the side of my head.

My blindfold was removed. One of the men took out a small, thin, coffee-coloured tube about eight centimetres long. He squeezed out some Johnson's lubricant jelly and rubbed it across its length. Someone else was touching and massaging my testicles and, to my alarm, an erection appeared. The small thin tube was then inserted into my urethra—a small bit was left to stick out—while someone else pushed a gun, with an extremely large barrel, up into my arse, rupturing the walls of my rectum and making it bleed.

I was crying with rage. I wanted to kill myself. I wanted to die.

There was something that looked much like a small tub. It rested on thick rubber wheels, and was about a metre deep and half a metre wide. Attached to the lower part was a hose with a nozzle at the end. They started filling the tub with water, adding a large quantity of soap powder.

A sergeant entered. I recognized him from the National Police in San Miguel. He was upset that I was without my blindfold because I might later be able to identify him. He checked the tub: he wanted to be certain there was enough foam: 'It's the foam that does it,' he said.

What follows is difficult to recall. For some time, I was given electric shocks until I felt that I really *was* going to have a heart attack. Through all this I still had the tube in my urethra; they had removed the gun. I was allowed to rest for about ten minutes, and then they slipped the nozzle from the tub into my mouth and opened the valve. I was forced to swallow the foamy liquid; my stomach contracted and heaved but still they forced the liquid down until the entire tub had been emptied: then promptly they sealed my mouth with a thick adhesive tape. I started to vomit, but because my mouth was sealed, I had to swallow everything. The pain was now in my head and my eyes.

It spread to my finger nails and I felt as if there were stones in my stomach. I then remember very little—vaguely a command from the sergeant: it seems they thought I was going to die.

Some time later a doctor gave me a drink and I evacuated everything: I began to vomit and defecate; foam was even coming out of my nose. Two soldiers entered and washed down the room with a hose. I was carried away and soon fell asleep.

When I awoke, it was the afternoon and I was wearing trousers. I was brought apple juice and some food. At around six in the evening, the blindfold was put back on. Someone said, 'We're going to take you somewhere where you can rest.'

The author, because of the intercession of the Red Cross, was released by the military and taken to a court of law where he was accused of being 'a leader of the Communist Party with daily contact among subversive associations.' He denied these charges and asked that the representative from the military leave the court. He informed the Red Cross that he had been released, and then told the court of his experience of the previous month. The judge presiding over the case granted official recognition of the beatings and punishment which the author suffered. The statement was made on 22 April 1982, and a copy of it can be found in the Court of El Salvador, San Salvador. The statement offered to the Commission of Human Rights in El Salvador—from which the above testimonial has for reasons of space, been extracted and edited—was made on 11 and 18 May, 1982. The author has been nominated for the Nobel Peace Prize.

Translated from the Spanish by Margaret Whitehead and
Margaret Jull Costa.

GRAHAM GREENE
*
MURIEL SPARK
*
WILLIAM TREVOR
*
ALEXANDER SOLZHENITSYN
*
ALLAN MASSIE
*
PETER DICKINSON
*
ROSEMARY SUTCLIFF
*
DAVID WHELDON
*
STEPHEN BENATAR
*
MORIS FARHI
*
VLADIMIR VOLKOFF

are all published by
THE BODLEY HEAD

GABRIEL GARCÍA
MÁRQUEZ
MYSTERY WITHOUT
END

Gabriel García Márquez

The light single-engine Piper PA 28, registration number HK2139P, piloted by the conservative politician Antonio Escobar Bravo, left Simón Bolívar Airport in Santa Marta, Colombia, at 7.45 a.m. on 28 April 1983—destination Paitilla Airport, Panama City, Panama. Seven minutes later it landed a few miles from the village of Ciénaga, on an old disused commercial runway where a group of ten people awaited it. Three got on board: two men and one woman. The tallest of the men, thin and rather gaunt, wearing a rough, blue cotton shirt and a sailing cap, was Jaime Bateman Cayón, commander-in-chief of M-19, who, for the past five years, had been the most wanted man in Colombia.

Only they and a few other members knew that the plane was meant to make one further clandestine landing, at yet another disused airport just outside the town of Montería—still in Colombia—to meet delegates from the Popular Liberal Army to discuss a number of problems involved in a joint plan of action. Afterwards, Jaime Bateman and his two colleagues would be flown to Panama where they believed they were about to meet a personal emissary of the President of Colombia, Belisario Betancur, to begin peace talks. The plane made its last contact with air control when it was fifty-five nautical miles from Paitilla Airport in Panama, exactly two hours and seventeen minutes after first taking off. It never landed. This is

---

Jaime Bateman was the leader of M-19, the Colombian left-wing guerrilla force formed on 19 April 1974, after a presidential election that many suspected to have been rigged. Throughout the seventies, M-19 was responsible for a great deal of terrorist activity—as various as stealing Simon Bolivar's sword from a museum outside Bogota, invading Colombia by sea, and the kidnapping of diplomats and journalists. M-19 called for greater recognition of the plight of the poor, lifting of the state of seige, repeal of the harsh Colombia security laws, and the freeing of political prisoners. In 1982, Colombia President Belisario Bentancur, elected in part on the pledge to stop terrorist violence, pardoned 4,000 political prisoners and granted amnesty to all guerrillas prepared to give up their arms. Among those who did not was Jaime Bateman, certain in the belief that, if it had the opportunity, the government would kill him.

the only fact we know with any certainty—nine months after Jaime Bateman's disappearance and after a comprehensive search by land, air and sea that lasted for seventy days. Everything else is speculation.

The most widely-held view—contrary to all the evidence—is that he is not dead. Everyone has their own particular justification, however irrational, for sustaining this self-deception. The same happened, of course, after the deaths of Emiliano Zapata in Mexico and Adolf Hitler in Germany, and after the deaths of hundreds of others who ended up devoured by their own legends.

Those, however, who believe beyond all possible doubt that Bateman *is* dead are his childhood friends who were with him in Santa Marta during the days immediately before his disappearance. Their certainty, though, also has no rational basis. On the contrary. It derives entirely from the Caribbean belief that there are certain people who have the supernatural distinction of being able to return, in the days before they die, to those places for which they have the greatest affection and in which they are able to relive, even if briefly, their happiest times. It is said then that the person is *retracing his steps*. And this in fact, in the very last week of his life, is precisely what Bateman did.

He had arrived on the Caribbean coast, somewhere near Cartagena, on 19 April to give what was to be his last press conference on the day of this organization's thirteenth anniversary. Five days later, he had his own birthday—an occasion usually so insignificant he was known to forget about it altogether. This 24 April was different. He insisted on celebrating his birthday in Santa Marta, the city in which he was born and which, for obvious reasons, he had not visited for almost seven years. The risk of returning to a city in which he was so well known—not only to the inhabitants but to every member of the security services of the region—was of course enormous. But Santa Marta contained all the people and places Bateman had loved in his youth, people and places which invoked, according to close friends, profound feelings of homesickness and nostalgia.

The person he missed most, curiously enough, was his mother, that brave woman Clementina Cayón for whom he felt the same extraordinary passion that Father Camilo Torres and Che Guevara were known to feel for theirs. She was perhaps the only person from Santa Marta whom he saw on a regular basis, and they met often, always in different and secret places, as her house had been under a constant security-watch for years. That security-watch, however, was never a genuine threat, and was usually as benign and unoffending as the brave woman who had to tolerate it and as the Caribbean city itself which was meant to enforce it. Clementina Cayón, for instance—out of kindness or guile, who knows?—would watch the poor policeman on duty on the corner in that terrible midday sun. She'd offer him a chair—why should someone have to stand in that horrible tropical heat?—and later she might fetch him some guanaba juice or perhaps a plate of stew. Later still she'd be buying him cigarettes and, in what seemed to be no time at all, she'd be treating him like one of the family, and he would have to be replaced.

At dawn on 20 April, the group that attended the press conference set out from Cartagena to Santa Marta by car. It was the dry season along the Caribbean coast and in the burning air the scent from the guava trees was strong. According to Álvaro Fayad and Carlos Toledo Plata, two of his passengers that morning, Bateman had been acutely nostalgic. Every point along the road seemed to evoke for him some noteworthy memory. Very near the place where, a week later, Bateman was to board the ill-fated plane, they passed through a village and he ordered them to stop at a roadside café for a breakfast of fried fish and slices of banana. He then drove the rest of the way to Santa Marta, with one more stop for a morning beer in the town of Rodadero.

Neither then, nor at any other moment in the days that followed, did Bateman do anything to disguise his identity. In Santa Marta, he visited all the places that still retained some meaning, however slight. He asked for news of the most unlikely old friends and of various forgotten girlfriends. He particularly asked after his fellow students at the local school (where his rebellious behaviour had deprived him of his school certificate) and each of them, when possible, was invited to his forty-fourth birthday party.

In a city where everyone knows everyone else and where there are secret agents everywhere—from the military, the police and the security forces—it's hard to believe that he was not found out. If in fact it is the case that he wasn't discovered, one reason may well have been that Bateman was simply well liked: who in his hometown was likely to denounce him? There was, many believe, another reason. One of Bateman's several brothers was so similar in looks he could have passed for his twin and was, like Bateman, a great practical joker. Ever since the first photographs of Bateman began appearing in the press, his brother had done everything possible to enhance the likeness: the Afro haircut, the sparse moustache, the blue shirt, the riding boots—even the sailing cap. He fooled the local police, sowed general confusion in public places in Santa Marta and thoroughly enjoyed himself until everyone just got used to him as an impostor. So when Jaime Bateman himself appeared no one took any notice, and many people confessed subsequently that they assumed that it was not Bateman they saw but his brother. Anyway, it was just not possible that the real Bateman would dare walk the streets undisguised.

The birthday party itself was strange. Bateman had rented a house at one of the beaches near Santa Marta to which access by car was possible but very difficult. April is the season for mangos, and, in addition to the many, many boxes of them brought beforehand, his guests brought along even more as presents, knowing it was Bateman's favourite fruit. There was unlimited rum and whisky but the official drink was also Bateman's favourite: *piña colada*.

The strict security made the party even stranger. Overall there were about one hundred guests but never more than ten at any one time. The only way to reach the party was by one of the hired boats on the other side of the bay, in which no more than eight people could fit. As one boat arrived another left, so the party never became over-crowded. There was, in any case, a number of speedboats near the house, as well as a whole column of guerrilla security forces capable of fending off any surprise attack.

In his own way, Bateman was a party lover. He enjoyed dancing the *salsa* and the *vallenato*. Like a true Caribbean, he was shy and prone to melancholy, which he concealed beneath his attractively explosive affability. On his birthday, he wore bathing trunks to receive his guests, and drank a toast with each one. He talked and laughed out loud, danced a little to the hired band and ate mangos.

Then suddenly he'd dive into the water and swim a long way out into the bay, while his guests carried on with the party. Around midday Clementina Cayón, arriving with a fresh supply of *piña colada,* animated the party even further. In a break in the music, someone cried out, 'Clementina Cayón—God, you're a wonderful woman.'

Until then, Bateman had no plans to go to Panama. He had intended to travel across country to talk to the second-in-command of M-19, Iván Marino Ospina, in charge of the guerrillas in Caqueta. Álvaro Fayad, meanwhile, had three appointments—in Bogotá, Toledo Plata, and Cali—and they all expected to meet up again three months later in the Putumayo jungle for a full meeting of the high command. These plans changed abruptly when Bateman received an unexpected message from Panama which said a personal emissary of Columbian President Betancur wanted talks with Bateman. The message, it seems, was not very explicit; it suggested, though, that a high-ranking person was involved. Bateman had been waiting for such an opportunity for some time. In less than twenty-four hours he changed all his immediate plans and decided to make the unforeseen journey which would lead ultimately to disaster.

Bateman's desire to meet Betancur face to face had become an obsession, but various incidents had convinced him that the government was not interested. The last such incident, on 3 April, was fairly unambiguous. President Betancur, on returning from talks in Cancún with the other presidents of the Contadora group, made a brief stop in Panama. Bateman had waited for him there. He waited expectantly all day only a few blocks from where Betancur talked for more than an hour with Colonel Manuel Antonio Noriega, the Chief of Security Services of Panama's National Guard. Betancur and Noriega discussed, among many other things, the activities of M-19 in Panama, but the possibility of meeting Bateman was never even raised. Disappointed once more, Bateman wrote the President a letter in which he insisted on the urgency of a truce in order to begin peace talks. The letter was delivered to the President of Panama, who read it over the phone to Betancur on 21 April, when Bateman was in Santa Marta. Perhaps Bateman thought sending a presidential emissary to Panama represented an answer to his letter. However, no Colombian source has been able to confirm that any such emissary was even sent in the first place.

During his week in Santa Marta, Bateman had several meetings with an old friend, the conservative politician Antonio Escobar Bravo. Few people knew at the time that Escobar had recently become a pilot. It should be noted, however, that an expert pilot is assumed to have flown 3,000 to 4,000 hours. Escobar had flown only eight hundred including lesson-time.

His plane was well-equipped: it had a dual system of VHF radio and VOR navigation which allows a plane's position to be determined from the ground; it also had a system of radio help for making instrument landings. He did, however, lack radar which, at the time of the emergency, would have been the most useful equipment of all, but very few light aircraft come equipped with it. Nevertheless, Bateman had confidence in him as a pilot and when the urgent trip to Panama became necessary, Bateman phoned Escobar at the beach where he had a house and they agreed to fly down the next day.

The ten people who were waiting for Escobar's plane at the airfield near Ciénaga included the following: Bateman, Toledo Plata, Nelly Vivas, Conrado Marín, two members of the national leadership and four members of M-19 security forces. They arrived before dawn in different cars and waited in a discreet corner for the plane to appear. It landed at 7.52 a.m., more or less as expected. Jaime Bateman boarded first, followed by Nelly Vivas and Conrado Marín who were both going to Caqueta by way of Panama. Nelly Vivas was a biologist from Cali who had spent eight years in Paris as a postgraduate; she had joined M-19 about six years before and was now one of the high command. Conrado Marín, once a peasant from Florencia, was now the regional leader of the guerrillas in Caqueta. He had been one of the first to take advantage of President Betancur's amnesty offer. Four of his comrades in Florencia followed his example, but then, over a period of a few months, each was killed by unknown gunmen. Shortly thereafter, Marín rejoined the organization, certain that he was meant to be the next victim.

Bateman had little luggage: a small case with a change of clothes,

$2,000 in cash, a cassette of two Colombian rock bands and the Spanish edition of Brazilian writer Jorge Amado's novel, *Doña Flor and her two husbands.* When they travelled by car he always carried a Browning revolver tucked in his belt under his shirt, and insisted on having a machine gun and at least one hand grenade within easy reach. Before that last flight, however, Bateman had given the machine gun to Álvaro Fayad, who took it with him on his drive to Bogotá. Bateman carried only the revolver and two grenades. He also carried a walkie-talkie with a range of eleven miles, which was necessary for communicating with M-19 ground troops but which Bateman intended to use before landing in Panama just to make sure there were no unpleasant surprises awaiting him. He also had a Colombian passport, with an assumed name. The most unusual object was a flare gun for being lost in the jungle or at sea. Bateman had bought it on his last trip to Panama. There was of course nothing inherently strange about this purchase. But later, after the long and fruitless searches in the jungle, Bateman's flares must have assumed the significance of a premonition. Later, too, the knowledge that Bateman had this emergency device contributed to the rescue team's conviction that Bateman could be found. But when the plane left the old airport at Ciénaga, nobody gave it a thought: it was a cloudless sky and it was certain to be a safe journey. Nevertheless, at that time exactly, a US meteorological satellite was relaying photographs of a vast area from Uraba to Nicaragua. They showed thick, threatening clouds just beginning to cover it.

After a long night on the road, Álvaro Fayad arrived in Bogotá the next afternoon. By that time, he assumed, Bateman would be safely in Panama. He was glad Bateman's change of plans had meant he had been unable to join him on the long overland drive, because the car had been stopped six times by different patrols—from the army and from the customs and drug squads. Why suddenly were there so many roadblocks? Each time he had been asked to identify himself and on at least three occasions he had been frisked and a torch was shone into his face. Bateman would not have made it: he was too well known. In any case, he certainly wouldn't have survived the friskings because of his right leg. Owing to an accident made worse by the life he had to lead in the jungle, he had a gangrenous limb; the skin on his shinbone, for instance, had shrunk to a taut layer of parchment, ulcerating at the slightest bump or bruise. It was impossible to disguise, and it was so well-known that whenever police agents suspected anyone of being Bateman, they would first grab his right leg and immediately roll up his trousers. On the one occasion that it really was Bateman, the soldier, obviously excited and confused, was unable to tell the difference between right and left, and looked up the wrong leg.

That night Fayad went to sleep without any news of Bateman. Very early the next day, two members of the Bogotá communications team told him Escobar's plane had not arrived, but they thought that perhaps the flight had been delayed. A little later, it was confirmed that the plane had left Santa Marta but had not stopped at Montería and had never reached Panama. Fayad then called Toledo Plata who, still in Santa Marta, confirmed the news: the day before at 12.28 the plane had been declared missing by the Civil Aviation in Panama. An air search had begun immediately. Until then, twenty-four hours later, nothing had been found. Days later, talking with some friends, Fayad expressed the impact of that day: 'It was as if suddenly my whole life went black.' On 30 April, the newspaper *El Tiempo* published a photo of Escobar on page nine with the news that his plane had been lost over Panamanian territory. At most about twenty people knew that behind that news item lay something much more sensational. And even though it was impossible to keep secrets in Santa Marta, no one knew anything there for twenty-two days when, by the most extraordinary coincidence, the editor-in-chief of the regional Cartagena newspaper, *El Universal,* found out. Shortly before, however, the Howarr Base at the Panama Canal, whom the Colombian Civil Aviation Authority had asked to help in the search for Escobar's plane, intimated just how much was known about that flight. 'That plane was not carrying drugs,' their cable read, 'but another kind of contraband.'

It has only been possible to piece together what actually happened after the plane left the old runway near the village of Ciénaga from the recordings of Escobar's radio contacts with the Panamanian air control. Contact was first made at 9.52. Having identified himself, Escobar was asked the time he had left Santa Marta, and replied: 'At

7.51.' That was not true. In fact he had left six minutes before but had added the six minutes so as to pick up his passengers at the secret airport without leaving traces of the clandestine landing. It was the only lie he told. He never said that he was flying alone—as was later reported—although no doubt he would have said so had he been asked. As regards the stop in Montería, we will never know why they did not make it.

In his first contact, Escobar informed air control that he was ascending from 6,000 feet—the authorized height for flying above the sea—to 9,000 feet. He must have been able to see the Darien Heights ahead of him, the highest point in Panama. Given his direction and his flying height, he should have arrived at Paitilla airport at 9.57. He made contact again to say that the weather was getting bad. The flight controller suggested he go up to 10,500 feet where there was better weather and stay there while he consulted radar control to ascertain the best route for him in the light of the changing conditions. The problem at that point was that Escobar's plane did not appear on the radar because he did not have adequate equipment on board, though he could be located on the direction finder through a radio signal emitted by the plane.

At 10.04 Escobar informed them that he was flying at 10,500 feet and there was still bad weather ahead, but that there were some breaks in the cloud through which he might be able to pass. His voice was calm, and his calculations and decisions were those of a good navigator. Then the flight controller asked him to press the radio button so that they could locate him on the direction finder. Escobar did so for just a moment before his signal was lost for ever. At that instant they were fifty-five miles northeast of Cerro de Ancón, which marks the boundary of Panama City with the Canal Zone. That means they had enough fuel to fly for another two hours and forty minutes but they were still over the Atlantic and thirty miles away from the Darien Heights. If the accident happened at the moment the radio signal was interrupted then the plane must have crashed into the sea. There is no evidence for this.

The Panamanian Civil Aviation Authority made a routine air search that lasted eight days. Lucio Escobar, one of the leaders of M-19, carried on looking for several more weeks. The M-19 patrols divided up an immense territory of almost 30,000 square miles into smaller units which they searched, inch by inch, for seventy days: the uninhabited universe of the Uraba tropical jungle—from Montería to the tip of Darien, with the Colombian border on one side and on the other, the frontier of Panama. In that last area alone nearly thirty planes have crashed since the Second World War: only four have been found. One of the patrols looking for the Escobar plane came across the remains of a plane that had disappeared in 1963: it was tangled up in the undergrowth only forty feet from a busy road. Others found communication equipment which the US Army had lost—heaven knows how long ago—in a kingdom of leaves and swamps where scarcely a ray of sun ever penetrates and which immediately envelops any object—including airplanes—unfortunate enough to fall into its depths.

From the start, M-19 believed that if Bateman and Marín were unhurt, they would need fifteen days at most to get out—the time it takes to cross the whole Panama jungle. If they were alive but badly injured, they would have made a camp and could have waited for up to a month and a half. Even a man of Bateman's physical and psychological strength could not have survived beyond that time. That Escobar was not a well-known politician helped the members of M-19 in their search. They divided it into two parts—air and land. For the first they hired two helicopters and private planes to fly over the jungle for twenty-five days. The land search began ten days after the accident, and was conducted by teams of fifteen men, each with one leader. Only the leaders knew whom they were looking for. It was felt to be important that no one, or at least as few people as possible, knew about Bateman's disappearance: it represented too significant a loss. In every other respect, though, it was classic guerrilla-search, characterized throughout by a network of codes and secret procedures. Communication, for instance, was conducted by beating the roots of trees—far more efficient than firing shots into the air or sending up red and blue flares like the ones Bateman carried and which were never seen. Every so often—at certain locations situated at the end of a sequence of signs which it was hoped that Bateman and his friends might come across and follow—they left a small encampment complete with radio, dry wood, food for three days and an extensive first-aid kit.

Around this time, on 20 May, the editor-in-chief of Cartagena's *El Universal,* Ángel Romero, picked up his phone at 7 p.m. to make a routine call and got a crossed line. It was a conversation between a man and a woman, talking openly about their deep concern over the disappearance of Bateman who, according to them, had been the victim of a plane crash, under mysterious circumstances, in Panama. Romero flew to Bogotá the next day and tried to contact M-19 there. He got nowhere. A military source, however, told him that Bateman had disappeared but that the plane-crash story was just a cover invented by M-19 to conceal the truth. It seems that the army's intelligence had quite a bit of information that supported a theory of its own: that Bateman had been killed in the village of Pajuil on 9 May and that M-19 wished, for no reason that makes immediate sense, to hide the fact of his death. Perhaps this is why, even now, the army continues to treat this case with a discretion verging on incredulity.

Following his own intuitions, however, Ángel Romero preferred the hypothesis of the coincidental telephone conversation and, on 30 May published the news of Bateman's death on the front page. It was greeted with indifference by the rest of the country's media—especially the larger papers who dismissed it as pure speculation. It was these same papers, months later, who published a story without any substantiation whatsoever—the source is still uncertain—that Bateman had fled the country with all of M-19's funds.

Long after this news reached the press, M-19 still refused to make a public statement. They wanted the crash kept as secret as possible if for no other reason than that it prevented army patrols from suddenly stumbling upon the trail of the search parties. But, more important, they simply refused to abandon a hope that had been reinforced by the visions of two clairvoyants. No one paid much attention to the unsolicited revelations of the first one in Panama. Later, however, a Colombian clairvoyant, independently of the first, revealed that he had had an identical vision. Even the most rational revolutionaries were shaken a little by doubt. Both visions spoke of three people in the heart of the jungle—two very weak and the other very strong, but the strong one was scared to move for fear of being discovered. And so the tireless search went on. But eventually even the most determined had to face up to reality. Only then, nine weeks after the accident, did the members of M-19 take the unanimous decision to announce Bateman's death officially. All that was lacking was the approval of his successor, Iván Marino Ospina, who, deep in the heart of the Caqueta jungle, was one of the last to hear the news. His reaction arrived at the very last moment, written on a crumpled, sweaty piece of paper smuggled to Bogotá in someone's shoe. Marino Ospina approved the publication of the news and sent his first order: 'Keep talking....'

Translated from the Spanish by Margaret Jull Costa

Mario Vargas Llosa
Cheap Intellectuals

I recall a remark made by James Baldwin, the black American novelist: 'Whenever I'm in a group of white intellectuals, I have a method for discovering the racists. I talk nonsense. Utter unqualified rubbish. I then support it with theories of the most grotesquely absurd nature. If the whites around me listen with respect and at the end overwhelm me with applause and praise, I have no doubt: they're racist pigs.'

Baldwin's anecdote describes a special kind of intellectual condescension: one that assumes that its victim—obviously 'crippled' by race or class or upbringing—is so mentally limited as to deserve little more than an amused pity. The anecdote came to mind recently. I was at a conference on the Latin-American novel. It was being held in Denmark—at the Museum of Modern Art—but it could well have taken place anywhere in Europe. The conference was organized around a series of seminars, and during each one a fellow Peruvian writer interrupted the proceedings and asked to speak. And every time, he was not merely given permission; he was veritably ushered to the podium. His first speech took me by surprise; it also took by surprise the two women who were expected to translate his curiously colloquial Spanish—full of the slang peculiar to the streets of Lima—into a language that future Danish readers might understand. He gesticulated. He shouted. It was, really, as if we were at a street-rally. And eventually he explained how his novels were special. They were not published by bourgeois publishers but by the trade unions. And the trade unions were also responsible for their distribution. He wrote, he told us, not to satisfy personal vanity or greed. He wrote to raise the revolutionary consciousness of the Peruvian masses. And therefore he never accepted royalties, preferring to donate them to popular movements.

It was, I think, at this point that someone in the audience asked about sales figures, and my compatriot unhesitatingly quoted a number of so many thousands that it was high enough to give the other novelists present an acute sense of vertigo. Another man spoke up—obviously a publisher from Copenhagen—and asked if my compatriot's moral reservations about capitalist publishing houses concerned only those in Peru, or did they apply equally to all publishers—even those, say, in Denmark? The question had a curious effect; the Peruvian was visibly agitated. He was, he informed us, not at all dogmatic. What would be the point? For as the great Latin-American Marxist theoretician Mariategui has pointed out, Marxism should never be a mindless reiteration of ideas, but was meant always to be a heroic creation. We must—he urged us to recognize—always make our decisions in strict accordance with the perceived objective conditions of each situation, since to do otherwise would represent a fall into subjectivism, the dangers of which have been pointed out from the very beginning by Marx and Engels and Lenin—and a long list of others whom I'm unable to recall.

The Danes listened with the greatest attention. Some took notes. Everyone applauded, passionately.

What exactly was the fascination? The image, I assume, of an effervescent Peru in which writers, instead of being the hired clowns of the bourgeoisie, were transubstantiated into political heroes by the working classes who printed, reprinted and purchased—in enormous quantities—all the copies of their books. It was, however, more than fascination. Or at least it appeared to be. Because no one tried to silence or contradict my compatriot. There was a time when young Peruvian writers attending international conferences were so overwhelmed by a sense of their own cultural inferiority that they said nothing. This has obviously now changed. The difficulty of Peru's champion of the proletariat was not that he said nothing; but that there seemed to be no time when he did. He spoke from beginning to end. He denounced enemy after enemy— so many enemies that even I wasn't able to identify most of them: they were obviously groups or individuals at the university in Peru with whom he had fallen out (it must have been an especially curious list to the Danes, many of whom, I know, had enough difficulty identifying exactly where you might find Peru on a world-map.) But this was not all. There were also the clichés and the jargon and the catchphrases and—perhaps worst of all—the rhetorical flourish with which my compatriot finished each speech, raising his arms (fists clenched) in anticipation of his applause. His speeches were grotesque; and they were tragic. They were tragic because they turned not just a country but even the continent into an unreality. Latin America emerged at the end of our seminars as so deformed that even the crimes of Pinochet or the repression in Argentina or the horrors of Central America appeared, like the thousands of trade unionists clamouring for his books, as nothing more than the stuff of fairy tales.

How could this be allowed to happen? Danish writers had brought this man from the other side of the world, preferring him to many others who would have given a more lucid and honestly representative account of Latin America. One of the organizers of the conference explained why: 'It was important that a writer of the proletariat participated in the symposium.' What could I say in reply? They knew so little about us that anyone, disguised as the literary mouthpiece of the exploited, could win a trip to the other side of the globe. Europeans are so filled with beautiful intentions— they want to help our poor continent of victims so much—that, on this occasion, they were prepared to sit day after day and endure, impassively, uncritically, the deceitful perorations of a confused Peruvian and, at the end of each session, to sign all the petitions and telegrams he passed around.

On reflection, however, I think I have a clearer understanding of these beautiful intentions. The Danish writers were not surprised by those extraordinary speeches: the speeches were what they expected. More important, they were what they wanted. The Peruvian proletariat was not there by accident or by his own self-aggrandizing designs. He was there because his hosts knew he would say exactly what we heard: because that is what Europeans want to hear from Latin Americans.

Why? Because Europeans want a fictitious Latin America on to which they can project their own desires. They want a Latin America which satisfies a longing for political engagement that is not possible in their own countries. In Latin America, they see the convictions by which they want to live their own lives, even though these very convictions are, day after day, demonstrated to be illusory and impossible in their own countries. They are frustrated and inadequate, and so Europeans turn to us—in Latin America— to see exactly what they want to see, an image distorted by their own fantasies, like the wicked Queen's magic mirror in *Snow White*. And what they see is not the complexity and diversity of our continent, in which there are many things other than suffering, exploitation, and oppression—misfortunes, incidentally, that cannot be understood or remedied by an easy populist rhetoric—but the grandiloquent, puerile, and sentimental image that my compatriot confirmed for them in his most fervent and passionate speeches, never suspecting that he was playing a part written for him by the intellectual patrons of a sophisticated culture. His function, fulfilled brilliantly even if naively, was to provide vicarious compensation for the unfortunate Europeans, who—poor things—must live in a democracy, must work in a country with a long and established cultural tradition, and must write for a population whose trade unionists prefer not to publish consciousness-raising novels by revolutionaries, but to stay at home and watch their television sets.

In one of her short stories, Isak Dinesen describes the practice, common among women of the eighteenth-century Danish aristocracy, of bringing African monkeys to grand parties. The monkeys served the double purpose of satisfying high-society's demand for the exotic, while perversely rendering the women themselves, framed by their hairy escorts, infinitely more beautiful than they might otherwise appear on their own. Ever an admirer of historical continuity, I derive great comfort from the awareness that this refined custom of the women of the Danish aristocracy is carried on today among their descendants.

Translated from the Spanish by Margaret Jull Costa

The Year of Miracle and Grief

LEONID BORODIN

'A miracle is something which occurs in spite of and contrary to everything. According to the rules, it does not happen. Consequently, when a miracle does take place, it does so in defiance of the rules.'

From time to time a novel is published that perfectly captures the mystery and panic of falling in love. Such novels linger around in the reader's mind long after the book has been read. Some novels even change our perceptions of reality. The Year of Miracle and Grief is such a novel. That this book has been written at all is a miracle.

Leonid Borodin was born in Siberia in 1938. He was arrested in 1967 and released after a protracted hunger strike in 1973. Re-arrested in 1982, he is now serving ten years' hard labour followed by five years' internal exile.

£7.95 Illustrated

QUARTET BOOKS LIMITED
A member of the Namara Group   27/29 Goodge Street   London W1

The British Council publishes British Book News, the monthly review with the best coverage of books published in Britain.

DON DELILLO
HUMAN MOMENTS IN
WORLD WAR III

A note about Vollmer. He no longer describes the earth as a library globe or a map that has come alive, as a cosmic eye staring into deep space. This last was his most ambitious fling at imagery. The war has changed the way he sees the earth. The earth is land and water, the dwelling-place of mortal men, in elevated dictionary terms. He doesn't see it any more (storm-spiralled, sea-bright, breathing heat and haze and colour) as an occasion for picturesque language, for easeful play or speculation.

At two hundred and twenty kilometres we see ship wakes and the larger airports. Icebergs, lightning bolts, sand-dunes. I point out lava flows and cold-core eddies. That silver ribbon off the Irish coast, I tell him, is an oil slick.

This is my third orbital mission, Vollmer's first. He is an engineering genius, a communications and weapons genius, and maybe other kinds of genius as well. As mission specialist, I'm content to be in charge. (The word *specialist,* in the standard usage of Colorado Command, refers here to someone who does not specialize.) Our spacecraft is designed primarily to gather intelligence. The refinement of the quantum-burn technique enables us to make frequent adjustments of orbit without firing rockets every time. We swing out into high, wide trajectories, the whole earth as our psychic light, to inspect unmanned and possibly hostile satellites. We orbit tightly, snugly, take intimate looks at surface activities in untravelled places. The banning of nuclear weapons has made the world safe for war.

I try not to think big thoughts or submit to rambling abstractions. But the urge sometimes comes over me. Earth orbit puts men into philosophical temper. How can we help it? We see the planet complete, we have a privileged vista. In our attempts to be equal to the experience, we tend to meditate importantly on subjects like the human condition. It makes a man feel *universal,* floating over the continents, seeing the rim of the world, a line as clear as a compass arc, knowing it is just a turning of the bend to Atlantic twilight, to sediment plumes and kelp beds, an island chain glowing in the dusky sea.

I tell myself it is only scenery. I want to think of our life here as ordinary, as a housekeeping arrangement, an unlikely but workable setup caused by a housing shortage or spring floods in the valley.

Vollmer does the systems check-list and goes to his hammock to rest. He is twenty-three years old, a boy with a longish head and close-cropped hair. He talks about northern Minnesota as he removes the objects in his personal-preference kit, placing them on an adjacent Velcro surface for tender inspection. I have a 1901 silver dollar in my personal-preference kit. Little else of note. Vollmer has graduation pictures, bottle caps, small stones from his backyard. I don't know whether he chose these items himself or whether they were pressed on him by parents who feared that his life in space would be lacking in human moments.

Our hammocks are human moments, I suppose, although I don't know whether Colorado Command planned it that way. We eat hot dogs and almond crunch bars and apply lip balm as part of the pre-sleep check-list. We wear slippers at the firing panel. Vollmer's football jersey is a human moment. Outsize, purple and white, of polyester mesh, bearing the number 79, a big man's number, a prime of no particular distinction, it makes him look stoop-shouldered, abnormally long-framed.

'I still get depressed on Sundays,' he says.

'Do we have Sundays here?'

'No, but they have them there and I still feel them. I always know when it's Sunday.'

'Why do you get depressed?'

'The slowness of Sundays. Something about the glare, the smell of warm grass, the church service, the relatives visiting in nice clothes. The whole day kind of lasts for ever.'

'I didn't like Sundays either.'

'They were slow but not lazy-slow. They were long and hot, or long and cold. In summer my grandmother made lemonade. There was a routine. The whole day was kind of set up beforehand and the routine almost never changed. Orbital routine is different. It's satisfying. It gives our time a shape and substance. Those Sundays were shapeless despite the fact you knew what was coming, who was coming, what we'd all say. You knew the first words out of the mouth of each person before anyone spoke. I was the only kid in the group. People were happy to see me. I used to want to hide.'

'What's wrong with lemonade?' I ask.

A battle-management satellite, unmanned, reports high-energy laser activity in orbital sector Dolores. We take out our laser kits and study them for half an hour. The beaming procedure is complex, and because the panel operates on joint control only, we must rehearse the sets of established measures with the utmost care.

A note about the earth. The earth is the preserve of day and night. It contains a sane and balanced variation, a natural waking and sleeping, or so it seems to someone deprived of this tidal effect.

This is why Vollmer's remark about Sundays in Minnesota struck me as interesting. He still feels, or claims he feels, or thinks he feels, that inherently earthbound rhythm.

To men at this remove, it is as though things exist in their particular physical form in order to reveal the hidden simplicity of some powerful mathematical truth. The earth reveals to us the simple awesome beauty of day and night. It is there to contain and incorporate these conceptual events.

Vollmer in his shorts and suction clogs resembles a high school swimmer, all but hairless, an unfinished man not aware he is open to cruel scrutiny, not aware he is without devices, standing with arms folded in a place of echoing voices and chlorine fumes. There is something stupid in the sound of his voice. It is too direct, a deep voice from high in the mouth, slightly insistent, a little loud. Vollmer has never said a stupid thing in my presence. It is just his voice that is stupid, a grave and naked bass, a voice without inflection or breath.

We are not cramped here. The flight deck and crew quarters are thoughtfully designed. Food is fair to good. There are books, videocassettes, news and music. We do the manual check-lists, the oral check-lists, the simulated firings with no sign of boredom or carelessness. If anything, we are getting better at our tasks all the time. The only danger is conversation.

I try to keep our conversations on an everyday plane. I make it a point to talk about small things, routine things. This makes sense to me. It seems a sound tactic, under the circumstances, to restrict our talk to familiar topics, minor matters. I want to build a structure of the commonplace. But Vollmer has a tendency to bring up enormous subjects. He wants to talk about war and the weapons of war. He wants to discuss global strategies, global aggressions. I tell him now that he has stopped describing the earth as a cosmic eye he wants to see it as a game board or computer model. He looks at me plain-faced and tries to get me in a theoretical argument: selective space-based attacks versus long, drawn-out, well-modulated land-sea-air engagements. He quotes experts, mentions sources. What am I supposed to say? He will suggest that people are disappointed in the war. The war is dragging into its third week. There is a sense in which it is worn out, played out. He gathers this from the news broadcasts we periodically receive. Something in the announcer's voice hints at a let-down, a fatigue, a faint bitterness about—*something.* Vollmer is probably right about this. I've heard myself in the tone of the broadcaster's voice, in the voice of Colorado Command, despite the fact that our news is censored, that they are not telling us things they feel we shouldn't know, in our special situation, our exposed and sensitive position. In his direct and stupid-sounding and uncannily perceptive way, young Vollmer says that people are not enjoying this war to the same extent that people have always enjoyed and nourished themselves on war, as a heightening, a periodic intensity. What I object to in Vollmer is that he often shares my deep-reaching and most reluctantly-held convictions. Coming from that mild face, in that earnest resonant run-on voice, these ideas unnerve and worry me as they never do when they remain unspoken. I want words to be secretive, to cling to a darkness in the deepest interior. Vollmer's candour exposes something painful.

It is not too early in the war to discern nostalgic references to earlier wars. All wars refer back. Ships, planes, entire operations are named after ancient battles, simpler weapons, what we perceive as conflicts of nobler intent. This recon-interceptor is called *Tomahawk II.* When I sit at the firing panel I look at a photograph of Vollmer's granddad when he was a young man in sagging khakis and a shallow helmet, standing in a bare field, a rifle strapped to his shoulder. This is a human moment, and it reminds me that war, among other things, is a form of longing.

We dock with the command station, take on food, exchange cassettes. The war is going well, they tell us, although it isn't likely they know much more than we do.

Then we separate.

The manoeuvre is flawless and I am feeling happy and satisfied, having resumed human contact with the nearest form of the outside world, having traded quips and manly insults, traded voices, traded news and rumours—buzzes, rumbles, scuttle-butt. We stow our supplies of broccoli and apple cider and fruit cocktail and butterscotch pudding. I feel a homey emotion, putting away the colourfully-packaged goods, a sensation of prosperous well-being, the consumer's solid comfort.

Vollmer's T-shirt bears the word INSCRIPTION.

'People had hoped to be caught up in something bigger than themselves,' he says. 'They thought it would be a shared crisis. They would feel a sense of shared purpose, a shared destiny. Like a snowstorm that blankets a large city—but lasting months, lasting years, carrying everyone along, creating fellow feeling where there was only suspicion and fear. Strangers talking to each other, meals by candlelight when the power fails. The war would ennoble everything we say and do. What was impersonal would become personal. What was solitary would be shared. But what happens when the sense of shared crisis begins to dwindle much sooner than anyone expected? We begin to think the feeling lasts longer in snowstorms.'

A note about selective noise. Forty-eight hours ago I was monitoring data on the mission console when a voice broke in on my report to Colorado Command. The voice was unenhanced, heavy with static. I checked my headset, checked the switches and lights. Seconds later the command signal resumed and I heard our flight-dynamics officer ask me to switch to the redundant sense frequencer. I did this but it only caused the weak voice to return, a voice that carried with it a strange and unspecifiable poignancy. I seemed somehow to recognize it. I don't mean I knew who was speaking. It was the tone I recognized, the touching quality of some half-remembered and tender event, even through the static, the sonic mist.

In any case, Colorado Command resumed transmission in a matter of seconds.

'We have a deviate, Tomahawk.'

'We copy. There's a voice.'

'We have gross oscillation here.'

'There's some interference. I have gone redundant but I'm not sure it's helping.'

'We are clearing an outframe to locate source.'

'Thank you, Colorado.'

'It is probably just selective noise. You are negative red on the step-function quad.'

'It was a voice,' I told them.

'We have just received an affirm on selective noise.'

'I could hear words, in English.'

'We copy selective noise.'

'Someone was talking, Colorado.'

'What do you think selective noise is?'

'I don't know what it is.'

'You are getting a spill from one of the unmanneds.'

'If it's an unmanned, how could it be sending a voice?'

'It is not a voice as such, Tomahawk. It is selective noise. We have some real firm telemetry on that.'

'It sounded like a voice.'

'It is supposed to sound like a voice. But it is not a voice as such. It is enhanced.'

'It sounded unenhanced. It sounded human in all sorts of ways.'

'It is signals and they are spilling from geosynchronous orbit. This is your deviate. You are getting voice codes from twenty-two thousand miles. It is basically a weather report. We will correct, Tomahawk. In the meantime, advise you stay redundant.'

About ten hours later Vollmer heard the voice. Then he heard two or three other voices. They were people speaking, people in conversation. He gestured to me as he listened, pointed to the headset, then raised his shoulders, held his hands apart to indicate surprise and bafflement. In the swarming noise (as he said later) it wasn't easy to get the drift of what people were saying. The static was frequent, the references were somewhat elusive, but Vollmer mentioned how intensely affecting these voices were, even when the signals were at their weakest. One thing he did know: it wasn't selective noise. A quality of purest, sweetest sadness issued from remote space. He wasn't sure, but he thought there was also a background noise integral to the conversation. Laughter. The sound of people laughing.

In other transmissions we've been able to recognize theme music, an announcer's introduction, wisecracks and bursts of applause, commercials for products whose long-lost brand names evoke the golden antiquity of great cities buried in sand and river silt.

Somehow we are picking up signals from radio programmes of forty, fifty, sixty years ago.

Our current task is to collect imagery data on troop deployment. Vollmer surrounds his Hasselblad, engrossed in some microadjustment. There is a seaward bulge of stratocumulus. Sun glint and littoral drift. I see blooms of plankton in a blue of such Persian richness it seems an animal rapture, a colour change to express some form of intuitive delight. As the surface features unfurl I list them aloud by name. It is the only game I play in space, reciting the earth names, the nomenclature of contour and structure. Glacial scour, moraine debris. Shatter-coning at the edge of a multi-ring impact site. A resurgent caldera, a mass of castellated rimrock. Over the sand seas now. Parabolic dunes, star dunes, straight dunes with radial crests. The emptier the land, the more luminous and precise the names for its features. Vollmer says the thing science does best is name the features of the world.

He has degrees in science and technology. He was a scholarship winner, an honours student, a research assistant. He ran science projects, read technical papers in the deep-pitched earnest voice that rolls off the roof of his mouth. As mission specialist (generalist), I sometimes resent his non-scientific perceptions, the glimmerings of maturity and balanced judgement. I am beginning to feel slightly pre-empted. I want him to stick to systems, onboard guidance, data parameters. His human insights make me nervous.

'I'm happy,' he says.

These words are delivered with matter-of-fact finality, and the simple statement affects me powerfully. It frightens me, in fact. What does he mean he's happy? Isn't happiness totally outside our frame of reference? How can he think it is possible to be happy here? I want to say to him, 'This is just a housekeeping arrangement, a series of more or less routine tasks. Attend to your tasks, do your testing, run through your check-lists.' I want to say, 'Forget the measure of our vision, the sweep of things, the war itself, the terrible death. Forget the over-arching night, the stars as static points, as mathematical fields. Forget the cosmic solitude, the welling awe and dread.'

I want to say, 'Happiness is not a fact of this experience, at least not to the extent that one is bold enough to speak of it.'

L aser technology contains a core of foreboding and myth. It is a clean sort of lethal package we are dealing with, a well-behaved beam of photons, an engineered coherence, but we approach the weapon with our minds full of ancient warnings and fears. (There ought to be a term for this ironic condition: primitive fear of the weapons we are advanced enough to design and produce.) Maybe this is why the project managers were ordered to work out a firing procedure that depends on the co-ordinated actions of two men—two temperaments, two souls—operating the controls together. Fear of the power of light, the pure stuff of the universe.

A single dark mind in a moment of inspiration might think it liberating to fling a concentrated beam at some lumbering humpbacked Boeing making its commercial rounds at thirty thousand feet.

Vollmer and I approach the firing panel. The panel is designed in such a way that the joint operators must sit back to back. The reason for this, although Colorado Command never specifically said so, is to keep us from seeing each other's face. Colorado wants to be sure that weapon personnel in particular are not influenced by each other's tics and perturbations. We are back to back, therefore, harnessed in our seats, ready to begin, Vollmer in his purple and white jersey, his fleeced pad-abouts.

This is only a test.

I start the playback. At the sound of a pre-recorded voice command, we each insert a modal key in its proper slot. Together we count down from five and then turn the keys one-quarter left. This puts the system in what is called an open-minded mode. We count down from three. The enhanced voice says, *You are open-minded now.*

Vollmer speaks into his voice-print analyser.

'This is code B for *blue-grass.* Request voice-identity clearance.'

We count down from five and then speak into our voice-print analysers. We say whatever comes into our heads. The point is simply to produce a voice-print that matches the print in the memory bank. This ensures that the men at the panel are the same men authorized to be there when the system is in an open-minded mode.

This is what comes into my head: 'I am standing at the corner of Fourth and Main, where thousands are dead of unknown causes, their scorched bodies piled in the street.'

We count down from three. The enhanced voice says, *You are cleared to proceed to lock-in position.*

We turn our modal keys half right. I activate the logic chip and study the numbers on my screen. Vollmer disengages voice-print and puts us in voice circuit rapport with the onboard computer's sensing mesh. We count down from five. The enhanced voice says, *You are locked in now.*

As we move from one step to the next a growing satisfaction passes through me—the pleasure of elite and secret skills, a life in which every breath is governed by specific rules, by patterns, codes, controls. I try to keep the results of the operation out of my mind, the whole point of it, the outcome of these sequences of precise and esoteric steps. But often I fail. I let the image in, I think the thought, I even say the word at times. This is confusing, of course. I feel tricked. My pleasure feels betrayed, as if it had a life of its own, a child-like or intelligent-animal existence independent of the man at the firing panel.

We count down from five. Vollmer releases the lever that unwinds the systems-purging disc. My pulse-marker shows green at three-second intervals. We count down from three. We turn the modal keys three-quarters right. I activate the beam sequencer. We turn the keys one-quarter right. We count down from three. Blue-grass music plays over the squawk box. The enhanced voice says, *You are moded to fire now.*

We study our world-map kits.

'Don't you sometimes feel a power in you?' Vollmer says. 'An extreme state of good health, sort of. An *arrogant* healthiness. That's it. You are feeling so good you begin thinking you're a little superior to other people. A kind of life-strength. An optimism about yourself that you generate almost at the expense of others. Don't you sometimes feel this?'

(Yes, as a matter of fact.)

'There's probably a German word for it. But the point I want to make is that this powerful feeling is so—I don't know—*delicate*. That's it. One day you feel it, the next day you are suddenly puny and doomed. A single little thing goes wrong, you feel doomed, you feel utterly weak and defeated and unable to act powerfully or even sensibly. Everyone else is lucky, you are unlucky, hapless, sad, ineffectual and doomed.'

(Yes, yes.)

By chance, we are over the Missouri River now, looking towards the Red Lakes of Minnesota. I watch Vollmer go through his map kit, trying to match the two worlds. This is a deep and mysterious happiness, to confirm the accuracy of a map. He seems immensely satisfied. He keeps saying, 'That's it, that's it.'

Vollmer talks about childhood. In orbit he has begun to think about his early years for the first time. He is surprised at the power of these memories. As he speaks he keeps his head turned to the window. Minnesota is a human moment. Upper Red Lake, Lower Red Lake. He clearly feels he can see himself there.

'Kids don't take walks,' he says. 'They don't sunbathe or sit on the porch.'

He seems to be saying that children's lives are too well supplied to accommodate the spells of reinforced being that the rest of us depend on. A deft enough thought but not to be pursued. It is time to prepare for a quantum burn.

We listen to the old radio shows. Light flares and spreads across the blue-banded edge, sunrise, sunset, the urban grids in shadow. A man and a woman trade well-timed remarks, light, pointed, bantering. There is a sweetness in the tenor voice of the young man singing, a simple vigour that time and distance and random noise have enveloped in eloquence and yearning. Every sound, every lilt of strings has this veneer of age. Vollmer says he remembers these programmes, although of course he has never heard them before. What odd happenstance, what flourish or grace of the laws of physics enables us to pick up these signals? Travelled voices, chambered and dense. At times they have the detached and surreal quality of aural hallucination, voices in attic rooms, the complaints of dead relatives. But the sound effects are full of urgency and verve. Cars turn dangerous corners, crisp gunfire fills the night. It was, it is, wartime. Wartime for Duz and GrapeNuts Flakes. Comedians make fun of the way the enemy talks. We hear hysterical mock German, moonshine Japanese. The cities are in light, the listening millions, fed, met comfortably in drowsy rooms, at war, as the night comes softly down. Vollmer says he recalls specific moments, the comic inflections, the announcer's fat-man laughter. He recalls individual voices rising from the laughter of the studio audience, the crackle of a St Louis businessman, the brassy wail of a high-shouldered blonde just arrived in California, where women wear their hair this year in aromatic bales.

Vollmer drifts across the wardroom upside-down, eating an almond crunch.

He sometimes floats free of his hammock, sleeping in a foetal crouch, bumping into walls, adhering to a corner of the ceiling grid.

'Give me a minute to think of the name,' he says in his sleep.

He says he dreams of vertical spaces from which he looks, as a boy, at—*something*. My dreams are the heavy kind, the kind that are hard to wake from, to rise out of. They are strong enough to pull me back down, dense enough to leave me with a heavy head, a drugged and bloated feeling. There are episodes of faceless gratification, vaguely disturbing.

It's almost unbelievable when you think of it, how they live there in all that ice and sand and mountainous wilderness.

'Look at it,' he says. 'Huge barren deserts, huge oceans. How do they endure all those terrible things? The floods alone. The earthquakes alone make it crazy to live there. Look at those fault systems. They're so big, there's so many of them. The volcanic eruptions alone. What could be more frightening than a volcanic eruption? How do they endure avalanches, year after year, with numbing regularity? It's hard to believe people live there. The floods alone. You can see whole huge discoloured areas, all flooded out, washed out. How do they survive, where do they go? Look at the cloud build-ups. Look at that swirling storm centre. What about the people who live in the path of a storm like that? It must be packing incredible winds. The lightning alone. People exposed on beaches, near trees and telephone poles. Look at the cities with their spangled lights spreading in all directions. Try to imagine the crime and violence. Look at the smoke pall hanging low. What does that mean in terms of respiratory disorders? It's crazy. Who would live there? The deserts, how they encroach. Every year they claim more and more arable land. How enormous those snowfields are. Look at the massive storm fronts over the ocean. There are ships down there, small craft, some of them. Try to imagine the waves, the rocking. The hurricanes alone. The tidal waves. Look at those coastal communities exposed to tidal waves. What could be more frightening than a tidal wave? But they live there, they stay there. Where could they go?'

I want to talk to him about calorie intake, the effectiveness of the earplugs and nasal decongestants. The earplugs are human moments. The apple cider and the broccoli are human moments. Vollmer himself is a human moment, never more so than when he forgets there is a war.

The close-cropped hair and longish head. The mild blue eyes that bulge slightly. The protuberant eyes of long-bodied people with stooped shoulders. The long hands and wrists. The mild face. The easy face of a handyman in a panel truck that has an extension ladder fixed to the roof and a scuffed licence plate, green and white, with the state motto beneath the digits. That kind of face.

He offers to give me a haircut. What an interesting thing a haircut is, when you think of it. Before the war there were time slots reserved for such activities. Houston not only had everything scheduled well in advance but constantly monitored us for whatever meagre feedback might result. We were wired, taped, scanned, diagnosed, and metred. We were men in space, objects worthy of the most scrupulous care, the deepest sentiments and anxieties.

Now there is a war. Nobody cares about my hair, what I eat, how I feel about the spacecraft's décor, and it is not Houston but Colorado we are in touch with. We are no longer delicate biological specimens adrift in an alien environment. The enemy can kill us with its photons, its mesons, its charged particles faster than any calcium deficiency or trouble of the inner ear, faster than any dusting of micrometeoroids. The emotions have changed. We've stopped being candidates for an embarrassing demise, the kind of mistake or unforeseen event that tends to make a nation grope for the appropriate response. As men in war, we can be certain, dying, that we will arouse uncomplicated sorrows, the open and dependable feelings that grateful nations count on to embellish the simplest ceremony.

A note about the universe. Vollmer is on the verge of deciding that our planet is alone in harbouring intelligent life. We are an accident and we happened only once. (What a remark to make, in egg-shaped orbit, to someone who doesn't want to discuss the larger questions.) He feels this way because of the war.

The war, he says, will bring about an end to the idea that the universe swarms, as they say, with life. Other astronauts have looked past the star points and imagined infinite possibility, grape-clustered worlds teeming with higher forms. But this was before the war. Our view is changing even now, his and mine, he says, as we drift across the firmament.

Is Vollmer saying that cosmic optimism is a luxury reserved for periods between world wars? Do we project our current failure and despair out towards the star clouds, the endless night? After all, he says, where are they? If they exist, why has there been no sign, not one, not any, not a single indication that serious people might cling to, not a whisper, a radio pulse, a shadow? The war tells us it is foolish to believe.

Our dialogues with Colorado Command are beginning to sound like computer-generated tea-time chat. Vollmer tolerates Colorado's jargon only to a point. He is critical of their more debased locutions and doesn't mind letting them know. Why, then, if I agree with his views on this matter, am I becoming irritated by his complaints? Is he too young to champion the language? Does he have the experience, the professional standing to scold our flight-dynamics officer, our conceptual-paradigm officer, our status consultants on waste-management systems and evasion-related zonal options? Or is it something else completely, something unrelated to Colorado Command and our communications with them? Is it the sound of his voice? Is it just his *voice* that is driving me crazy?

Vollmer has entered a strange phase. He spends all his time at the window now, looking down at the earth. He says little or nothing. He simply wants to look, do nothing but look. The oceans, the continents, the archipelagoes. We are configured in what is called a cross-orbit series and there is no repetition from one swing around the earth to the next. He sits there looking. He takes meals at the window, does check-lists at the window, barely glancing at the instruction sheets as we pass over tropical storms, over grass fires and major ranges. I keep waiting for him to return to his pre-war habit of using quaint phrases to describe the earth: it's a beach ball, a sun-ripened fruit. But he simply looks out of the window, eating almond crunches, the wrappers floating away. The view clearly fills his consciousness. It is powerful enough to silence him, to still the voice that rolls off the roof of his mouth, to leave him turned in the seat, twisted uncomfortably for hours at a time.

The view is endlessly fulfilling. It is like the answer to a lifetime of questions and vague cravings. It satisfies every child-like curiosity, every muted desire, whatever there is in him of the scientist, the poet, the primitive seer, the watcher of fire and shooting stars, whatever obsessions eat at the night side of his mind, whatever sweet and dreamy yearning he has ever felt for nameless places far away, whatever earth sense he possesses, the neural pulse of some wilder awareness, a sympathy for beasts, whatever belief in an immanent vital force, the Lord of Creation, whatever secret harbouring of the idea of human oneness, whatever wishfulness and simple-hearted hope, whatever of too much and not enough, all at once and little by little, whatever burning urge to escape responsibility and routine, escape his own over-specialization, the circumscribed and inward-spiralling self, whatever remnants of his boyish longing to fly, his dreams of strange spaces and eerie heights, his fantasies of happy death, whatever indolent and sybaritic leanings, lotus-eater, smoker of grasses and herbs, blue-eyed gazer into space—all these are satisfied, all collected and massed in that living body, the sight he sees from the window.

'It is just so interesting,' he says at last. 'The colours and all.'

The colours and all.

How to make
a year
last 13 months!

Buy a subscription to **The Times Literary Supplement** for a friend or relative as a gift and take advantage of our special offer of a 13-month subscription (56 issues) for the price of 12. Simply complete the coupon below and send it with your cheque or postal order made payable to Times Newspapers Limited.

If more than one subscription is required, please enter details on a separate sheet of paper. Offer applies to U.K. only. Details of overseas subscriptions are available on request from the address below.

TLS
The Times Literary Supplement

Please send a year's subscription to The Times Literary Supplement to:

NAME_____

ADDRESS_____

_____

_____

_____

I enclose my cheque for £30.00 (Cheques made payable to Times Newspapers Ltd.)

SIGNATURE_____ DATE_____

Address this coupon with your cheque to:
FRANCES GODDARD, The Times Literary Supplement, Priory House, St John's Lane, London, EC1M 4BX.

GRA

REDMOND
O'HANLON
DEEPER INTO THE
HEART OF BORNEO

The next day the river became more difficult still: an unending series of rapids and snags and boulders. The dugout seemed to increase its weight with every mile; the one-hundred-and-twenty-five-degree heat was not easy to struggle through, and there were less laughs at lunch-time. The river was too low, said Dana, the going too tough. Only Leon, immensely strong, cheerful and affectionate, was undaunted. He was obviously a champion river-hunter, too: while we lay, exhausted, in the shade of a jungle-chestnut tree, he disappeared, swimming underwater up an adjacent creek. Half-an-hour later he returned, towing a fresh trophy. It was much longer than he was: a big water monitor, a black and yellow prehistoric dragon with a long forked tongue which it protruded like a snake. Dana and Leon pulled it up the bank, the harpoon stuck through its side. It stood four-square, hissing, and lashing its long tail. Dana drew his parang and killed it with a blow to the head.

The lizard lashed into the dugout, we set off again. It was too arduous to notice much. But then, hours later, the country began to open out, and the big trees stepped back from the bank. Rolling hills stretched away to a forest horizon. The Iban looked about them, uneasily. There was no mark of all this on our secret government maps.

A little further on, four men, in two small canoes, were setting nets.

'Kayan?' shouted Dana.

'Kenyah!' shouted the men, much insulted. They yelled instructions above the noise of the water, pointing upriver.

'Can you understand them, Leon?'

'No,' said Leon, uncharacteristically quiet. 'These are not our peoples.'

The river meandered and then entered a very long straight reach. A paradise was disclosed. An inland kingdom, secluded almost beyond reach—of padi fields and banana trees, palms and coconuts lay in its own wide valley, surrounded by jungle hills. A huge longhouse, its atap roof blending into the landscape, was set back from the bank of the river, about three miles off. It took us two hours to manhandle the heavy dugout up to the beach beneath the

Redmond O'Hanlon and James Fenton, led by their two Iban guides—Leon and Dana—journeyed into Borneo from February to April of last year.

longhouse.

I was about to wade ashore, when Dana stopped me emphatically, pointing me to my place on the duckboards.

'We must waits,' said Leon, 'this not our country.'

About sixty children watched us silently from the bank. Some of their mothers, their ear-lobes weighted by brass rings dangling down below their shoulders, watched too. In about a quarter-of-an-hour, after much to-ing and fro-ing, the Chief's son arrived and formally invited us to set foot on his tribal lands.

The settlement was obviously large and well-organized. Even the dogs looked young and healthy. And the longhouse, when we reached it, was spectacular. Massively constructed on tree-trunk piles and a forest of lesser stilts, it was about three hundred yards long, the main floor set fifteen feet from the ground. Dark, hairy, boar-like pigs rootled and grunted among the garbage between the poles; chickens scratched about among the pigs; and favourite dogs, stretched out on the side of the verandah, lolled their heads over the edge of the bamboo platform and observed our arrival with mild interest.

Climbing a slippery notched log with a sixty-pound Bergen on one's back is not easy, and I went up the muddy track almost on all fours, holding on hard with both hands.

The Iban and the Chief's son paused while James and I took our shoes off. We then crossed the outer apron and the roofed verandah and were ushered into the Chief's quarters. His room stretched, at a right angle, back from the line of the longhouse for about a hundred feet. It was cross-beamed and triangularly roofed like a barn, the huge timbers cross-cut into one another and lashed with rattan. The Chief's son, smaller, fairer-skinned than the Iban, but just as muscular and just as dignified, indicated a patch of floor where we might sleep. Dana and he, to their mutual delight, began to talk, albeit with no great fluency.

'The son of the chief says he very sorries,' Leon said, translating. 'Almost all the people are in the fields, but they come back tonight. The Chief is away on the Mahakam. We have fun tonight.'

I awoke instantly from a passing reverie.

'Hey Leon,' I said, a little too anxiously, 'step outside a minute, will you? I've something very important to tell you.'

'Eh?'

'Come on.'

Out on the verandah, I grabbed his tattooed arm. 'Look, don't tell James, because he wouldn't like it, he's so modest. But, in England, he's *very* famous. He is the poet of all the tribe, the chief poet in all England. His *whole life* is making songs. That's what he does all day. You understand? He *sings songs.* And he dances. He knows *all* the dances.'

Leon was genuinely excited, immensely impressed.

'So look Leon, between now and tonight, tell everyone—or else James will just sit there—you tell everyone, via Dana, that James is the greatest poet in all England and that when it's our turn to dance and sing, they must shout for James. OK? Will you do that?'

'He very great man,' said Leon, 'very old. Very serious man. I tell Dana.'

We began to unpack; and a crowd started to gather. The oldest woman I had yet seen in Borneo, squatting on the floor, her wrinkled breasts and her ear-lobes hanging forlornly, her attitude one of exaggerated distress, was alternately touching my leg and theatrically placing her hands over her eyes. I assumed that, sensibly enough, she found the sight of me painful beyond endurance and wanted this white tramp out of her drawing-room, fast. After all, with a half-grown beard, river-and-sweat-soaked shirt, water-frayed trousers and socks, and already inescapably possessed of the sweet, fetid, rotting smell of the jungle, I was even less of a truffle for the senses than usual. But I suddenly realized that she was asking for help. Her old eyes were bloodshot, her eyelids swollen. Feeling useful and needed, I pulled out my medicine pack and found the antibiotic eye-drops. Smiling broadly, she disclosed her gums. Not a tooth to be seen. I squeezed in some drops and she clapped her hands.

A mother pressed forward, holding up her baby's arm. There was an angry red mound of infection on it, just below the shoulder-joint. Perhaps this was the ringworm that Harrisson wrote about.

'Kurap?' I asked.

She nodded, impatiently. I put Savlon and a dressing on the wound, covering up the skin which was split like a rotten tomato, and weeping like one. A queue of mothers and children formed. We dressed hundreds of cuts that had gone septic, small ulcers, patches of skin fungus, rashes. And then the men began to trickle in. They mimed, with a suppleness, a balletic grace that would have impressed Nijinsky, excruciating, disabling back-pain; with eyes as big and bright as those of a fox hunting in the dusk they indicated that they were suffering from the kind of headaches that amount to concussion; with contortions that would have torn Houdini into spare ribs they demonstrated that their stomachs had ceased to function, that they were debilitated almost beyond assistance.

'Multivite,' I announced, with great solemnity.

I put two bright orange pills in each extended palm. Some swallowed. Some chewed. Everyone looked happy.

'Alka-Selzer,' said James, as one who practised it.

Eight tablets, as white and round and efficacious as sacred slices of pig tusk, sat in the bottom of James's mess-tin. Gurgle, gurgle, went his upturned water bottle, and the roundels spun and bubbled and talked to each other. Throwing up spray, foaming like the river in a rapid, the water rose up in the tin. The Kenyah crowded round tight, and looked in.

'Drink,' said James, handing it to the first man and staring at him like a shaman.

The patient shut his eyes, mumbled something, and took a mouthful. 'Aaah!' he gasped, passing it on, wiping the fizz from his lips.

'Aaah!' said everyone in turn, straightening out at once, squaring their powerful shoulders. There would be no backache tonight.

Some minutes later an old man clutched me by the arm. He pointed at the medicine bag and tugged at my shirt. He was obviously much distressed and I followed him out, carrying the first-aid kit.

To my surprise he led me right to the far end of the longhouse, past a group of older women who were weaving mats from strips of split rattan and two who were weaving cloth on six-foot-long wooden frames. We clambered down the notched log and set off along a path shaded by the huge leaves of planted banana trees. Rounding a corner, we came to a group of huts, all built on stilts, like a longhouse in single sections, and the old man climbed the notched pole into the first one and beckoned to me to do likewise.

It was dark inside, and the stench seemed to soak into me. A circle of people—I assume the old man's family—stood round an old woman, presumably his wife. She was sitting on a stool, a bundle of tied sticks in her hand, fanning her foot. As my eyes adjusted, I looked where everyone was looking: at her foot. My stomach turned. The top surface was an open pool of fluid with a clearly-defined, raised shoreline of indented flesh. She moved slightly as she fanned herself and, as she did so, yellow and black and red islets of infection slithered gently to new positions on the watery surface of the wound. The sons and daughters looked at me, inquiringly. An earnest young man mimed someone entering the river and treading on—a fish. She had stepped on a fish spine. Her sarong was pulled up to her waist and her leg was a dark reddish-brown right up to her thigh, about six inches above the knee.

She looked at me, her face resigned and dignified despite the pain, but her eyes big and brown and pleading. It was a terrible moment. She had, I supposed, gangrene. And she needed massive doses of penicillin, far more than we possessed. I gave her two tubes of Savlon, two packets of multivitamins, and a roll of bandages. In return, the old man gave me three sweet potatoes, which I took. It was the nastiest transaction of my life.

Distractedly, I walked off into the secondary jungle, the nearby land on its fifteen-year rest between crops, to be alone. A Spiderhunter called somewhere, and I thought I saw an orange-bellied flowerpecker, a small burst of flame dancing from bush to bush. I sat down, half-way up the hill, in sight of the longhouse, beside some kind of large, purple-flowering orchid. Ought we to forget the Tiban range and take the woman to hospital in Kapit, a river's-length away? What ought we to do? So this was how the people of the far interior died—exactly as we had been told—of septicaemia, of one misjudged cut with a parang in a clearing, of a scratched mosquito-bite that became a boil, of a fish-spine in the foot. No wonder the population was so perpetually young, so beautiful. Perhaps Lubbock had got it the wrong way round in his *Prehistoric Times*. Perhaps it was not so much the 'horrible dread of unknown evil' which 'hangs like a cloud over savage life, and embitters every pleasure' but the very sensible dread, in this climate, of every passing accident, of every present micro-organism. They were certainly very stable societies, but perhaps this was exactly why they were so stable. The Niah caves excavation tells us that the Borneo peoples of the true Stone Age ate the same kind of animals and made the same kind of boats as their probable descendants do today; and that the large mother-of-pearl fastenings on the ceremonial belts of Dana's daughters in the longhouse at Kapit are exactly the same as those worn by their ancestors forty thousand years ago.

I returned to a packed longhouse and tried to resume our unpacking and, most pressing of all, to change into my dry clothes. I dislodged the sealed bag of picture-postcards of the Queen on horseback, trooping the colour. An idea presented itself: the Sovereign would save me from undue scrutiny in the transition between pairs of trousers.

'Look,' I said, 'this is for you. Here is our *Tuai Rumah*, our Chief in England.'

'Inglang!' said the children. The cards were sheeny and metallic, the kind that change the position of their subjects as their own position is changed against the light.

I gave one to a little boy. He looked at it with amazed delight: he turned it this way and that; he scratched it and waited to see what would happen; he whipped it over, to catch a glimpse of Her Majesty from the back. Small hands thrust up like a clump of bamboo; a woman, annoyed, demanded a pile for herself. If the children had one each, the men wanted more than one each. In five minutes, four hundred mementoes of the Empire disappeared.

There was now such a large number of people in the room that I really wanted a portrait: with, I imagined, great stealth, I held a Fuji to my stomach, pointed it in the right direction, looked the other way myself, and pressed the button. Chaos ensued. Children howled, the women pulled their sarongs over their breasts, the men looked annoyed.

'Quick, quick—get the Polaroid,' hissed James.

With an elaborate enactment of deep apology, followed by circus-gestures promising fun to come, great tricks, something quite different, and not at all offensive, I drew out the Polaroid and loaded it. The grey box would take away their image, I tried to suggest with both hands, and then give it back again. They looked dubious. I had behaved badly once, and was not really to be trusted.

The Polaroid flashed; we waited; the box whirred: the tray slid forward and proffered its wet card. I laid it on the floor, waving their fingers away. Slowly, it grew colours, like bacteria in a dish of culture. The room was very silent. They watched the outlines of heads and shoulders appear; features became defined. Suddenly they pointed to the card and to each other. Wild hilarity erupted. They clapped and clapped. They ran off to change into their best clothes and we, at last, put on our dry trousers. Only the old woman was left to grimace in astonishment, or disgust, at the whiteness or the hairiness of our legs.

Proudly wearing garish sarongs or Chinese shorts and tee-shirts, which had been traded downriver in the rainy season, presumably, for turtles or deer or pig, for camphor or guttapercha or rattan or pepper, they arranged themselves into family groups, forcing me to shuttle their images in and their pictures out, until the Polaroid grew hot and all the film was finished.

'What a lot of children everyone has,' I observed to Leon.

'No, no,' said Leon, 'the mothers and the fathers—they die. My own parents, they die too, sickness, or cutting trees, *shick-shick*,' said Leon, miming the curving descent of a parang blade, 'or in the river, bang heads on the rocks, or poison-fish, or in the jungle, hunting. They have cut. They have boil. Very painful. They die. Then you must be adopted.'

So these magnificent warrior-farmers, I thought, looking round at so much health and so much glowing muscle, at so many beautiful faces and breasts and smiles and jangling ear-rings, are the product of evolution by natural selection in almost its crudest sense.

The Chief's son appeared. We must be hungry, he said (we were); his mother and his sisters had cooked the monitor lizard (perhaps we were not quite that hungry). At the far end of the room there was a fire of split logs with a massive piece of ironwood for a hearth. A series of pots were suspended above it, and the smoke made its way out through a propped-open flap in the roof.

The girls left our mess-tins and plates in a circle round a piled bowl of rice and the hindquarters of the monitor lizard, and then withdrew. Dana served me a helping of tail—the last ten inches of it or thereabouts; and the resin lamps flickered, and the sows and boars and piglets grunted and squealed on the rubbish and pig-shit below the floor-boards; and the geckoes *chick-chacked* to each other in the roof space like mating sparrows; and I realized that the yellow-and-black-skinned monitor lizard tail would not disappear from my tin, as custom demanded, until I ate it myself.

'Makai! Makai!' said Dana.

The flesh was yellow and softish and smelled bad, very like the stray chunks of solid matter in the effluvia one sees in England on an unwashed pavement outside a public house late on a Saturday night. I eased it off the small vertebrae, mixed it into the sticky rice, and told myself that even this particular meal would all be over one day.

The Iban ate fast and went out for a swim and a wash in the river. We finished our supper, more or less, but felt far too sick to swim in the dark. The girls cleared everything away. Returning, looking very clean, Dana and Leon and Inghai put on their most dazzling trousers and tee-shirts.

We were very tired. It was all confusing; and the river seemed to have spun cat's-cradles of pain out of all the muscle fibres in my calves and back; and the monitor-lizard's tail began gently whisking, from side to side, in my stomach. I took a long pull at the *arak*-can and lay down on the floor of the Chief's room. The huge cross-beams of the roof bucked and twisted and stuck fast on some celestial river flowing over my head: I fell asleep.

'Come on,' shouted James, from a bank far away to my right, 'get up! There's going to be a welcome party.'

Staggering out, wanting to sleep as never before, I looked around, and wished I were somewhere else. The gallery was packed. The lamps had been lit. *Tuak* was being drunk. A long, uninviting space had been cleared in front of part of the line of longhouse doors; and around its three sides sat an expectant audience. Leon, looking fresh and eager, beckoned us to the back row. We were given a glass of *tuak*, and a tray of huge cone-shaped cheroots—Kenyah tobacco wrapped in leaves that were tied together with a bow of leaf-strips—was passed round: a sinuous young girl put ours in our mouths and lit them with a taper. I noticed that Leon was wearing his large and flashy, supposedly waterproof digital watch. After its first celebratory dive with Leon into the depths of the Rajang, this watch had ceased to tell the time, but it would still, if shaken violently enough, and to Leon's unvarying delight, sound its alarm.

The musicians sat in front of us. An old man held a *keluri,* a dried gourd with six bamboo pipes projecting in a bundle from its bulb; a group of young men sat ready with a bamboo harp, a bamboo xylophone, a bamboo flute, and a single-stringed instrument, a sounding box the size of a dugout canoe with a string so heavy it had to be pulled with an iron hook.

The Chief's son entered, transformed. On his head he wore a war-helmet, a woven rattan cap set with black and yellow and crimson beads, topped with six long black and white plumes from the tail of the helmeted hornbill. He was dressed in a war-coat, the skin of the largest cat in Borneo, the clouded leopard. His head appeared in the opening at the front of the skin, and the bulk of it stretched down his back. Around his waist, slung on a silver belt and sheathed in a silver scabbard, was a *parang* to outshine all other *parangs.* In his left hand, he carried a long shield, pointed at both ends, and from the centre of which a huge mask regarded us implacably, its eyes red, its teeth the painted tusks of the wild boar.

Laying the ancient, and presumably fragile, shield carefully against the wall, the warrior took up his position at the centre of the floor. He crouched down and, at a nod from the man on the bass string, a hollow, complicated, urgent, rhythmic music began. With exaggerated movements, his thigh muscles bunching and loosening, his tendons taut, a fierce concentration on his face, the Chief's son turned slowly in time with the music; first on one foot and then on the other, rising, inch by inch, to his own height, apparently peering over some imaginary cover. Sighting the enemy, he crouched again, and then, as the music quickened, he drew his bright *parang* and leaped violently forward, weaving and dodging with immense exertion, cutting and striking, parrying unseen blows with his mimed shield. For a small second, his ghostly foe was off-guard, tripped on the shingle, and the heir to the Lordship of all the Kenyah of Nanga Sinyut claimed his victory with one malicious blow.

Everyone clapped and cheered, and so did I, spell-bound. Five young girls rushed forward to take off the hero's hornbill helmet, and war-coat, and *parang.* It was wonderful. The girls were very beautiful. All was right with the world. And then I realized, as a Rajah Brooke's birdwing took a flap round my duodenum, that the beautiful girls, in a troop, were coming, watched by all the longhouse, for me.

'You'll be all right,' said James, full of *tuak*. 'Just do your thing. Whatever it is.'

Strapped into the war-coat and the *parang*, the hornbill feathers on my head, I had a good idea. It would be a simple procedure to copy the basic steps that the Chief's son had just shown us. There really was not much to it, after all.

The music struck up, sounding just a little bit stranger than it had before.

I began the slow crouch on one leg, turning slightly. Perhaps, actually, this was a mistake, I decided. Ghastly pains ran up my thighs. Terminal cramp hit both buttocks at once. Some silly girl began to titter. A paraplegic wobble spread down my back. The silly girl began to laugh. Very slowly, the floor came up to say hello, and I lay down on it. There was uproar in the longhouse. How very funny, indeed.

Standing up, I reasoned that phase two would be easier. Peering over the imaginary boulder, I found myself looking straight into the eyes of an old man on the far side of the verandah. The old fool was crying with laughter, his ridiculous long ears waggling about. Drawing the *parang,* which was so badly aligned that it stuck in the belt and nearly took my fingers off, I advanced upon the foe, jumping this way and that, feeling dangerous. The old man fell off his seat. There was so much misplaced mirth, so much plain howling, that I could not hear the music, and so perhaps my rhythm was not quite right.

'Redsi!' came an unmistakable shout, 'why don't you improvise?'

Stabbed in the back just as I was about to take my very first head, I spun round violently to glare at the Fenton. I never actually saw him, because the cord of the war-helmet, not used to such movements, slipped up over the back of my head, and the helmet itself, flying forward, jammed fast over my face. Involuntarily, I took a deep gasp of its sweat-smooth rattan interior, of the hair of generations of Kenyah warriors who had each been desperate to impress the girls of their choice. It was an old and acrid smell.

The boards were shaking. The audience was out of control. And then, just in time, before suffocation set in, the five girls, grossly amused, set me free.

'Go and get James,' I spluttered, 'you go and get James.'

'Now you sing song,' shouted Leon.

206

'No, no—James sing songs.'

'Jams!' shouted Leon, remembering his mission.

'Jams!' The longhouse reverberated. 'Jams! Jams!' Leon had done his work well.

With great theatrical presence, offering almost no resistance to the five young girls, James proceeded on to the stage. The Kenyah fell silent. T.D. Freeman, in his work on Iban augury, tells us that the King of the Gods, Singalang Burong, may well be encountered in dreams. There is no mistaking him. He is almost as old as the trees, awe-inspiring, massive of body and—a characteristic which puts his identity beyond doubt—completely bald. Judging by the slightly uneasy, deferential, expectant faces around me, Bali Penyalong, the High God of the Kenyah, was but a different name for the same deity.

The attendants withdrew. James, resplendent in leopard skin and hornbill feathers, looked even more solemn than is his habit. With the accumulated experience of many thousands of evenings at the theatre, of years of drama criticism, he regarded his audience. His huge brown eyes appeared to fix on everyone in turn. There was some backward shuffling in the front row. A dog whimpered.

The music began, a little shakily. James, in time with the music, began to mime. He was hunting something, in a perfunctory way. He made rootling movements with his head, and grunted. He was hunting a pig. Evidently successful, he butchered his quarry, selected the joint he had in mind, hung the carcase from a hook in the roof and betook himself to his ideal kitchen. Passion entered the show. James began to concentrate; his gestures quickened and the mesmerized musicians increased their tempo. He scored the pork; he basted it; he tied it with string; he made extraordinarily complex sauces; he cooked potatoes and sprouts and peas and beans and broccoli and *zucchini*, I think, until they were *fritti*. After many a tasting and many an alchemical manoeuvre with a *batterie de cuisine* decidedly better than Magny's, James deemed the gravy to be perfect. The apple sauce was plentiful. The decanted Burgundy was poured into a glass. James looked fondly at his creation and began to eat. The crackling crackled between his teeth. The warriors of the Kenyah, as if they had been present at a feast of the Gods, rose to their feet and burped. Everybody cheered.

'Jams very hungry,' said Leon to me confidentially, 'he must eat more rices.'

James held up a hand. Everyone squatted down again, cross-legged.

'And now,' he announced, 'we will have a sing-song.'

'Inglang song! Inglang song!' shouted Inghai, wildly excited, and full of *arak*.

And then James really did astonish me. To the beat of the big string he launched into a rhyming ballad, a long spontaneous poem about our coming from a far country, about our entering the Rajang from the sea, about the pleasures of the Baleh and the danger of the rapids and the hospitality of the strongest, the most beautiful people in all the world, the Kenyah of Nanga Sinyut.

I clapped as wildly as Inghai. 'Bravo Jams!' I shouted.

'Bravo Jams!' mimicked Inghai.

'Bravo! Bravo!' sang the Kenyah.

The Chief's son then stood up and announced something. The long gallery became quiet again. He pointed to about fifteen men, in turn, who followed him on to the floor. They were all young and eager, bodily alert, absurdly fit. Long-backed, with fairly short, lavishly-muscled limbs, they looked like athletes at the peak of their careers, assembling at the Olympics for the men's pentathlon.

'They all bachelors,' whispered Leon. 'They not yet picked their womens.'

The men formed into a single line, by order of height. And a completely different kind of music began, violent, aggressive, with a menacing and insistent beat. They walked slowly forward, unsmiling, stamping their feet, looking rhythmically to either side, intent. With the delight of discovery, I realized that this was the dance described in Hose, albeit the protagonists were wearing shorts and singlets:

> The bigger boys are taught to take part in the dance in
> which the return from the warpath is dramatically
> represented. This is a musical march rather than a dance. A
> party of young men in full war-dress form up in single line
> which advances slowly up the gallery.

After five march-pasts, as I was deciding that this would not be a sensible longhouse to attack even if one really was in the SAS, everyone relaxed, and we were invited to join the line. James picked up the rhythm at once, but I found even these steps difficult, falling over my boots. All the girls giggled.

'Redmon,' said Leon, when we sat down again, 'you so big—your feet too far from your head.'

'That's it. That's exactly what it is.'

There was a pause.

'Or, maybe,' said Leon, 'you so fats you can't see them.'

Leon, with gross bad manners, uncrossed his legs, lay flat out on the floor, and laughed at his own joke, re-directing his attention, sharply, only when the unmarried girls stood up.

Gracefully, shyly, the young girls aligned themselves.

'Look at that one,' said Leon, 'look at that one in the pink sarong, Redmon. Just *look* at that one.'

'Behave yourself,' I said, testily, 'this is no time for one of your jumps. You'll get us all killed.'

'She the moon in the sky,' said Leon.

The girls—to a delicate, lilting dance-tune—began their own movement across the long stage and back again. Lithe, slender, very young, they were indeed lovely to look at, and their dance was deliciously fragile after the violence of the men. The forward step of the beat outlined the legs beneath their folded-down sarongs. The gentle, backward swaying on the pause revealed the tight breasts beneath their tee-shirts.

Leon's eyes were wide, as wide as they had been when he shot his turtle. I blew in his ear.

'Shush,' said Leon. 'You be quiets. Now we watch.'

Looking round to poke Inghai, I saw that he was asleep, curled up on the floor, still holding his *arak* mug in both hands. All the men were very quiet.

Far too soon, the dance was over. We clapped, adoringly, sentimentally, soppily, feeling a little weak. The girls, blushing, scurried to their seats and giggled. But the girl in the pink sarong returned, carrying two huge bunches of hornbill feathers. Her features were strikingly beautiful, certainly; her hair, about a foot longer than that of the other girls, was combed down—loose and fine, black and silky—to her waist. Her looped ear-lobes, weighted with rings, hung down only to the base of her smooth neck. The tattoos on her arms were only half-complete and, as tattooing begins in a girl's tenth year and continues in small bouts at regular intervals, she could not be, I calculated, very old.

'Leon,' I said, 'she's far too young. She's only fourteen.'

'What is it?' said Leon. 'What is it? You sit stills. You be quiets. Now we watch.'

However young, she danced with tremulous invitation: a slow, yearning, graceful dance, the long fan feathers sweeping over her body in alternating curves, a dance that began from a crouching position and opened gradually upwards as she rose, inch by inch.

'This is really something,' whispered James, holding his head in both hands, gazing at her. And then, perhaps remembering his professional self, his column inches, 'She *really, really* knows what she's doing.'

The two fans of the tail feathers of the rhinoceros hornbill, at the end of her outstretched arms, joined above her head. She stood at her full height, little, curved, lissome, beautiful. We clapped and clapped.

And then, suddenly looking straight at us, giving us a small charge of our own internal electricity, a conger eel uncurling in the guts, she walked into the audience with every eye upon her and pulled Leon to his feet.

Leon's brown face grew browner and browner. He was blushing. He was suffusing uncontrollably with blood and surprise, with fright and pride, with increasing vigour and overpowering lust.

She tied him, very slowly, into the helmet and the war-coat, lingering over every knot, staring steadily into his eyes, hanging the belt around his waist with both her hands, arranging the silver *parang* so that it hung neatly down the outside of his right thigh.

Leon, taller and darker than the Kenyah, and just as fit, stood like a warrior; and this was his reward, I realized. For Leon, conqueror of the river, as she must have heard, had proved his manhood and his spontaneous, natural courage as surely as if he had arrived at Nanga Sinyut with a severed head. In our eyes, and probably in theirs, he had done much better: he had saved one, and a particularly fine specimen, too, a Bald Godhead rescued from among the rocks.

Still fired with inspiration, his face growing even darker, his body a furnace of Iban desire, he nodded to his little muse in lordly fashion as she returned to her seat. He then, I am sure, executed the finest dance of his life. To the frantic music of open combat, he somersaulted backwards; he cartwheeled from side to side; he cut heads like corn; he lunged and feinted and dodged behind his

flying spears. For his new love, he topped whole armies. He moved
with such energy that black and white banded wheels, images of
hornbill feathers, arcs and lines, seemed to hang in the murk all
around him, fading and appearing in the flicker of the lamp.

Leon, shiny with sweat, strode to the side of his beloved. In the
stunned, short pause before the clapping began, I heard an odd noise.
It was not a gecko. It was Leon's watch. It was as shaken and over-
excited as he was. *Beeeep-beeeep-beeeep*, it said.

The formal gathering broke up into small groups drinking and
laughing and telling stories. The largest circle grew around
James. The Kenyah sat at his feet in rings, listening to his
bizarre tales of life in England. They studied his expressive face and
his agitated gestures, laughing at the right moments; tingling, when
required, at the voice from the Hammer House of Horror, just as if
they knew where Rugley was, or were connoisseurs of murder, or
understood two words of what he said.

Maybe the *arak* and *tuak* were beginning to tell on me. My legs
seemed to have contracted elephantiasis. It was difficult to focus. The
longhouse pitched a bit, like an anchored canoe. Or maybe I was
simply coming to the end of the longest day I ever hope to traverse.

As if from a long way off, I heard James issue a solemn warning to
his audience: 'The butcher bird, or red-backed shrike,' he said,

Should not be trusted with your bike
The pump and light he whips away
And takes the spokes to spike his prey.

It was an entirely new, unpublished Fenton poem, I realized
dimly. But whatever it was, it was too much. It was crazy. And so
were the Kenyah. I staggered, luckily, the right way off the verandah,
through the correct *bilek* door, and found my patch of board.
Through the wooden wall I could hear James singing songs,
parcelling out the verses, teaching the Kenyah English. I fell asleep.

Jay McInerney
The Night Shift

Y ou are not the kind of guy who would be at a place like this at this time of the morning. But you are here, and you cannot say that the terrain is entirely unfamiliar, although the details are a little fuzzy. You are at a night club talking to a girl with a shaved head. The club is either Heartbreak or the Lizard Lounge. All might come clear if you could just slip into the bathroom and do a little more Bolivian Marching Powder. Then again, it might not. A small voice inside you insists that this epidemic lack of clarity is a result of too much of that already. The night has already turned on that imperceptible pivot where two a.m. changes to six a.m. You know that moment has come and gone, but you are not yet willing to concede that you have crossed the line beyond which all is gratuitous damage and the palsy of unravelled nerve endings. Somewhere back there you could have cut your losses, but instead you rode past that moment on a comet trail of white powder and now you are trying to hang on to the rush. Your brain at this moment is composed of brigades of tiny Bolivian soldiers. They are tired and muddy from their long march through the night. There are holes in their boots and they are hungry. They need to be fed. They need the Bolivian Marching Powder.

Something vaguely tribal about this scene—pendulous jewellery, face paint, ceremonial headgear and hair styles. You feel that there is also a certain Latin theme—something more than the piranhas cruising your bloodstream and the fading buzz of marimbas in your brain.

You are leaning back against a post which may or may not be structural with regard to the building but which feels essential to your own maintenance of an upright position. The bald girl is saying this used to be a good place to come before the assholes discovered it. You do not want to be talking to this bald girl, or even listening to her, which is all you are doing, but just now you do not want to test the powers of speech or locomotion.

How did you get here? It was your friend, Tad Allagash, who powered you in here, and now he has disappeared. Tad is the kind of guy who would be at a place like this at this time of the morning. He is either your best self or your worst self, you're not sure which. Earlier in the evening it seemed clear that he was your best self. You started on the Upper East Side with champagne and unlimited prospects, strictly observing the Allagash rule of perpetual motion: one drink per stop. Tad's mission in life is to have more fun than anyone else in New York City, and this involves a lot of moving around, since there is always the likelihood that where you aren't is more fun than where you are. You are awed by his strict refusal to acknowledge any goal higher than the pursuit of pleasure. You want to be like that. You also think he is shallow and dangerous. His friends are all rich and spoiled, like the cousin from Memphis you met earlier in the evening who would not accompany you below Fourteenth Street because he said he didn't have a lowlife visa. This cousin had a girlfriend with cheekbones to break your heart, and you knew she was the real thing when she absolutely refused to acknowledge your presence. She possessed secrets—about islands, about horses, about French pronunciation—which you would never know.

You have travelled in the course of the night from the meticulous to the slime. The girl with the shaved head has a scar tattooed on her scalp. It looks like a long, sutured gash. You tell her it is very realistic. She takes this as a compliment and thanks you. You meant as opposed to romantic.

'I could use one of those right over my heart,' you say.

'You want I can give you the name of the guy did it. You'd be surprised how cheap.'

You don't tell her that nothing would surprise you now. Her voice, for instance, which is like the New Jersey State Anthem played through an electric shaver.

The bald girl is emblematic of the problem. The problem is, for some reason you think you are going to meet the kind of girl who is not the kind of girl who would be at a place like this at this time of the morning. When you meet her you are going to tell her that what you really want is a house in the country with a garden. New York, the club scene, bald women—you're tired of all that. Your presence here is only a matter of conducting an experiment in limits, reminding yourself of what you aren't. You see yourself as the kind of guy who wakes up early on Sunday morning and steps out to cop the *Times* and croissants. Who might take a cue from the Arts and Leisure section and decide to check out an exhibition—Costumes of the Hapsburg Court at the Met, say, or Japanese Lacquerware of the Muromachi Period at the Asia Society. The kind of guy who calls up

215

the woman he met at a publishing party Friday night, the party he did not get sloppy drunk at. See if she wants to check out the exhibition and maybe do an early dinner. A guy who would wait until eleven a.m. to call her, because she might not be an early riser, like he is. She may have been out late, perhaps at a night club. And maybe a couple of sets of tennis before the museum. He wonders if she plays, but of course she would.

When you meet the girl who wouldn't et cetera you will tell her that you are slumming, visiting your own six a.m. Lower East Side of the soul on a lark, stepping nimbly between the piles of garbage to the gay marimba rhythms in your head. Well, no, not *gay*. But she will know exactly what you mean.

On the other hand, almost any girl, specifically one with a full head of hair, would help you stave off this creeping sense of mortality. You remember the Bolivian Marching Powder and realize you're not down yet. No way, José. First you have to get rid of this bald girl.

In the bathroom there are no doors on the stalls, which makes discretion tricky. But clearly, you are not the only person here to take on fuel. Lots of sniffling going on in the stalls. The windows are blacked over, and for this you are profoundly grateful.

Hup, two, three, four. The soldiers are back on their feet. They are off and running in formation. Some of them are dancing, and you must follow their example.

Just outside the door you spot her: tall, dark and alone, half-hidden behind a pillar at the edge of the dance floor. You approach laterally, moving your stuff like a Bad Spade through the slalom of a synthesized conga rhythm. She jumps when you touch her shoulder.

'Dance?'

She looks at you as if you had just suggested instrumental rape. 'I do not speak English,' she says, when you ask again.

'*Français?*'

She shakes her head. Why is she looking at you that way, as if there were tarantulas nesting in your eye sockets?

'You are by any chance from Bolivia? Or Peru?'

She is looking around for help now. Remembering a recent encounter with a young heiress's bodyguard at Danceteria—or was it the Red Parrot?—you back off, hands raised over your head.

The Bolivian Soldiers are still on their feet, but they have stopped singing their marching song. You realize that you are at a crucial juncture with regard to morale. What you need is a good pep talk from Tad Allagash, but he is not to be found. You try to imagine what he would say. *Back on the horse. Now we're really going to have some fun.* Something like that. You suddenly realize that he has already slipped out with some rich Hose Queen. He is back at her place on Fifth Ave, and they are doing some of her off-the-boat-quality drugs. They are scooping it out of tall Ming vases and snorting it off of each other's naked bodies. You hate Tad Allagash.

Go home. Cut your losses.

Stay. Go for it.

You are a republic of voices tonight. Unfortunately, that republic is Italy. All these voices waving their arms and screaming at each other. There is an *ex cathedra* riff coming down from the Vatican: *Repent. Your body is the temple of the Lord and you have defiled it.* It is, after all, Sunday morning, and as long as you have any brain cells left there will be a resonant patriarchal basso echoing down the marble vaults of your church-going childhood to remind you that this is the Lord's Day. What you need is another over-priced drink to drown it out. But a search of pockets yields only a dollar bill and change. You paid twenty to get in here. Panic gains.

You spot a girl at the edge of the dance floor who looks like your last chance for earthly salvation. You know for a fact that if you go out into the morning alone, without even your sunglasses—which you have neglected to bring, because who, after all, plans on these travesties?—the harsh, angling light will turn you to flesh and bone. Mortality will pierce you through the retina. But there she is in her pegged pants, a kind of doo-wop Retro ponytail pulled off to the side, as eligible a candidate as you are likely to find this late in the game. The sexual equivalent of fast food.

She shrugs and nods when you ask her to dance. You like the way she moves, the oiled ellipses of her hips and shoulders. After the second song she says she's tired. She's on the point of bolting when you ask her if she needs a little pick-me-up.

'You've got some blow?' she says.

'Is Stevie Wonder blind?' you say.

She takes your arm and leads you into the Ladies. After a couple of spoons she seems to like you just fine and you are feeling very likeable yourself. A couple more. This woman is all nose.

'I love drugs,' she says, as you march towards the bar.

'It's something we have in common,' you say.

'Have you ever noticed how all the good words start with D? D and L.'

You try to think about this. You're not quite sure what she's driving at. The Bolivians are singing their marching song but you can't quite make out the words.

'You know. Drugs. Delight. Decadence.'

'Debauchery,' you say, catching the tune now.

'Dexedrine.'

'Delectable. Deranged. Debilitated.'

'Delinquent.'

'Delirium.'

'And L,' she says. 'Lush and luscious.'

'Languorous.'

'Librium.'

'Libidinous.'

'What's that?' she says.

'Horny.'

'Oh,' she says, casting a long, arching look over your shoulder. Her eyes glaze in a way that reminds you precisely of the closing of a sand-blasted glass shower door. You can see that the game is over, although you're not sure which rule you broke. Possibly she finds *H* words offensive. A purist. She is scanning the dance floor for a man with a compatible vocabulary. You have more: *detumescence*, for instance. Personally, you feel like a Q. But you can play her game: *drowning* and *depressed*; *lost* and *lonesome*. It's not that you're really going to miss this girl who thinks that *decadence* and *Dexedrine* are the high points of the language of Kings James and Lear. But the touch of flesh, the sound of another human voice... You know there is a special purgatory waiting for you out there in the dawn's surly light, a desperate half-sleep which is like a grease fire in the brain pan.

The girl waves as she disappears into the crowd. There is no sign of the other girl, the girl who would not be here. There is no sign of Tad Allagash. The Bolivians are mutinous. You can't stop their treacherous voices.

I t is worse even than you expected, stepping out into the morning. The light is like a mother's reproach. The sidewalk sparkles cruelly. Visibility unlimited. The downtown warehouses look serene and restful in this bevelled light. An uptown cab passes and you start to wave, then realize you have no money. The cab stops.

You jog over and lean in the window. 'I guess I'll walk after all.'
'Asshole.' He leaves rubber.

You start north, holding a hand over your eyes. Trucks shudder up Hudson Street, bearing provisions into the sleeping city. You turn east. On Seventh Avenue an old woman with a hive of rollers on her head walks a German shepherd. The dog is rooting in the cracks of the sidewalk, but as you approach he stiffens into a pose of terrible alertness. The woman looks at you as if you were something that had just crawled out of the ocean trailing ooze and slime. An eager, tentative growl ripples the shepherd's throat. 'Good Pooky,' she says. The dog makes a move but she chokes it back. You give them a wide berth.

On Bleeker Street you catch the scent of the Italian bakery. You stand at the corner of Bleeker and Cornelia and gaze at the windows on the fourth floor of a tenement. Behind those windows is the apartment you shared with Amanda when you first came to New York. It was small and dark, but you liked the imperfectly patched pressed-tin ceiling, the claw-footed bath in the kitchen, the windows that didn't quite fit the frames. You were just starting out. You had the rent covered, you had your favourite restaurant on MacDougal where the waitresses knew your names and you could bring your own bottle of wine. Every morning you woke to the smell of bread from the bakery downstairs. You would go out to buy the paper and maybe pick up a couple of croissants while Amanda made the coffee. This was two years ago, before you got married.

D own on the West Side Highway, a lone hooker totters on heels and tugs at her skirt as if no one had told her that the commuters won't be coming through the tunnels from Jersey today. Coming closer, you see that she is a man in drag.

You cross under the rusting stanchions of the old elevated highway and walk out to the pier. The easterly light skims across the broad expanse of the Hudson. You choose your steps carefully as you walk out to the end of the rotting pier. You are none too steady and there are holes through which you can see the black fetid water underneath.

You sit down on a piling and look out over the river. Downriver, the Statue of Liberty shimmers in the haze. Across the water, a huge Pepsi sign welcomes you to New Jersey.

You watch the solemn progress of a garbage barge, wreathed in a cloud of screaming gulls, heading out to sea.

Here you are again. All messed up and no place to go.

You see yourself as the kind of guy who appreciates a quiet night at home with a good book. A little Mozart on the speakers, a cup of cocoa on the arm of the chair, slippers on the feet. Monday night. It feels like Thursday, at least. Walking from subway to apartment, you tell yourself that you are going to suppress this rising dread which comes upon you when you return home at night. A man's home, after all, is his castle. You let yourself in the front door and gingerly unlock the mailbox. No telling what might be inside. One of these days there could be a letter from Amanda explaining her desertion, begging forgiveness, or asking you to send the rest of her stuff to a new address.

Tonight there is an overdue notice from VISA; a solicitation from Recording for the Blind; a letter from Jim Winthrop in Chicago, college roommate, best man at your wedding; and something corporate for Amanda White. You open Jim's letter first. It starts 'Hey stranger,' and ends with 'regards to Amanda.' The letter to Amanda is a printout on an insurance company letterhead, her name typed into the salutation:

> Let's face it—in your business, your face is your greatest asset. Modelling is an exciting and rewarding career. In all likelihood, you have many years of earning ahead of you.
>
> But where would you be in the event of a disfiguring accident? Even a minor injury could spell the end of a lucrative career and the loss of hundreds of thousands of dollars in potential income.

You ball up the letter and arc it into the wastebasket beside the elevator. You press the button. *Where would you be, for instance, if a spurned husband threw acid in your face?* No. Stop this. This is not your better self speaking. This is not how you feel.

The sound of the tumblers in the locks of your apartment door puts you in mind of dungeons. The place is haunted. Just this morning you found a makeup brush beside the toilet. Memories lurk like dustballs at the backs of drawers. The stereo is a special model that plays only music fraught with poignant associations.

You close the door and stand in the foyer, listening. For some time after Amanda left, you would pause here in the hope that you would hear her inside, that she had returned, that you would discover her, penitent and tender, when you stepped into the living room. That hope is mostly gone, but still you observe this brief vigil inside the door, gauging the quality of the silence to see if it is only the melancholy silence of absence, or whether it is full of high register shrieks and moans. Tonight you are uncertain. You step into the living room and throw your jacket on the love seat. You hunt up your slippers and read the spines of the books in the shelves, determined to make a go of this quiet-night-at-home idea. A random sampling of titles induces vertigo: *As I Lay Dying, Under the Volcano, Anna Karenina, Being and Time, The Brothers Karamazov.* You must have had an ambitious youth. Of course, many of these spines have never been cracked. You have been saving them up.

Fuck it. You need to relax. After all, you've been busting ass all day. You check the fridge; no beer. A finger of vodka in the bottle on the sink. Maybe you will step out and get a sixpack. Or wander over to the Lion's Head, as long as you're going out, to see if there's anybody you know. It's not impossible there to meet a woman at the bar—with hair, minus tattoo.

The intercom buzzes while you're changing your shirt. You push the Talk button: 'Who is it?'

'Narcotics squad. We're soliciting donations for children all over the world who have no drugs.'

You buzz him up. You're not sure how you feel about the advent of Tad Allagash. While you could use company, Tad can be too much of a good thing. His brand of R and R is nothing if not strenuous. By the time he gets to the door, you're glad to see him. He's looking *très sportif* in J. Press torso and punked-out red Soho trousers. He presents his hand and you shake.

'Ready to roll?'

'Where are we rolling?'

'Into the heart of the night. Wherever there are dances to be danced, drugs to be hoovered, women to be Allagashed. It's a dirty job but someone's got to do it. Speaking of drugs, are you in possession?'

You shake your head.

'Not a single line for young Tad?'

'Sorry.'

'Not even a mirror I can lick?'

'Suit yourself.'

Tad goes over to the mahogany-and-gilt framed mirror that you inherited from your grandmother, the one Amanda was so afraid your cousin was going to nab. He runs his tongue over the glass.

'There's something on here.'

'Dust.'

Tad smacks his lips. 'In this apartment the dust has better coke content than some of the shit we buy by the gram. All us coke fiends sneezing—it adds up.'

Tad runs his finger across the length of the coffee table. 'It looks like you could teach a course in dust here. Did you know that ninety percent of your average household dust is composed of human epidermal matter? That's skin, to you.'

Perhaps this explains your sense of Amanda's omnipresence. She has left her skin behind.

He walks over to the table and leans over the typewriter. 'Doing a little writing, are we? *Dead Amanda*. That's the idea. I told you you'd get more nookie than you can shake a stick at if you tell the girls that your wife died. It's the sympathy vote. More effective than saying she fit you with horns and kited off to Paris. Avoid the awful taint of rejection.'

Tad's first reaction, when you told him about Amanda's departure, contained a grain of genuine sympathy and regret. His second reaction was to tell you that you could make a fine erotic career for yourself by repeating the story just as you had told it to him, adding touches of pathos and cruel irony. Finally, he advised you to say that Amanda had died in a plane crash on her way home from Paris on the day of your first anniversary.

'You're sure there aren't any drugs around here? I'm disappointed in you, Coach. I've always thought of you as the kind of guy who saves something for a rainy day. The temperate sort.'

'I've fallen in with bad companions.'

'Let's get on the phone,' Tad says. 'We must locate party fuel.'

All the people who might have drugs aren't home. The people who are home don't have drugs. There is a pattern here. Tad hangs up and checks his watch, which tells him the time in selected major cities of the world, including New York and Dubai, Persian Gulf, Oman. 'Eleven-forty. A little too early for the Odeon, but we might be able to bushwhack someone there with the goods. Ready?'

'Have you ever experienced this nearly overwhelming urge for a quiet night at home?'

Tad reflects for a moment. 'No.'

The glittering, curvilinear surfaces inside the Odeon are reassuring. The place makes you feel reasonable at any hour, often against bad odds, with its good light and clean luncheonette-via-Cartier deco décor. Along the bar are faces familiar under artificial light belonging to people whose daytime existence is only a tag—designer, writer, artist. A model from Amanda's agency is sitting at the bar. You do not want to see her. Tad goes right over and kisses her. At the other end of the bar you order a vodka. You finish it and order a second before Tad beckons. The model is with another woman. Tad introduces them as Elaine and Theresa. Elaine, the model, has a punk high-fashion look: short, razor-cut dark hair, high cheekbones, eyebrows plucked straight. Metallic and masculine are the adjectives that come to mind. Theresa is blonde, too short and busty to model. Elaine looks you over as if you were an impulse purchase that she might return to the department store.

'Aren't you Amanda Ross's boyfriend?'

'Husband. I mean, I was.'

'She was in Paris showing the fall collections,' Tad says, 'and she got caught in a crossfire between Palestinian terrorists and the French police. Totally fluke thing. Innocent bystander. Senseless death. He doesn't like to talk about it.' Tad's delivery is entirely convincing. You almost believe him yourself. His air of being privy to dark secrets and inside stories gives credence to outrageous statements.

'That's terrible,' Theresa says.

'Tragic is what it is,' Tad says. 'Excuse me, but I've got to do some business. Back in a minute.' He moves down the bar to a potential supplier.

'Is that true?'

'Not really.'

'What is Amanda doing these days?' Elaine asks.

'I don't know. I think she's in Paris.'

'Wait a minute,' Theresa says. 'Is she alive?'

'We just sort of split up.'

'Too bad for you,' Elaine says. 'She was yummy.' She turns to Theresa. 'Sort of this slinky-girl-next-door look. Farm fresh. Very ingenuous.'

'I don't understand this,' Theresa says.

'Me neither,' you say. You'd just as soon change the subject. You don't like this role of bird with broken wing, especially since that is exactly how you feel. The lame duck husband. You'd rather be an eagle or a falcon, pitiless and predatory among the solitary crags.

'Aren't you some kind of writer?' Elaine says.

'I do some writing. I'm sort of an editor actually.'

'Oh, God,' Theresa says, when you mention the name of the magazine. 'I've been reading it all my life. I mean my parents get it. I always read it at the gynaecologist. What's your name? Should I know you?' She asks you about writers and artists on the staff. You dish up a standard portion of slander and libel.

Without getting too specific you imply that your job is extremely demanding and important. In the past you could often convince yourself as well as others of this. But your heart is no longer in it. You hate this posturing, even as you persist, as if it were important for these two strangers to admire you for all the wrong reasons. It's too much, this menial job in a venerable institution, but it's all you've got left.

Even now, as you puff yourself up with tales of high adventure in magazine publishing, you can see Elaine's eyes wandering out over the room, leaving you behind. She's drinking champagne. As you watch, she dips her tongue into the tulip bowl and moves it around inside the glass.

A woman who looks vaguely famous glances up from her table and waves. Elaine waves back. Her smile goes sour when the woman turns away.

'Look at that,' Elaine says. 'Silicone implants.'

You look. 'I don't know. She looks pretty damn flat to me.'

'Not the boobs—the cheeks. She's got fucking silicone implants to make it look like she has cheekbones.'

Tad comes back, looking pleased with himself. 'Bingo,' he says.

It's somewhere past midnight. Anything that starts now is not going to end at a reasonable hour. You think about slipping out and heading home. All sorts of beneficial effects are rumoured to accrue from a good night's sleep. On the other hand, you wouldn't mind a test of that toot. Just enough to boost your morale.

In a moment you are all en route to the bathroom downstairs. Tad lays out some fat lines on the toilet seat. Elaine and Theresa take their turns. Finally, Tad hands you the bill. The sweet nasal burn hits like a swallow of cold beer on a hot August day. Tad fixes another round and by the time you all troop out of the bathroom you are feeling omnipotent. You are moving into a zone of anticipation. Certainly something excellent is bound to happen.

'Let us locomote out of here,' Tad says.

'Where to?' Theresa says. 'Where the boys are?'

'Where the girls are,' Elaine says. You're not sure if this is just having fun with movie allusions or something more pointed.

Your merry band decides that Heartbreak is the destination. A cab is procured for the short hop uptown.

Outside the door there is a small crowd of would-be Heartbreakers with a uniform outer-borough look. Ted pushes through the supplicants, confers with the bouncer, and then waves the three of you in. Elaine and Theresa are chatting away when it comes time to pay, so you cover one and Tad covers the other. Inside, there is still room to move.

'It's early,' Tad says. He is disappointed. He hates to arrive before everyone else is in place. He takes pride in his timing, being on time by being the latest.

Elaine and Theresa disappear and you don't see them for fifteen minutes. Tad discovers some friends, advertising people, at a table. Everyone is discussing the new *Vanity Fair*. Some are for and some against. 'Utter confusion,' says Steve, a copywriter. 'It's the Abstract Expressionist approach to publishing. Throw ink at paper. Hope for pattern to emerge.'

You go off to buy a drink, keeping both eyes peeled for lonely women. There don't seem to be any at the moment. Everyone knows everyone else. You are on the anti-clime of your first rush. You are also experiencing the inevitable disappointment of clubs. You enter with an anticipation that is entirely unjustified on the basis of your past experience. You always seem to forget that you don't really like to dance. Since you are already here, though, you owe it to yourself to make a sustained assault on the citadel of good times. The music pumps you up, makes you want to do something, not necessarily dance. The drugs make you feel the music and the music makes you want to do more drugs.

At the bar someone thumps your shoulder. You turn around. It takes you a minute to place the face, but in the time it takes to shake hands you come up with a name: Rich Vanier. He was in your dining club at college. You ask what he's been doing. He's in banking, just back from South America tonight, after saving a small country from bankruptcy.

'What the hell, I restructured the economy, gave the generals a few more months of high living. So what are you doing to keep body and soul together. Still the poet?'

'I do a little business in South America myself.'

'I heard a rumour you married an actress.'

'*Activist*. I married a beautiful activist. She was the illegitimate daughter of Che Guevara. A few months ago she went home to visit her mother and got herself arrested and tortured by a series of rich South American generals. She died in prison.'

'You're kidding, right?'

'Do I look like I'm kidding?'

Rich Vanier can't get away from you fast enough. He says you'll have to have lunch sometime.

Walking back to the table you see Theresa and Elaine heading off with Tad. You catch up with them—just outside the Men's Room. The four of you occupy a stall. Elaine sits on the tank and Theresa sits on the seat.

'Seems like I spend half my life in bathrooms,' Theresa says as she blocks off a nostril.

Later you run into a woman you met at a party. You can't remember her name. She acts embarrassed when you greet her, as if something shameful had once passed between you, though all you can remember is a discussion about the Talking Heads. You ask her if she wants to dance and she says sure.

Out on the floor, you invent your own dance step. You call it the New York Torque. 'Some Girls' segues to 'Shattered'. You keep outstripping the prevailing tempo. Your partner sways back and forth metronomically. When you look at her, she seems to be studying you sympathetically. After you have soaked through your shirt you ask her if she wants to take a break. She nods her head vigorously.

'Is there something the matter?' You have to shout in her ear to be heard.

'Not really.'

'You seem nervous.'

'I heard about your wife,' she says. 'I'm so sorry.'

'What did you hear?'

'About what happened. About the, you know, leukaemia.'

You are riding the Bolivian Local up through the small mountain villages into the lean oxygen of the Andean peaks.

'We've got Terrain and Elisa eating out of our hands,' Tad says. 'I think it's time we suggested that we all slip out to some place more comfortable.'

You are in the bathroom, again. Elaine and Theresa are in the Ladies' on legitimate business.

'I do not appreciate this leukaemia bit,' you say. 'Not funny.'

'Just trying to boost sales. Consider me your agent.'

'I'm not amused. Bad taste.'

'Taste,' says Tad, 'is a matter of taste.'

You are dancing with Elaine. Tad is dancing with Theresa. Elaine moves with an angular syncopation that puts you in mind of the figures on Egyptian tombs. It may be a major new dance step. Whatever it is, she is making you feel self-conscious. She's a tough act to accompany. You feel like you were just transplanted from the junior prom. You are not particularly attracted to Elaine, who's too hard-edge in your view. You do not even think she is a particularly nice person. Yet you have this desire to prove that you can have as good a time as anyone, that you can be one of the crowd. Objectively, you know that Elaine is desirable, and you feel obligated to desire her. It seems to be your duty to go through the motions. You keep thinking that with practice you will eventually get the knack of enjoying superficial encounters, that you will stop looking for the universal solvent, stop grieving. You will learn to compound happiness out of small increments of mindless pleasure.

'I really enjoyed Amanda,' Elaine says between songs. 'I do hope I see her again.' There is something confidential in her manner, as if you shared a secret with regard to Amanda. You would be happier if she had said she didn't like Amanda. Being still unable to think the worst of her, you need other people to think it and speak it for you.

Tad and Theresa have disappeared. Elaine excuses herself and says she will be right back. You feel abandoned. You consider the possibility of conspiracy. They have planned to meet at the door and ditch you. You are doing bad things to their mood. Or, worse yet, maybe you are missing out on drugs. You get yourself a drink. You wait five minutes and then decide to reconnoitre. You check the Men's Room first and then the Ladies'. A woman in a leather jump suit is teasing her hair at the mirror. 'Plenty of room,' she says. You hear sounds coming from one of the stalls. Giggling. Looking down, you see Elaine's pumps and Theresa's sandals under the door.

'Save a little for me,' you say, pushing on the door of the stall, which yields just enough to allow you to stick your head in and discover Elaine and Theresa engaged in an unnatural act.

'Want to join the party?' Elaine asks.

'*Bon appétit*,' you blurt, and you lurch out of the Ladies' Room. You emerge into a din of bodies and music.

It is very late.

GREGOR VON REZZORI

MEMOIRS OF AN ANTI·SEMITE

A NOVEL IN FIVE STORIES

Hardback £7.95

PICADOR

Paperback £2.50

The Society of Authors

★ gives individual advice to members on any business matter connected with authorship (e.g. publishing contracts, copyright, public lending right etc.)

★ takes up complaints on members' behalf and institutes legal proceedings when issues of general concern to the profession are at stake

★ sends to members free of charge the Society's quarterly journal, *The Author* — an unrivalled source of information for writers

★ publishes guides on authors' agents, copyright, income tax, publishing contracts, VAT etc

★ invites members to business meetings and social occasions

★ gives members access to the Retirement Benefit Scheme, group medical insurance schemes, and other fringe benefits

★ administers trust funds for the benefit of authors

★ organises special interest groups (e.g. broadcasters, children's writers, educational writers, medical writers, technical writers, translators)

★ pursues campaigns on behalf of the profession (e.g. PLR, improved publishing contracts, changes in copyright legislation, returns from photocopying etc.)

It is common for members to report that, through the help that they have been given, they have saved more — sometimes substantially more — than their annual subscription to the Society.

For a booklet and further information please write to:
The Membership Secretary
The Society of Authors
84 Drayton Gardens
London SW10 9SB

NOTES FROM ABROAD

Notes from Chile
Ariel Dorfman

P ablo Neruda once declared that if he had not been a poet, he would have built houses. He might have added that he did build houses. Before he died on 23 September 1973, exactly twelve days after the death of the democratic Chile that he loved so dearly, he had managed to buy three houses in three different locations, and had spent years enlarging them, appending spires and rooms, galleries and watchtowers, guest-houses and libraries.

The house in Valparaíso was ransacked after his death, and Matilde, his widow, has refused to fix it. It remains as it was the day the soldiers decided to call: the windows shattered, the doors broken, the furniture splintered, the paintings slashed. Matilde wanted that ravished home to be a symbol. If Pinochet's men treated Chile's Nobel Prizewinner in that way, treated the greatest poet in the Spanish language that way, the world could well imagine, Matilde said, the way in which they would be treating Neruda's readers: the poor, the unprotected, the unknown.

The second house is in Santiago. When Matilde returned to it from the hospital with Neruda's dead body, the house was flooded. Troops had broken in, and left the water in the kitchen and bathrooms running. Neruda's coffin—not a black one, he hated that colour—was placed on a table in the middle of the overflowing mud and rubble.

His third house is the most famous; his home in Isla Negra, a tiny coastal hamlet of rocks, surf and gulls sixty miles west of Santiago. It also was invaded by soldiers, but not ravaged. This may have been due to the fact that the poet was there, dying of cancer, when they came. They were looking for weapons, for guerrillas, for communists: they opened each book, original editions of Whitman and Rimbaud; they clicked their flashlights into his unique collection of shells and of frigates in bottles; they looked behind his seventeenth-century maps of America and behind the figureheads of schooners that he had carried back with him from all the corners of the earth; they even searched a small-sized, many-coloured locomotive that he had in his front yard, one of the delights for the children who came to visit.

When he finally confronted the poet in bed, the major in charge of the operation was flustered, and excused himself: 'I'm sorry, sir, but we have been informed that there is something dangerous here.'

Legend has it that Neruda answered: 'Very dangerous indeed. It's called poetry.'

The major coughed, and then withdrew his men from the search.

It was after this military operation, that Neruda's illness worsened. The physician who had been taking care of him was arrested. Neruda left for Santiago, never to return to Isla Negra. On the way back, his ambulance was searched, and then delayed for three hours. Matilde says it was the only time in her life that she saw Neruda cry.

During all my years of enforced exile, I have been unable to visit any of Neruda's houses. So one of my first acts, upon arriving in Chile, was to visit Isla Negra. If Chile were democratic, it would have been natural not only that I should have gone, but that I should have slept and worked there: Neruda had left his house to Chile's poets, young and old, so we could live and write by the sea with all our expenses paid. He had made the Chilean Communist Party, of which he was a prominent member, the executor of that clause in his will. When the Junta confiscated all the possessions of left-wing parties, Neruda's magic house had also fallen into their hands. Just as the major had been disconcerted by the sight of Neruda, so the government had not known what to do with his house. Even the absurd General Pinochet found it unreasonable that he should open this house to the very writers he had spent the last ten years persecuting and beating up, censoring, kicking out of jobs and sending into exile. So the government did the only thing it could do: shut the house up and let it deteriorate. After all, the police must have thought, how much harm can an abandoned house do?

At first glance, this surmise seems correct. The room is boarded up where Neruda used to munch cheese and write verse watching the waves burst on to the shore. The round-eyed fish he painted along the outside walls—along with many other symbols—are peeling. Inside, one can imagine the books growing mouldy.

It is, nevertheless, a heartening sight. A fence surrounds the house, and on each of its slats, messages have been scribbled—hundreds, thousands of messages. People have come from all over Chile, and from all over the world, to write something on that fence. They speak to Neruda directly, calling him Pablo, and using the familiar *tú* instead of the more distant *usted*. Some are political slogans, but most are declarations of love, short poems, random thoughts. Sometimes it is a couple of lovers who sign, lovers who have used Neruda's verses as a bridge between them; very often it is groups of teenagers; and also whole families. I stopped and was particularly moved by one list of ten people, all with the same surname. At the bottom someone had scratched: *And also Pablito (2 years old).*

Scores of ordinary people had felt that they could not be silent; that their words had enough significance to be left as a gift for others. By pledging their troth, by scrawling their names, by thanking a dead man for interceding in heaven, they were telling Neruda how much they missed him, how far away he was. Some of the messages were carved in the wood, but most had been written with chalk or coal. When the rains came, they washed the phrases away and then other visitors came, to inscribe new vows.

This was how Chile survived ten years of dictatorship. Thousands had journeyed to Neruda's house; but many millions more had inscribed on other fences other kinds of words. They had somehow kept a part of themselves intact, and had been able to find minimal, marginal, anonymous ways of expressing that part to their fellow countryfolk. It had been dangerous.

The first act of the Junta, on 11 September 1973, had been to bomb the left-wing radio stations. Behind that act was the realization that, in order to govern the country, each of its citizens had to be isolated. The military had then systematically destroyed and reorganized the channels by which the people had always communicated. A television presenter, received in each home on 10 September 1973, might have found her- or himself on the 12th with a crayon, looking for a wall. Books were burned, trade unions were abolished, schools and universities were interfered with, art galleries were shut down, public and private speech were carefully monitored. And while the military went about the business of closing down channels of communication, its soldiers did not neglect to apply pressure to the communicators themselves.

The communicators, left only with their bodies and their memories, had reacted. At first, slowly, at the most primitive, elementary, individual level—rumours, information, jokes. And after this initial oral stage, had come the writing—graffiti on walls; messages on paper money; small, home-made bulletins. Then, as resistance gathered strength, clandestine organizations were able to bring out more regular reports and information. The quality of these publications became increasingly sophisticated. I can remember, over seven years ago—I was in Paris at the time—the awe with which I received the first underground book to be entirely made in Chile. Not mimeographed: printed.

A French friend, who had been a *résistant* against the Nazis during the Second World War, smiled in recognition. 'It was done on three different printing presses,' he said. 'It looks just like the ones we used to bring out.'

That sort of output continues, but it is not the most fundamental form of resistance. As the opposition movement to Pinochet started tentatively to surface, to discover what would or would not be tolerated, multitudes of semi-legal publications began to appear. Surveillance of this sort of material is only possible when the numbers are limited; when they become large, they cannot be controlled.

There is a place in Chile where many of those alternative initiatives in communication are being collected. Hundreds of mimeographed, poorly executed, painstakingly written, yellow-page journals fill a whole room. I leafed through some of them, and it was like taking a tour of a forbidden country. Most of the people—slum-dwellers, student activists, trade unionists, members of feminist groups and literary workshops—who bring out these bulletins do not have enough to eat, but somehow they have managed to test their voices, so similar, although more articulate and refined, to those who left their imprint on Neruda's fence.

'They don't think of their work as especially noteworthy,' I was told by Varlos Catalán, the executive secretary of CENECA, the study centre for Chilean culture which has been trying, over the course of the last ten years, to gather up each transitory issue, each piece of paper, each flyer, each counter-cultural endeavour. 'In fact, after using them, they just throw them away, as if they had no value. So we make a special effort to amass them in this one place. A time will come when people can visit this living memory of ours and remember what life was like.'

CENECA is one of dozens of small institutions that have timidly multiplied after the military takeover of the universities and the media, and that, together, constitute a sprawling, overlapping, informal network. If it were not for these groups, there would have been no significant intellectual production in Chile during these bleak years. The variety is enormous: art galleries and theatre groups, writers' workshops and *peñas* where protest music can be heard, alternative magazines brought out by professional journalists and cultural centres which offer courses in sculpture, weaving, the contemporary novel. The academic centres, like CENECA, are typical: they have tried to keep some semblance of critical discourse alive, publishing studies, stimulating discussions and exchanging experiences. Privately funded, perpetually in debt, they are threatened more by the possibility of bankruptcy than by harassment from the secret police, although its officers pay a visit from time to time. Until now, the groups have managed to subsist by keeping a low profile and working within relatively narrow limits. However, because they are public and therefore visible, they must always be wary.

One could suggest that if Chilean popular counter-culture can be likened to the messages on Neruda's fence at Isla Negra, these institutions, which are the product of élites engaged in more permanent and formal functions of communication, might very well be compared to Neruda's house itself. Just as the house has managed to survive untouched (although sullied), the literature, journalism, theatre, and music, have all established enduring identities, although beset by dangers and hostility. Most of the groups are actually located in separate old, large houses, set apart and far from the street, so that one must pass through a gate and then the interlude of a garden. There are economic reasons for this: these houses are cheap and available because Chile's current financial crisis has forced out the upper middle class who had originally constructed them for their numerous offspring and servants. In spite of knowing this, I felt that the groups' segregation was also, ultimately, emblematic. By remaining apart from society, they had kept going. They had been born stealthily, had learned not to overstep certain boundaries, disguising their language and their intentions. They had been careful to avoid confrontations, but they had always said a little more, not less, than was necessary to stay alive. Their autonomy cannot be confused with inactivity. The story of Chilean culture under Pinochet has been the story of how these groups have managed to extend their influence and grow. It has also been the story of the risks they took in order to break out of their isolation.

Americans may have problems understanding this. The law, and what it establishes, has no objective meaning in a place like Chile. The limit between what can and cannot be said under an authoritarian regime is always fluctuating, always up for re-interpretation. There is a whole zone, a sort of no man's land, where it is not clear what is prohibited and what permitted. In each case it does not depend on a set of agreed rules, but on shifting ground in which the opposition has to measure how much it can say without being suppressed, and the government has to measure how much it loses politically each time it represses and, instead of persuasion, uses coercion. It is in this insecure, wavering situation that Chileans have had to learn when to be silent, when to speak softly and subtly—and when to scream.

For years, Chilean artists have publicly referred to this process in military terms: it is 'occupying' or 'conquering' the 'open spaces'. In private, however, they will smilingly use another term, which they have borrowed from another sort of battlefield, that of the sexes. *Hay que meter la puntita,* they will say, which could be roughly translated as 'you've got to get the tip in.' Once you've manoeuvred yourself into that introductory position, Chileans say, the rest is a matter of patience and time.

Over the last six months, however, the change in political climate has made this metaphor obsolete. The country is in open rebellion against Pinochet. The ferment in the land has intensified the demands on intellectuals and journalists. What used to be sufficient—cultivating a flower-patch in the midst of an apparently barren landscape and trying to make it a permanent oasis—is no longer adequate and a furious need has developed for fertility and pollenization.

The opposition now faces two major problems.

One is the old problem of repression, but under a new guise. Just because the government is not strong enough to mount a general offensive against the democratic forces does not mean that it cannot terrorize some of them. The old rules of the game have been dissolved, and new ones are in the process of being created, changing with each skirmish and each gamble. I believe that this unstable, anguishing vulnerability will only vanish when Pinochet himself disappears from the face of Chile.

This silent war is evident in the fortunes of two magazines. *Apsi* began five years ago as a fortnightly journal dedicated to international affairs. This was the mask, the tip, the *puntita*. Slowly, it started to cover national affairs, and around a year and a half ago, after receiving many threats, it was forced to shut down. The government insisted that the magazine had the authority to speak on foreign affairs only. *Apsi* went to court and initially won its case. The government pressured the court to reconsider and the same justices that had upheld *Apsi*'s rights reversed their decision.

Apsi had no alternative but to comply, but in their next issues, the international window was used as a sly way of viewing national issues. When prior censorship was recently lifted, and it became possible to publish new magazines without having to ask for authorization, *Apsi* found itself in the absurd position of still only being allowed to print stories that referred to events outside Chile's borders. The journalists of *Apsi* went to see the new Minister of Internal Security, Onofré Jarpa, to ask him to find a solution. When I spoke to them in mid-September of 1983, they were still waiting for his reply, and had decided that in a forthcoming issue they would simply go ahead and speak out about Chile.

They may have to reconsider their plan. *Analisis,* another magazine, was originally published under the Church's protection. As it grew more outspoken and political, the Church—wanting to act as a bridge between the government and the opposition—withdrew its sponsorship towards the beginning of September. *Analisis* came out, while I was there, on 13 September, with a number dedicated to Salvador Allende. The number was quickly sold out, as was a second printing. Three days later (notice that the response was hesitant and not immediate), the government requisitioned the magazine and accused the director, Juan Pablo Cárdenas, of insulting the armed forces. Cárdenas had, indeed, miscalculated what was permissible in Chile. In an editorial, he had suggested that Chile's army had the dubious honour of having killed more of its compatriots than enemies in foreign wars. He is now awaiting what in all likelihood will be a three-year prison sentence. Strangely enough, it is because the old weapon of intimidation is no longer effective, and the old brutalizing terror no longer politically viable, that the government has been forced, for the first time, publicly to prosecute a journalist for his opinions.

But it is not only external, physical problems that Chilean culture is facing. By suddenly being forced into the open, artists and intellectuals are now coming up against an internal dilemma. Everywhere I went I found them obsessed, not with their safety, but with their language. They could now attempt to expand their influence, but it remained to be seen how their thinking and their use of words had been affected by years of hiding and fear. Chile's novelists and poets have spent much of their time writing hermetic, distressed parables and—almost for the first time—allegories.

Because few readers could understand what was criticized, most of these works managed to get through the Kafkaesque system of censorship. But meanwhile, a subtle process of internal accommodation and self-censorship had developed, until it had become almost automatic. Words were scrutinized, weighed, turned upside-down and inside-out, before being allowed to come into daylight. The way people had been forced to speak in public life, guardedly, full of *double-entendres* and allusions, seeped into their dreams and poisoned their privacy. This decade has deeply twisted and crushed the way in which people used to express themselves. A coded language has become the norm and people feel comfortable with it, suggest certain advantages to it.

Have Chilean art and literature lost their way, then? Such things are difficult to measure, and the question will probably not find an answer until democracy returns. Chileans have learned a lot about themselves in these bitter years, and they are not prepared to throw this wisdom away. They are obsessed with how to integrate the degrading experience and language of this decade into the new situation which asks for more clarity. How to keep what is valuable and uplifting from the past, and yet be open to the changed needs of the present?

My own experience, when I read stories and poems to different groups in Chile, tends to confirm this dilemma. People were pleased that I read with a loud resonant voice; and that I spoke 'in Spanish'—that is, that I alluded to reality quite directly and did not use subterfuge. But I could also sense their discomfort. They were not used to this sort of tone or literature. Even when I pointed out that, by publishing these works, I had been risking nothing more than adverse literary criticism and that, furthermore, within a few days I would be safely back in Washington DC, they were not satisfied. It did not matter under what 'protected' circumstances I had written. What puzzled and shocked them was a discourse that had, for so many years, been excised from their world. It was a meeting with themselves.

There is one area where this particular dilemma has been more triumphantly solved than elsewhere. Chilean theatre, perhaps because it has had to work in the open, has met the question head on, and has produced the best drama in our history. This has not been achieved without considerable pain. In 1974, one year after the coup, one of the most promising troupes presented a play in which the captain of a sinking ship went down foretelling better days. The audience, recognizing an allusion to Allende, flocked to see the performance. Unfortunately, so did the secret police. Oscar Castro, the director, and his sister Marietta, an actress, were tortured and then spent several years in a concentration camp. As a further reprisal, their mother and Marietta's husband, John McLeod, were kidnapped, and today are still among Chile's 2,500 *desaparecidos.*

Some years later, in 1977, Nicanor Parra, Chile's foremost living poet, brought out a play based on his verses in which the country was likened to a circus full of clowns. It was, appropriately, performed in a circus tent. The tent was burned down. (The secret police's artistic committee must have been presided over that year by a pyromaniac. A few weeks after this incident, someone set fire to a radio station in Osorno, a small town six hundred miles south of Santiago, because it had been educating the peasantry about human rights. And some months before, in January 1977, an arsonist had destroyed an art gallery.)

And yet, today, theatre is thriving. You can see any number of interesting plays in Santiago. *Lautaro* tells the story of an Indian youth who, during the Spanish Conquest, went over to the enemy's side, learned the tactics and then deserted, becoming a guerrilla warrior against the invader. Lope de Vega's famous *Fuente ovejuna* is being shown: in that seventeenth-century Spanish masterpiece, a local tyrant is killed by an irate populace. In the culminating scene, where torture is being applied to exact a confession, the answer by one and all is: We all did it, the whole town did it.

More interesting perhaps, are the works which refer more straightforwardly to Chile's current circumstances. Ictus, the major theatrical group in the country, has been consistently exploring contemporary problems. Its members call in a writer and elaborate the play as a collective. In previous years they have looked at the unemployed (*Pedro, Juan y Diego*), at groups of women who have to make a living by selling tapestries (*Tres Marías y una Rosa*) and at how censorship and fear shape the lives of journalists (*Cuántos Años Tiene un Día*). The two plays presently in repertory try to dissect some of Chile's most elusive myths. 'We want to look at some of our national traumas,' one of the actors explained to me. 'The reason why we have the troubles that we have. We try to let the audience identify those problems.'

Sueños de Mala Muerte, based on a short story by Chile's most renowned novelist, José Donoso, uses a squalid boarding-house to explore the obsessions of its transient inhabitants. The main characters, a pair of lovers, are intoxicated by the need to become proprietors of a house of their own. As in the ruined Chile of 1983, they cannot buy a real place to live; they use their savings to acquire another sort of place, a resting-place, an ancestral tomb. The play explores dramatically the fascination with property and death, two of Chile's most persistent preoccupations. In another play, *Renegociación Bajo la Lluvia,* Ictus savagely satirizes the Chilean ruling class. The setting is Santiago, when a recent torrential rain led to extensive flooding. A pair of rich brothers, not noticing how the river keeps rising, play tennis and, as they play, re-enact the history of murder and guilt which has surrounded their class all these years.

Ictus became aware several years ago, that though their works did well at the box office, they remained inaccessible to the majority of the Chilean people. They then took the conscious decision of working with video. Each of their plays has a videotaped version, and they have established a cautious circuit for the slums, trade unions and students. Other playwrights like David Benavente, have done something similar. Benavente has tried to blend sociology, journalism and theatre, by going out into Chilean society, interviewing people extensively about certain problems, and then allowing them to participate as critics in the various stages which lead to the play's creation.

This work with audiovisual media is more than an attempt to reach a wider audience. It is also a way of preparing for the day when television will once again be open to dissidents. The Junta has always kept a stranglehold on the mass media, knowing that the control of major outlets ensures ultimate ideological power.

It is in the cinematic field that the paralysis of Chilean culture is most alarming. Only two films have been commercially produced during these past ten years. There have been some illegal motion-pictures. I spoke to Pedro Cáceres (not his real name), whose half-hour clandestine documentary on the 'missing' and their families, *No Olvidar,* won the Grand Prize in the Bilbao Film Festival last year. His modesty is embarrassing. It is almost impossible to get him to talk about the dangers he and his crew went through to make the film. He had also made other sorts of sacrifices. In order to save enough money to finance it, he and his wife and children had to move into his parents' house for two years.

The irony is that Cáceres makes his living by filming advertisements for Chilean television. He does not seem to mind this Jekyll and Hyde existence: 'The whole country has been like this all these years,' he said. 'Why should movie-makers be any different?'

His dilemma illustrates the distance that still has to be travelled. While in his private life he writes and directs a vibrant denunciation of oppression, in his everyday, public life, he serves a television consumer culture. It is precisely this sort of culture, directly imported from the United States or produced by Chileans apeing US models, which is popular in my country. Pinochet can afford to ignore the intellectuals and the artists as long as he knows he can rely on American-oriented mass culture to stupefy and invade the dreams of his people. And we are stupefied, and we are invaded.

It is not a new situation. As in many Third World nations, we always imported most of our television and cinematic fare, but we had also developed, painstakingly, through the scantest of means, a series of mass-media alternatives which, though technically awkward, were able to compete for public attention with what came from abroad. It is painful and astonishing to note that in present-day Chile the most mediocre sit-coms and dramas bought from the States almost seem masterpieces compared to the sad imitations made in Santiago. If Pinochet's reliance on 'Dallas' is proof of his cultural bankruptcy, it is also true that when 'Dallas' begins to look, next to Chilean productions, like Fellini, it is not only the dictator who is in trouble, but the consciousness of the whole nation.

GRANTA

LETTERS

Facts

To the Editor

Mario Vargas Llosa's skilfully-constructed narrative of the murder of eight Peruvian journalists and their guide in the Andean village of Uchuraccay over a year ago raises a number of interesting points [*Granta* 9]. It looks like a straightforward factual representation of what happened from the time the reporters set out for Huaychao on 25 January 1983 until their bodies were dug up from shallow graves on a bare hillside a few days later. There is, however, more to it than that.

Just how much more is perhaps evident in the reception Mario Vargas Llosa's report received when published in Peru. Some of the more noteworthy critics include the following:

—The families of the dead journalists, who published an open letter accusing Vargas Llosa of 'distorting reality' and criticizing him for his 'unspeakable determination to deceive the world with deliberate lies.'

—The 15,000 people who marched through the streets of Lima on the anniversary of the massacre, unhappy with the conclusions Mario Vargas Llosa reached and which the government seems, on the whole, content to accept, and who demanded a speedy completion to the judicial investigation originally established to account for the journalists' deaths. That inquiry, meant to have been completed sixty days after the murder, was granted yet another two-month extension

last December. Some of the more peculiar features of the investigation include the fact that General Clemente Noel—Chief of the Political Military Command in the Emergency Zone in which the murders occurred—has informed the magistrates that they are not empowered to inquire into military activities, and the fact that of the seventeen Iquichano peasants who had been charged with the crime, only three have been detained. Even the President of the Supreme Court has said that those responsible for the Uchuraccay massacre will probably remain unpunished.

—Both the National Federation of Colleges of Lawyers and the Lima College of Lawyers that protested that the President's appointment of the commission which Mario Vargas Llosa headed contravened the Peruvian constitution: the matter was *sub judice* and the activities of the commission were seen, potentially, as attempts to interfere with the activities of the magistrate whose reponsibility the case was.

—The Peruvian Congress whose right to appoint its own commission of inquiry had been pre-empted by the President's prompt action.

—The noted historian Pablo Macera who said that by pre-empting a Congressional inquiry the President had also pre-empted the opportunity of establishing a commission which drew its members from all parties, including the left-wing opposition. The President's commission consisted instead of *only* three people: the ineffectual Mario Castro Arenas, Dean of the Peruvian College of Journalists; Dr

Abraham Guzman Figueroa, an eminent criminal lawyer, but—at eighty years of age—equally ineffectual; and Mario Vargas Llosa, friend and well-known admirer of the President.

—Luis Guillermo Lumbreras, the noted Ayacucho anthropologist and historian, who pointed out that Mario Vargas Llosa's report confined itself, amid so much contradictory evidence, to a single hypothesis, and that, throughout, there was a 'strong tendency, conscious or unconscious, to defend the system.'

—Dr Luis Piscoya Hermoza, Professor of Logic and Head of the Humanities at San Marcos University, who observed that Mario Vargas Llosa's report was virtually invalidated by rejecting so easily the notion that villagers' determination to 'defend themselves and kill' could not be part of the strategy of the political and military command in Ayacucho.

These represent only a small part of those people who felt that Mario Vargas Llosa's straightforward factual representation of what happened in Uchuraccay may not have been either entirely straightforward or reliably factual. Mario Vargas Llosa's own words invite us to regard his supposed objectivity as potentially suspect. His appointment to the three-man presidential committee just a few days after the tragedy was discovered was because—he states in the original Spanish version but not *Granta*'s—'The Government sought to counteract suspicions of official complicity in the journalists' death.' In other words, President Fernando

Belaúnde Terry's government expected the commission to demonstrate that the government's security forces bore no responsibility for what happened at Uchuraccay. It was feared the massacre might become a political issue that could be exploited by the left-wing opposition—a prospect that was apparent just days after the massacre was discovered when a big street demonstration in Lima accused the security forces of being involved in the incident. And of course the commission's report did, in fact, reach conclusions that were extremely sympathetic to the government, regardless of the protest those conclusions occasioned elsewhere. When the report appeared, it was hailed by the arch-conservative daily *El Comercio* as scotching 'rumours, lies and demagogic travesties bandied about by those who take advantage of the misfortunes of others to sling mud at Peruvian democracy both here and abroad.' The report suppressed all suggestion that the Peruvian security forces might be conducting—or at least condoning—an Argentine-style 'dirty war' against insurgents in the Andes and argued instead that the whole of Peruvian society was to be blamed, for having tolerated a backward and isolated and irresponsible group of citizens. Peru's government, the report tries hard to demonstrate, has nothing to hide.

The enormous protest generated by the report, however, is because the report simply fails to consider evidence that might have led to difficult or unpleasant conclusions.

Among the considerations it does not address are the following:

—The left-wing opposition in Lima and a number of foreign papers, including the Mexican *Excelsior* and *Le Monde* of Paris, have all reported that the counter-insurgency police known as *sinchis* had encouraged the Iquicha peasants to attack and kill all strangers arriving on foot. Those who arrived in helicopters—the security forces—were friends. Vargas Llosa does not address this possibility; the peasants, Vargas Llosa argues, acted completely on their own, deciding to take the law into their own hands to commit mass murder.

—That the *sinchis* have been organizing paramilitary peasant militias in the region for some time was confirmed by a clandestine radio broadcast of the *Sendero Luminoso* in Huanta, one of the towns closest to Uchuraccay. The left-wing publications *El Diario de Marka* and *Equis X* have both alleged that these paramilitary peasant militias are a key element in General Noel's anti-guerrilla strategy.

—In August 1983, Amnesty International wrote to President Belaúnde Terry arguing that the military authorities in Ayacucho had, by the end of December 1982, organized a network of community patrols—led mainly by the local government representative in each community—to defend the communities against the *Sendero Luminoso*: some of these patrols were reported to have led attacks on villages suspected of pro-guerrilla sympathies. Amnesty International

cast doubt on the commission's conclusion that the peasants of Uchuraccay, in a state of panic, rejected the journalists' press credentials and killed them; it suggests instead that the massacre—like the reported killing of the guerrillas before—was carried out by one of these paramilitary community patrols as part of an officially-approved strategy to 'interdict all movement of strangers through the area.'

—None of this, of course, was addressed by Mario Vargas Llosa. He has even suggested arguments of this sort show the influence of Marxist-Leninist propaganda.

—Vargas Llosa has denied that security forces were in the region at the time of the massacre, refuting thereby the possibility that the security forces were in the position to support or encourage the peasants who killed the journalists. As such, he fails to take into account that several newspapers had reported that large-scale clashes between guerrillas and military patrols had occurred around the Yanaorcco telecommunications post—the spot where the journalists left the road and set off on foot for Uchuraccay.

—Fortunato Gavilán is mentioned in Vargas Llosa's account briefly: he is identified by the guide's mother as the principal authority present after the massacre. What Vargas Llosa does not mention is that he was the lieutenant-governor of Uchuraccay and that he subsequently informed the President of the Uchuraccay community, Dionisio Morales, that the journalists had been killed not because of confusion or panic but because they 'had come to investigate.'—presumably the other killings that had occurred in the region. Moreover, he was the person who handed over the journalists' belongings and equipment to the military patrol immediately after the killings. Despite this, he has neither been arrested nor called in as witness in the investigation. He is, similarly, ignored by Vargas Llosa.

—Vargas Llosa does not address the different accounts for the disappearance of the guide, Juan Argumedo, who has still not been discovered. No one will admit to killing him and no one claims to know where he is buried. In the Lima daily, *El Observador,* Argumedo's widow claimed that her husband was shot, reinforcing a number of rumours that his body had disappeared because of bullet wounds: bullet wounds would have disproved the commission's claim that the villagers were armed with sticks and stones and would have suggested that outsiders—that is, the military—had taken part in the massacre. Argumedo—the only one to have died who was not a journalist—was not from the village and may have been feared as a witness. It is worth noting that, when they were about to board a plane in Lima to carry out more investigations into Argumedo's disappearance, the state prosecutor and his assistant were assaulted by soldiers at Ayacucho airport.

—The other potential witnesses have died mysteriously. Celestino Ccente, Silvio Chavez and Marcia Galvez de Gavilán, the wife of Fortunato Gavilán, have all died under strange circumstances after giving testimony to Judge Flores.

—There is little speculation about what happened to the rolls of film taken by the journalists' party: it disappeared, for some reason, between General Noel and Judge Flores, to reappear in part, without adequate explanation, months later. Nor is there any speculation about how some of it ended up in the pro-government Lima evening paper, *Ultima Hora,* and the equally pro-government *Caretas.*

There have been several massacres in Uchuraccay since the death of the journalists; up to one hundred villagers may have been killed. Many people have begun to wonder if somebody other than the guerrillas might be interested in removing those who had taken part in the killings. No such doubts trouble Vargas Llosa. To him, it is quite clear what happened at Uchuraccay, who did it, and why. When I put a few of the above points to him in a BBC Latin American Service radio programme in June, he lost his temper and accused me of being a propagandist. He later expanded this theory in a syndicated column published in most of the leading conservative newspapers of South America and Spain.

Vargas Llosa has since accepted, in general terms, that many of the elements of a 'dirty war' are present today in the Peruvian Andes. He recognizes the weight of Amnesty International's documented evidence of disappearances, massacres and tortures carried out by the security forces in their attempts to stamp out the *Sendero Luminoso* guerrillas. Even the Army itself has admitted that excesses sometimes happen. In November, General Noel agreed to set up an internal inquiry after Lima publications, including *Caretas,* obtained eye-witness evidence that thirty-five peasants had been murdered by the security forces at Soccos near Ayacucho. They included women and young children cut down by machine-gun bullets. All previous evidence of such incidents had been dismissed as propaganda.

Perhaps more to the point, Vargas Llosa now seems to be engaged in an ideological crusade against those who share his cultural background but not his political views. Eminent European intellectuals such as Gunter Grass and ignorant foreign journalists such as myself have come in for virulent criticism. We are responsible, it seems for portraying Latin America and particularly Peru, as a strange and barbarous place.

Vargas Llosa perhaps feels betrayed by those who persist in seeing Latin America as a place of guerrillas, revolutionaries and banana republics. Such people have been taken in. As he says: 'Guerrilla movements in Latin America are not "peasant movements". They are born in the cities, among intellectuals and middle-class militants who, with their schematic rhetoric, are often as foreign and incomprehensible to the peasant masses as *Sendero Luminoso* is to the men and women of Uchuraccay...

The fact of the matter is that Lima's middle-class Marxists are almost as bewildered and repelled by *Sendero Luminoso* as he is.

Vargas Llosa's theory of guerrilla movements in Latin America is antiquated and relevant only to the Peruvian tragicomedy of 1965, when middle-class militants took to the hills to create guerrilla *focos,* and even advertised their whereabouts in the Lima press. It is no help at all in trying to understand the phenomenon of Sendero Luminoso, or the FARC and ELN guerrillas in Colombia.

All these movements have lasted for years, in the face of determined counter-insurgency campaigns, and most certainly do in fact have a peasant base. If *Sendero Luminoso* were merely a gang of desperadoes preying on the Andean peasantry they would not have lasted five minutes, particularly once the *campesinos* were given carte blanche by the security forces to strike back at them. But they are still there, despite staggering casualty rates (if official figures are to be believed), and show few signs of losing their operational capacity. They have found support among at least some of the poor, Quechua-speaking peasants of the Andes and elsewhere.

To put forward such a hypothesis lays oneself open to further charges of being a propagandist. It assumes that the Maoist guerrillas are rational human beings rather than the fanatical madmen portrayed in military communiqués and the writings of Mario Vargas Llosa.

Sendero Luminoso has undoubtedly been guilty of many atrocities, many cruelties, and in some areas there is evidence that the peasants have turned against them, or never thought much of them to begin with. But to take the Vargas Llosa line is to succumb to wishful thinking. The poor peasants of the high Andes are not pining for liberal democracy, any more than they get excited about the fate of the Gang of Four. They want simple material things, and *Sendero*'s leaders appear to grasp this point very clearly.

Vargas Llosa's crusade has reached a stage at which such appeals to rationality probably count for little. A few months ago he was the guest speaker at a world media conference in Cartagena, Colombia, at which he again denounced the threat to democracy represented by people like me. The event was organized by the fanatically anti-communist and somewhat undemocratic religious and commercial conglomerate put together by the Rev. Sun Myung Moon, 'spiritual' leader of the moonies.

Colin Harding
London

Lies

To the Editor

Are we really expected to believe, for one moment, that Redmond O'Hanlon [Granta 10] really witnessed James Fenton reading Swift while barely surviving rapids, that O'Hanlon really was able to remember all the dialogue that he sets down as having actually occurred, that James Fenton really did disappear down a whirlpool,

that all this really happened? If it weren't for the pictures you included, I would be inclined to doubt that O'Hanlon and Fenton ever went to Borneo, for I find little that confirms that they were ever actually there. O'Hanlon writes in an amusing energetic way, but it's all lies.

And so, it seemed, was most of *Granta*'s travel writing. And in publishing such obvious and elaborated fabrications, *Granta* was missing the point of what travel writing is meant to be—at least for my generation which has grown up reading it: it is not about the author, it is about the place; it is not about perceptions or feelings or thoughts; it is a record of another land, another people, another experience.

J.M. Marshall
London

Socialism's Failure

To the Editor

Your collection of articles and photographs [Granta 9] organized around the tenth anniversary of the death of Allende seemed to romanticize and distort what occurred.

I left Chile in 1972, and I did so because it had become impossible to live there: it was economically impossible. The left had destroyed industry and it had destroyed agriculture. It had proceeded from the belief that change can be realized by planting a little Chilean flag on top of a factory and proclaiming that, from now on, it belonged to the people. That Allende's government did not fall earlier I attribute to Allende himself, who managed to resist, even if slightly, the constant pressure of his ministers: the pressure to destroy the capitalist economy completely as the only way of securing the advent of real socialism.

That was the real object of the revolution: to destroy the economy. The first year, 1971, was a year of euphoria: everyone spent money; everyone bought consumer goods; everyone ate only in restaurants. Allende, 'benevolent' and 'fair', raised everyone's salaries a full one hundred percent. Within no time, the gold reserves of the Central Bank were completely exhausted. And in no time, the economy was in shambles.

It is true that Allende was attacked from the very beginning: by the shameless meddlings of the CIA and ITT; by the skilful politicking of *El Mercurio*; and by the oligarchy of Chile's farmers. But the greatest adversaries were from the left itself, who were determined to break entirely with the past, who disregarded completely the established judicial system, and who bungled the few important reforms—for instance, the agrarian reform—they attempted to institute. Chile was trying to create a democratic socialism. But it was a failure. And its failure proves, once again, that Stalin was right: socialism is imposed not by the people, not by one class or another, not by democracy, but by military might.

Mauricio Wacquez
Spain

Complaints

To the Editor

I have received a copy of *Granta 8: Dirty Realism*. I am cancelling my subscription. Please do not send me another copy of your magazine. I do NOT want it. I don't share your enthusiasm for dirt, realistic or not.

John Brown
Winscombe
Avon

All letters are welcome and should be addressed to *Granta,* 44a Hobson Street, Cambridge CB1 1NL.

"The finest magazine for reading in the open air"
SPIKE MILLIGAN

Open your mind with
THE PLEASURES OF LISTENERING...

Think for yourself. It won't hurt. Well, not much. For those without minds of their own, they can rent one. Or borrow mine.

You start by ordering The Listener from your newsagent each week. Or you can take out a subscription by filling out the coupon

- A good crossword. And crosswords are better than cross words.
- Best smelling magazine on the news-stand.
- It works outdoors, indoors, everywhere.
- The great and famous are in it every week. So am I, sometimes.
- Invaluable Viewer/Listener guide.
- They say what they think about the programmes. Don't spare my feelings.
- It's on after the other stations have closed down. And before.

and sending it in quick.

It works out £1 less over the year. With the postage thrown in.

For that, they'll even get the postman to throw it through your letter box. And just look at what you'll get.

Notes on Contributors

The first part of *The Men's Club* by **Leonard Michaels** was published as a story in the first issue of *Granta*. **Slawomir Mrozek's** 'Letter' is from *Donosy* and was first published in Polish last autumn by Puls Publications in London; it is translated here by Timothy Garton Ash. **Raymond Tallis** is a doctor, living in Liverpool. 'Certain Thoughts arising on being Pointed out t by my Two-year-old Son' is his first published work of prose. **Ian McEwan's** most recent work was the film *The Ploughman's Lunch*. He is currently working on a novel. **Milan Kundera** lives in Paris. 'Soul and Body' will be included in his forthcoming novel *The Unbearable Lightness of Being* which Faber publishes early this summer. **Salman Rushdie** has contributed to *Granta 3* and *Granta 7*. He has just returned from a lecture tour in India. **Martha Gellhorn** contributed to *Granta 10: Travel Writing*. She is currently snorkelling around the world. **Gabriel García Márquez** has recently returned to Colombia, where he plans to start a new newspaper. **Mario Vargas Llosa** is a regular contributor. His new novel *The War of the End of the World* will be published here in the autumn. **Don DeLillo's** novel *The Names* was published here last autumn by the Harvester Press. **Redmond O'Hanlon's** first instalment of 'Into the Heart of Borneo' was written for *Granta 10: Travel Writing*. It has since developed into a book which he expects to finish this spring and which Salamander Press will publish in the autumn. **Jay McInerney's** fiction has appeared in the *Paris Review* and *Ploughshares*. This is his first work to be published in Britain. **Ariel Dorfman** is the author of *Widows*, a novel, and a collection of essays entitled *The Empire's Old Clothes* (Pluto Press). His previous contribution was in *Granta 6: A Literature for Politics*.

Photo credits: 'Milan Kundera' by Vera Kundera; 'Parkbench' by Marc Riboud (John Hillelson); 'Russian Soldier' by Ivan Kyncl; Wenceslas Square photos by J. K. (John Hillelson); 'City of Dissidents' by Marc Riboud (John Hillelson); 'Henry Kissinger' (Popperfoto); 'Monkey' (Topham); 'Redmond O'Hanlon in a Boat' and 'Redmond O'Hanlon, a remarkably strong man' by James Fenton.

NER/BLQ

New England Review and Bread Loaf Quarterly

"One of the best, and most essential, of America's literary magazines..."
—Raymond Carver

In the past year, *NER/BLQ* has been drawn international accolades for such offerings as the book-length *Writers in the Nuclear Age* (with contributions from **Grace Paley, Denise Levertov, Seamus Heaney,** and forty others), and a **Symposium on Poetic Form.** One of America's most beautiful and least doctrinaire journals, with a primary emphasis on publication of work by younger or less recognized writers, *NER/BLQ* is sure to challenge and surprise both general readers and literary connoisseurs.

Alongside dozens of new names you will find those of many of the most respected authors of our time. Upcoming numbers include excerpts of the screenplay for *Dostoevsky*, by **Raymond Carver** and **Tess Gallagher;** new poetry by **Hayden Carruth** and **Robert Penn Warren;** and a special feature on **Antonio Benítez-Rajo** and the Arts Cultures of the Caribbean. As well, look for passionate commentary about issues that matter: Ron Powers on *Literature and the Mass Media*; Jay Parini on books of essays by poets and fiction writers, including **Cynthia Ozick, Wendell Berry, Margaret Atwood, Alice Walker, William Bronk,** and others; and Michael Ryan on **Elizabeth Bishop.**

Neither academic nor self-consciously experimental, *NER/BLQ* provides an ideal sampler for British readers devoted to the highest calibre of current fiction and poetry.

NER/BLQ Box 170, Hanover, NH 03755   USA

1 year, $14_____   2 years, $25_____   3 years, $34_____ (foreign)
  (all foreign rates, postpaid)

Name:_____

Street:_____

City, Country, Code:_____